Outside the tunnel beneath Government House, Hong Kong, on the morning of December 25, 1941. Wally Skinner, myself and Vivian Garton. Both the men were employed by the Public Works Department and were working on Rescue and Demolition during the war. Japanese troops were about a mile away at that moment. We didn't know then that Hong Kong would surrender in the afternoon.

Tin Hats and Rice

A diary of life as a Hong Kong prisoner of war 1941-1945

Barbara Anslow

BLACKSMITH BOOKS

Tin Hats and Rice

ISBN 978-988-77927-4-1

Published by Blacksmith Books
Unit 26, 19/F, Block B, Wah Lok Industrial Centre,
37-41 Shan Mei Street, Fo Tan, Hong Kong
Tel: (+852) 2877 7899
www.blacksmithbooks.com

Layout by Pete Spurrier
Index by Mark Rossi

First printing August 2018
Second printing December 2018

Contents

Foreword

Barbara Anslow shouldn't have written this book. In 1940 she set sail for Australia as part of the wartime evacuation of Hong Kong. Her father stayed behind to continue his work in the Naval Dockyard, but Barbara, along with her mother and sisters, should have spent the war years safely in Australia.

Instead, during a stopover in Manila, they received shocking news. Barbara's father had died of a sudden heart attack shortly after they'd left him. The four women managed to find passage on a ship leaving Manila and returned to Hong Kong. Once back, they decided they'd stay.

It was a strange time. On the surface, daily life for Hong Kong's expatriates carried on unchanged, with the usual social round of dances, dinners, movies and sports. But as the evacuation shows, Hong Kong was well aware of the dangers it faced. The daily newspapers were full of the war in Europe and the growing tensions between Japan and the United States.

Barbara's diary entries from November 1941 show the tension building:

12th: "Churchill says if Japs and USA come to grips, Britain will follow USA 'within the hour.'". She added the prescient note, "I'm a bit afraid that Xmas won't come."

14th: "London (radio) news says that tanks are massing in the Canton area. Blackout. I am frightened."

30th: "Topper says we are as near war now as we have ever been, that Japan with her militarist Govt. can't very well back down now."

On the 8th of December, Barbara's fears were realized:

"Was raked out of bed this am at 6.30 – to be at office at 7am. When I got there Mr Bevan, Deputy Director of ARP, said war had been declared between Britain/America against Japan. Just after 8 o'clock air raid sirens sounded.

"It's hardly worth writing diary because I can't visualise us ever getting out of this, but I want to try to believe in a future."

Fortunately for us, Barbara did carry on writing her diary. She leads us through the fighting and surrender, the uncertain time that followed, then the move to Stanley Camp. She didn't know at the time, but she was to spend the next three and a half years there. Her diary records the dramatic incidents of internment like the bombing of the camp by American aircraft, but more often it details the daily activities and the ups and downs of life in cramped quarters. Struggles with roommates, hunger and sickness, and the worry that the Japanese wouldn't let the internees leave the camp alive all play a part.

I first read these diary entries in 2011, when Barbara posted extracts to an internet group about Stanley Camp. They started me thinking about how to get this valuable resource out to a larger audience. I thought I could use email to send daily extracts from wartime diaries. Subscribers would receive one email each day for the three years and eight months of the Japanese occupation. They'd re-live the diarists' experiences at the same pace they originally happened. Barbara kindly agreed, and I launched the first series in January 2012. Since then I've started a new series each December, and now the day's diary entries are sent to around 400 subscribers each morning.

The feedback from subscribers has been very positive, especially from those who had family members in Stanley:

- *MH from Australia:* I love to read them every day... I find them SO interesting. They give me much insight into a part of my father's life that he never spoke about. My adult children also are finding out about their beloved "Pa" and what his life was like during his time in "Stanley".
- *John Bechtel:* My father, also named John Bechtel, was in Stanley but we could never get him to talk about it. I took him back to Stanley several times but he found it difficult to discuss details with me. After reading the diaries I now am able to knit together the facts with his experience and life. Wish he could have read the information before he passed in 1981. Thank you so much.
- *Robert Millar:* I read the diaries every day. I don't contribute to the daily chats as being only 16 months old when I went into camp with my mother Doris and sister Gillian, and coming out soon after my 5th birthday, I don't unfortunately have much to offer. However from the diaries and also from various books I've been reading I have gained a lot of information about what went on around me in my early life.

Several subscribers asked if they could have a copy of the full diary to read, instead of the daily email format. So in October 2015, at a book launch for the wartime diary of Graham Heywood, I mentioned this to the publisher, Pete Spurrier. I put him in touch with Barbara, and I'm very pleased to see that the end result is this book!

Barbara – as well as congratulating you on the publication of your diary, let me thank you. First for being so generous in sharing your diary with us, as a diary is a private thing, and second for your endless patience in answering all my questions about it over the years. Thank you!

David Bellis
Gwulo.com

The three Redwood sisters: Olive, Barbara and Mabel, February 1940.

Introduction

I lived with my parents and sisters in Hong Kong from 1927 to 1929. In 1938, when I was 19, we returned there.

We Redwoods – my mother Mabel Winifred, 46, my sisters Olive, 25, Mabel Anne, 18, and myself, 23 – were living in a flat in Happy Valley when the Japanese attacked on 8th December 1941. My father William had died the previous year.

Olive was engaged to Sam (Topper) Brown, R.A., Mabel Anne's boyfriend was Sidney Hale of the Royal Scots Band to whom she was unofficially engaged. I had a comparatively new boyfriend (unserious) – Arthur Alsey, violinist and deputy leader of the Royal Scots Band.

Olive and I worked as stenographers with the Hong Kong Government, she in the Food Control Dept, I in the Air Raid Precautions Dept. Mabel Anne worked in an Army office. Mum had just started a job looking after six-month-old baby Jean Martin, whose mother had died.

During the battle, my mother was an auxiliary nurse in a wartime hospital, my younger sister was a VAD (Voluntary Aid Detachment) nurse in the Military Hospital; I worked with the Air Raid Precautions Dept, my elder sister worked with Food Control.

After the surrender of Hong Kong to the Japanese, all four of us ended up with some two thousand others in the civilian internment camp at Stanley, seven miles from the city, in cramped accommodation: camp beds with little bedding, no hot water for washing ourselves or our clothes. Food consisted of rice, vegetables and sometimes minute quantities of meat or fish; no desserts. Like most internees we had lost our homes and possessions through bombing and shelling – or looting after the surrender on Christmas Day.

Most of us survived three and a half years of hunger and deprivation, boosted by optimism, amateur concerts, talks, language classes and so on, and our tireless doctors and nurses; also our captors often allowed us to swim at a beach within the camp. Apart from the execution of several internees whom the Japanese found had wireless sets, most of the time the Japanese authorities did not bother us.

After VJ Day in August 1945 we were deliriously happy to leave Hong Kong for repatriation to the UK – yet a year later my mother, sisters and I were all back in the colony again!

Barbara Anslow
Kirby-le-Soken, Essex
July 2018

1941

12 Nov 1941

Churchill says if Japs and USA come to grips, Britain will follow USA 'within the hour.'

I'm a bit afraid that Xmas won't come.

Reply from Home Government about evacuation – no chance of people coming back yet.

13 Nov 1941

The rumour today is that the Japs are coming on Saturday.

14 Nov 1941

London news (radio) says that tanks are massing in the Canton area. Blackout. I am frightened.

15 Nov 1941

Newspaper says Japan is calling up her reserves.

16 Nov 1941

The Band came in from camp to play in two Canadian Battalions which have just arrived on grey ship and another. Arthur (Alsey, Royal Scots Band Sergeant) and Sid (H.S. Hale, pianist and clarinettist, Royal Scots Band) arrived about noon, and we went to King's Theatre – 'Buck Privates.'

17 Nov 1941

Once again Japs look like business, and they can't call it off every time. Mary Taylor phoned me about a possible new job, so at 5pm I went to 3rd floor, Hong Kong Bank Building, and met Elsie Cholmondeley, tall and fair, very blue eyes, employed there (Stabilization Board of China.) I was there until 7pm and everyone still working – wouldn't like that continuously.

Mr Fox interviewed me, he sprawled over a table... said he couldn't take anyone till he got more room. *((I seem to think he was American, and I don't think he was in Stanley Camp... none of the people on the Stanley list named Fox sound like him. Perhaps he got away before 8th Dec, he certainly spoke about going 'on a trip' when he interviewed me shortly before.))*

18 Nov 1941

Arthur came in from camp unexpectedly, and we had tea in Cecil Hotel.

Mum started work at Mr. Addis Martin's today. *((Mum had been interviewed by Mr Thomas Addis Martin the previous week. She had applied for the job of a live-out supervisor of his baby daughter Jean, then 7 months old. Mrs Addis Martin had cancer and died when Jean was about 5 months old. There were amahs in the house to do all the housework, washing, etc., but Mr A M wanted a motherly figure to supervise Jean's care. Mum loved the job from the start, she went there daily.))*

19 Nov 1941

Jap/USA situation isn't looking any better, it really doesn't seem as if anyone can bluff any longer, so I typed a long letter to Margaret *((a friend in the UK))*, whatever happens here I want her to know I'm happy these days.

Two of Patsy's pups taken to Mrs Hogg today.

21 Nov 1941

In morning, Mr Bevan (Michael Lee Bevan, Deputy Director of Air Raid Precautions) took Mrs. Marjorie Cook (stenographer) and I in Bevan's car to Bacteriological Institute to have blood tests. They won't take the actual blood until it is wanted. *((Mr Bevan is the artist whose Stanley sketches appeared postwar in 'London Illustrated' magazine.))*

23 Nov 1941

All to 9.30am Mass at St Margaret's. We still seem to be doing well in Libya, but I'm so afraid we may be crowing too soon.

24 Nov 1941

China Fleet Club dance. Some Canadians there.

25 Nov 1941

News from Cairo is rather more cautious.

27 Nov 1941

Asking myself what am I waiting for? i.e., starting new story. In a way, it's the political situation, but I will begin tomorrow morning. Mum and I went shopping tonight, I bought shoes for HK$12.50.

28 Nov 1941

Arthur phoned, he might get in on Sunday, but they will be 'manning' up to Christmas from now on.

29 Nov 1941

Arthur rolled up at 5pm. We had tea at home, then I went to office. Although Saturday there was a Defence exercise, we were working shifts and I was due for evening 6-11pm. I told Tony Cole of predicament, and he said he would do my shift for me! (A. Cole of Senior & Accounting Staff, HK Govt.) Arthur and I took Mum to see 'Sun Valley Serenade'.

Because of Exercise, there was blackout and no trams or buses during 'pretend' raids, so we had to walk most of the way to Central and back because air raid sirens blew from time to time. Saw a plane drop a 'pretend' parachute.

30 Nov 1941

Mum on practice duty as an ANS (Auxiliary Nursing Service) nurse at Jockey Club (designated as a war-time convalescent hospital.) They had real convalescent patients brought out from main hospitals – in this cold weather. Sid was in from camp yesterday but had to go back ready to play at camp church services – riding round on back of lorry with piano.

Arthur had to leave early today to play at the Officers' St. Andrews do. He gave me 'Human Being' by Christopher Morley for my birthday.

Topper says we are as near war now as we have ever been, that Japan with her militarist Govt. can't very well back down now. I don't know what to think, but I'm afraid – because I recklessly bought myself chocolates today at $2.30... perhaps as a treat lest it's the last of treats. *((Topper was Sam Brown, Army, Olive's fiance.))*

1 Dec 1941

My 23rd birthday. Mr Bendall (Senior & Accounting Staff, HK Govt.) gave me a Roget's Thesaurus, Olive and Topper stockings; Mabel – eau de cologne; Sid – hanks; Mary (Taylor) eau de cologne.

New girl started at work, Lily A. Medina (Portuguese).

Malaya mobilised. Even Mr Cole thinks there will be war this time. *((The Mr Cole referred to here is not Tony Cole, but Lieutenant George Reginald Cole, R.N, a colleague of my father's whose wife and son had been evacuated to Australia. When we Redwoods had to leave our Dockyard flat after my Dad died, Lieut. Cole had us live with him until we found a private flat. He was killed at Aberdeen on 16 Dec.))*

Even if this place isn't involved by 5th Dec. when the R.S. *((Royal Scots))* Band should be in, I don't expect... can't see that they will be allowed in under present circumstances.

At the Civil Service Club, Happy Valley, early in November 1941. Back row, left to right: my sister Olive; her fiance 'Topper' Brown, R.A.; my mum; Mr V. Garton and Mr W. Skinner (both Govt. servants). Front row: H. Hale ('Sid') of Royal Scots; my sister Mabel; Arthur Alsey of Royal Scots; myself.

Government advising further evacuation. Only hope seems to be that Japs now say they will keep on talks with USA in hope that USA will change viewpoint – that isn't thought likely. Began writing 'Vacation in Hong Kong.'

2 Dec 1941

Libyan news isn't so good. Germans 36 miles from Moscow.

HMAS 'Sydney' presumed lost, having sunk an armed raider merchantman, then no news. 700 men, apparently no survivors.

Japs now want to resume talks with USA 'until the last moment.' Suggestions are that Japs must continue talks for 2 weeks by which time their war preparations will be complete.

3 Dec 1941

Mary and I went to Peggy Wilson's house – St Joan's Court, Macdonnell Road. (Mary lodged there).

I like Lily Medina but I'm sorry because she's so pitifully poor.

Jap and USA talks evidently proceeding.

Battleship 'Prince of Wales' is in Singapore.

Olive and I each sent $5.00 to local Bomber Fund in lieu of Christmas cards. Perhaps we should do the same for presents, but I'm loath to make that sacrifice.

4 Dec 1941

So far, the Band due in for the Races on Saturday, but Far East situation so fluid that even that may be off.

HMS 'Prince of Wales' and more Fleet in Singapore, it's supposed/hoped it will help Japs to change their minds, though 'HULL HINTS HOPE ABANDONED' says placard of evening paper. I can't believe that. *((Cordell Hull was an eminent US politician)).*

5 Dec 1941

Japan's reply expected to be against USA policy, which should mean breaking off of diplomatic relations, then Japan going on her way re Indo China and Burma, then WAR.

6 Dec 1941

Sunny. Race Day.

Had just settled down to work in Puckle's office when Olive appeared with Arthur – unbeknown to Royal Scots, another Band had arranged to do the Races.

I left work at 7pm, then Arthur and I to Peninsula for tea, then to King's – 'My Life with Caroline.'

The Jap/USA situation is getting worse because Japan, though evasive in her reply, says she means to keep her troops in Indo China against the Chinese.

7 Dec 1941

HKVDC have been mobilised since this morning. *((Mabel and Sid were having lunch at Dairy Farm in town when someone called for silence and said that Army & Navy personnel should return to their barracks immediately.))*

Lots of people think there will not be things happening here at first.

Mum, Olive and I played tennis with Mr Bendall in afternoon, then to his house for dinner.

8 Dec 1941

Was raked out of bed this am at 6.30 – to be at office at 7am. *((My office, ARP HQ, was only about 300 yards away. A Chinese messenger brought me a handwritten note from my boss asking me to get to the office by 7am. Not knowing why, but fearing the worst – we'd been on alert for the past few days – I hurried off)).*

When I got there Mr Bevan said war had been declared between Britain/America against Japan. *((I had charge of a number of files labelled 'Bring up in an emergency' – so I duly brought them up!))*

Just after 8 o'clock air raid sirens sounded *((The sirens were activated from our offices)).*

About 10.30 all clear went, it was said 1 bomb had been dropped in Shamshuipo (Kowloon) causing many casualties.

At 1.30pm sirens went again; quite a lot of AA fire. I saw 3 planes high up, being chased away to Lyemun.

It's hardly worth writing diary because I can't visualise us ever getting out of this, but I want to try to believe in a future.

Kai Tak has been bombed and I'm thinking of Arthur and Sid. *((Out fighting on the border between China and Kowloon)).*

Mabel is at CSO *((Colonial Secretary's Office. She had first reported this morning to her Army Office, but was told no females allowed in Fortress HQ now, so she went to CSO and offered her typing services there.))*

Mum nursing at Jockey Club hospital. I'm home now until 7pm. Scared and gloomy. I'm sure we'll have raids every night and day, and the night much worse than in the day. Tony Cole is coming here *((to our flat))* to eat *((he lived in Kowloon.))*

9 Dec 1941

2 false alarms, 1 last night and one early this am, and 6 more throughout the morning. Not much damage, mostly propaganda leaflets dropped, which means I fear that we may expect heavier raids in due course.

Mabel is sleeping at Women's International Club in town *((for wartime billet, not far from CSO))*. Olive staying overnight on 4th floor of Gloucester Hotel *((her Food Control Office nearby))*. Olive phoned me and I rang Mabel, she heard there is one Royal Scot in Military Hospital.

Japs are said to be at Taipo, according to the London news. Also some Japs were ambushed and mostly annihilated on Castle Peak Road – where the boys are. Can't properly imagine it.

Wrote to Arthur, though have little hope of his getting the letter, expect they're too busy to see about such things. Topper called at flat but none of us in. Mr Bendall also called, and Mr. Hall came home for a few hours. *((Mr. Hall was a colleague of my Dad's; his wife, evacuated to Australia, had written and asked Mum if he could lodge with us, which he did. We left a writing pad on the table in our flat, so that anyone calling while we were out could leave a message.))*

Libya and Moscow news brighter.

Singapore/Malaya news not good, and raids at Manila.

10 Dec 1941

Sid has been wounded. Bullet through shoulder. He told Hospital to phone Mum at the Jockey Club *((we didn't have a phone at home))* and she went to see him.

In afternoon I had a few hours off: went into town; alarm signal on way, I went into Battery Path tunnel – more orderly than I had expected *((despite large numbers of interested rather than frightened Chinese))*, and quite cool.

I left clothes at International Club for Mabel, where met Virginia Beaumont *((a VAD friend of Mabel's))* and we got lifts to Bowen Road Military Hospital and I was able to get in to see Sid. He is very shocked and upset, and didn't look like his old self. He's worried about the 2 men he had with him – no news of them – they went on ahead when he got entangled in a creeper plant and was sniped. He says Arthur is at HQ.

Peaceful last night, but 3 raids in afternoon. News that Japs have sunk 'Prince of Wales' and 'Repulse' by bomb – hard to believe. Japs seem to be starting well, though here we have sunk boats in an attempted landing at Tide Cove.

11 Dec 1941

8.30am. – On duty in office from 7 pm last night till 7 this morning, but actually slept *((fully-dressed, on camp bed behind screen in main office where all ARP staff were))* from 4.30am to 6.45am.

No raids during night, but shells are coming over now, but so far not doing much damage.

Slept some of morning at home, and a little in afternoon, when they dropped about 17 bombs in Wanchai area, one near Football Club (about 200 yards from our flat). Amah took me downstairs to flat below *((where I sat drooping on a chair in the hall among lots of kindly Chinese neighbours))*.

Then I went to office and worked until about midnight when had chance to doss down. It seemed so queer, me retiring behind screen on camp bed, with Tony Cole on bed nearby, and Gillies (Police), both sleeping. I slept well after 2 am until 7am Friday.

Our office might be moving to CSO tunnel beneath Government House.

12 Dec 1941

The rumour about Jordan *((Royal Scots Band Leader))* was confirmed today – he was shot by one of our own sentries – being deaf, he apparently didn't hear the challenge.

Mum got to Bowen Road to see Sid this morning, he is walking about now and hopes to be back with his unit within a few days.

Mabel has joined the VADs and sleeps below the military hospital in air raid shelter. Sid told her as far as he knows Arthur is all right and at Taikoo *((on the island))*.

We have apparently abandoned Kowloon, and unless a miracle happens, are going to be shelled to bits.

There is talk that Chinese guerillas are coming up behind the Japs and are now at Taipo, but I'm afraid to believe anything so heartening. I can see absolutely no escape, but we didn't have to stay in Hong Kong, and at least this IS something and we are in the war with the folks at home.

ARP HQ moving to CSO Tunnel – I'm to go tomorrow at 7 am and live in Dina House, but if shelling starts I doubt if that will last for long.

Usual raids throughout the day. Peggy Wilson joining our office staff, also Bonnie Penny and Mrs Bird (known as 'Charles'). *((Both had just come from Kowloon when evacuated. Bonnie Penny nee Winifred Agnes Robinson had recently married an Army lad who was killed.*

Because my next-day move to Dina House would leave Mum alone in the flat apart from the amahs, I asked her to consider staying at the Jockey Club hospital in future, or going to a nearby billet with other ANS ladies: our men folk no longer called, most people were becoming marooned at their places of duty through uncertain transport. Mum insisted she felt quite safe with the amahs at night at present. That night Mum and I slept in our lounge, Mum on the settee, I in an armchair. The amah made us laugh because she insisted on putting a layer of cushions beside the settee 'in case Missie fall off.'))

13 Dec 1941

Walked from home with Mum just as it was getting light, and went to office *((Mum to Jockey Club hospital.))* Much shelling by Happy Valley in night.

Mr Puckle (Director of ARP) gave me a lift to the CSO tunnel *((beneath Government House, we entered by entrance in Lower Albert Road opposite*

CSO building; the tunnel had another entrance from Government House)). Peggy Wilson had already arrived.

((We secretaries worked in two shifts – Peggy and I, then Bonnie and Charles. Our job was to keep a log of events, mostly messages per phone calls, and also to make out identification cards for ARP people.

Boiling hot in the tunnel, I was glad of short-sleeved jumper. Strong smell of raw wood from the props round the earthy walls etc. Various Govt. departments stationed in the tunnel which had been made with sections at all angles. An alcove just inside the entrance was I think meant to be for toilets, but these were not present – just a few chairs without seats. There may well have been toilets in other sections, but for calls of nature we ran over Lower Albert Road to the ones in the CSO building.))

Off duty at 3pm, had meal at Parisian Grill *((my pass allowed me to eat there free of charge.))* Bought lemonade as an excuse to stay longer when the siren sounded. Got into conversation with a stranger, Mr Robinson of Metals Control Office. Then went to find Dina House, 2nd floor, as instructed, to get a billet, but couldn't get any satisfaction about where I was to sleep. Phoned Olive's office for help, and she and Topper (who was then visiting her) came and carried me off. Had dinner with them at Gloucester, where met Eric Kennard *((Govt. clerk))* and he and one other escorted me back to Dina House where I met up with Mr G. P. Murphy and he directed me to a camp bed in a room with two ARP girls, Janet Broadbridge and Lillian Hope (both from Kowloon). Hardly slept because it was so cold, also had no nightwear as my luggage hadn't arrived.

14-15 Dec 1941

((Diary not available from this date until 22nd January 1942, but the following was written up from brief notes of that period when diary was recovered.))

Had to get up while it was dark *((as working from 7am to 3pm))*. Went to Parisian Grill for breakfast with Mr G. P. Murphy, Lillian and Janet. *((P.G. was only a short walk from Dina House))*. It was bacon and beautiful chips, and bread and butter and coffee. Then to tunnel. Central Police Station was bombed badly in afternoon, 15th Dec., several killed. Felt the concussion even in the tunnel.

Peggy Wilson invited me to stay with her in MacDonnell Road flat so moved there after shift. 'Uncle Sidney' (not a real uncle, but friend of Peggy's family) also lodging there, he is S.S. Harris, Gas Detection Officer. *((All three of us slept in the same room, felt safer that way.))* We had cold meat and salad.

I'm very mixed up over the next few days. Raids most of daylight hours, and shelling day and night. Peg & I got up at half past 5 and dressed in the drying-room as could have electric light on there as no windows. To conserve Peggy's food stocks I went to breakfast at P.G. before going (with tin hat and respirator) to tunnel. Peggy drove a truck or lorry where required after finishing her shift at 3pm. I admired her a lot for that.

16 Dec 1941

Mr Garton (Vivian Garton of Public Works Dept.) and W. Skinner and Mr Bendall – family friends – were in and out of the tunnel re their war work. One day Mr Garton appeared and said he'd got someone to see me – and there was Sid, in khaki shorts and tin helmet. I went into corridor and we sat on chair frames *((still no seats on them))* with his mate Cooper. He said he was feeling more confident now, and appeared completely recovered. Cooper had been in hospital with foot trouble. Of Mabel, Sid said 'You'll find her much older in the head.' *((Then both went off to war again.))* I gave Sid a note for Arthur in case he saw him.

The P. Grill was dark and tiffin generally soup, then some hash, and maybe a potato or macaroni or spaghetti; and tea. If no soup, there was generally salad. One day a delicious hot cake. Enjoyed the meals until those who fed at Cafe Wiseman started saying what they were having – whole oranges, and bread and jam in addition to other rations. But I was scared to change because it was a longer walk to Cafe Wiseman, and by

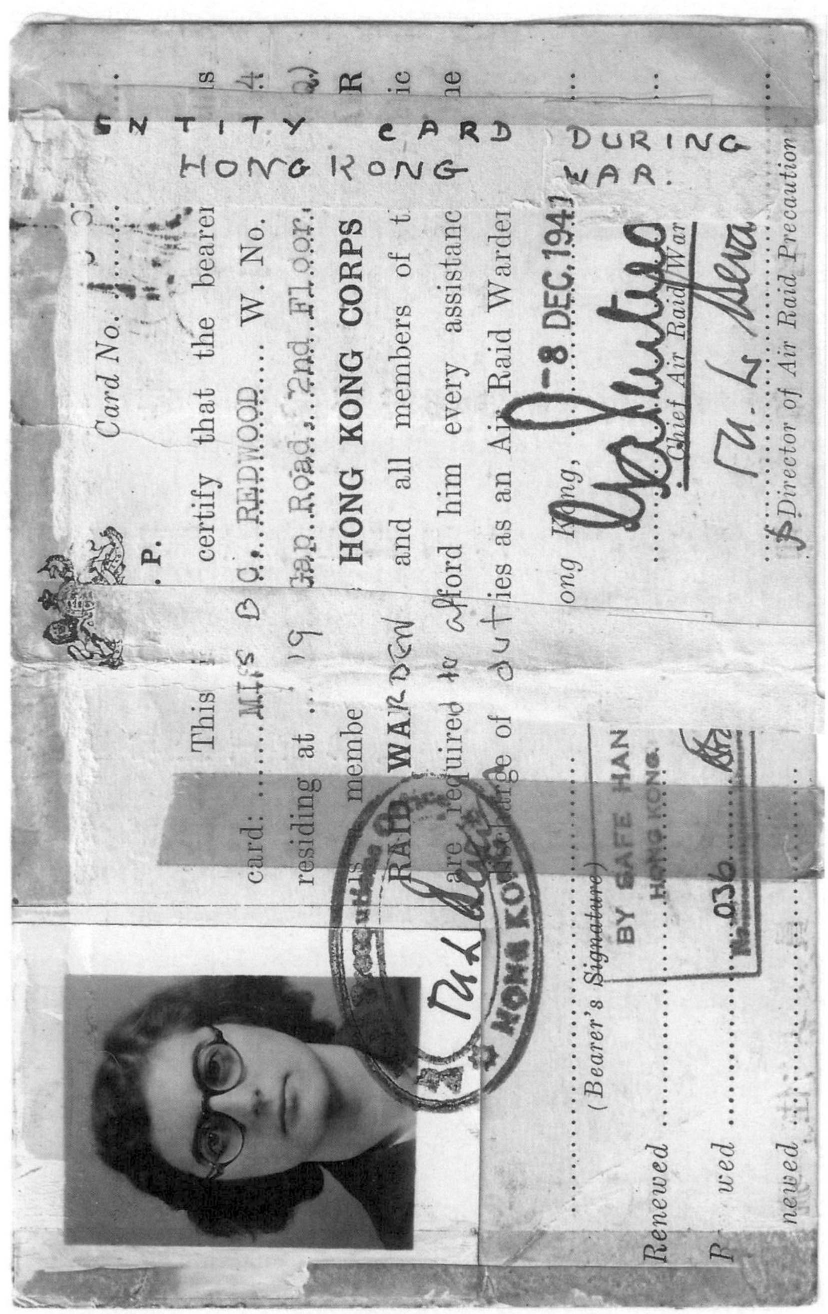

ENTITY CARD
HONG KONG DURING WAR.

Card No. ....

P.

This ... certify that the bearer ...s

card: ...MISS D.C. REDWOOD.... W. No. ...

residing at ...19 Gap Road, 2nd Floor, ...

memb... HONG KONG CORPS ...

RAID WARDEN and all members of t...

are required to afford him every assistanc...

...ge of duties as an Air Raid Warden

...ong Kong, -8 DEC 1941

Chief Air Raid War...

Director of Air Raid Precaution

(Bearer's Signature)

BY SAFE HAN...
HONG KONG
No. 036

Renewed ....

...wed ....

...newed ....

My ARP identity card

this time shells were bursting all over the place spasmodically. After eating at P.G. I usually went to see Olive in her office in Holland House.

One afternoon I arrived too late at P.G. for tiffin, so got a cup of tea at Hong Kong Hotel, then waited in a queue at Lane Crawfords, bought half a pound of bread, 2 oz butter, a jar of paste and a jar of jam. Had to carry the bread in my fist, no bags. Went to Olive's office for a knife. There an unknown lady gave me some lettuce with which I made a delicious sandwich.

17 Dec 1941

Met Olive, she said Mr. Cole had been killed at Aberdeen. *((Not Tony Cole of ARP staff, but George Cole)).*

On way back to Macdonnell Road, a great crater had been made directly across it. The only damage to Peggy's flat was a window pane broken, and the bathroom door broken off, but that was the end of the electric light and the water and telephone. Gas had been turned off previously when a fire threatened the gas mains.

At dusk Peg and I stood on verandah and watched the Japs shelling the Naval Dockyard – the flag was at half-mast for Mr Cole and others.

18 Dec 1941

Bombs fell in vicinity of the tunnel. The concussion made our hair go up on end and wave backwards and forwards. The CSO garages were burnt out or bombed. A lot of Indian policemen were injured and carried into the tunnel. I wished so much that I knew something about first aid, to see these great bleeding people groaning. All I could do was tear up a sheet someone produced into bandages. Bombing in the middle of Garden Road and Volunteer HQ as well.

((My colleague Barbara Budden in the tunnel was looking terrible as her father had phoned a little earlier saying he was on his way to the tunnel to see her, and she feared he had been caught in the bombing. But he hadn't. Sadly, he and his only son, Gilbert, both died as prisoners of war in Shamshuipo Camp.))

Uncle Sidney and I had a hectic time going back to Macdonnell Road in the evening. Shells were concentrated on the Garden Road district so we took shelter in a military post under the Lower Peak Tram Station for a while. Avoiding the road, we went up the steps to Macdonnell Road but they were in a blasted mess, sticky red clay all over the place. I was always scared of making that journey at dusk, and when Mum rang me (from Jockey Club Hospital) and said she'd feel happier if I didn't stay up at Macdonnell Road, I decided next day I would move back to Dina House, so I did.

19 Dec 1941

Japs started landing at North Point *((but we were given to understand that most of them had been mopped up.))* Heard rumours that Mabel *((with other VADs from Bowen Road Hospital))* had been sent to Stanley to nurse... was pretty worried, thinking of a 7-mile journey perhaps under fire.

20-22 Dec 1941

Paper said more landings had been made. Tales that Chinese planes had been engaging Jap planes over Kowloon.

I re-installed myself at Dina House, slept first night in room with Janet and Lillian since Mrs Pryde and Mrs Bebbington, who had moved in, were on night duty. Next day moved to large room with Mrs Hilda Hutchinson (who is expecting soon), Mrs Boulton (American), Edith Palmer from Shanghai, and Marjorie Cook and Edith and Ivy Batley (three Eurasians working with ARP). At night Mrs H. told us stories about the BBC where she had worked (telephonist); and Edith told us of her many travels.

Had dinner with Mr Murphy and Janet and Lillian at the Hong Kong Hotel. We were said to have sunk a cruiser off Stanley. Mrs. Boulton very nice, she wasn't in any of the essential services so wasn't eligible for meals at the Parisian Grill or Cafe Wiseman, so I used to buy bread and butter for her in Lane Crawford's – with her money.

No. 12,971 Saturday, December 20, 1941 One Penny

THE JAPS GO FORWARD ● BRITISH GARRISON ON INVADED HONGKONG ISLAND REPORTED TO BE MAKING LAST STAND AT VICTORIA PEAK, FORTIFIED PICNIC RESORT. PENANG ISLAND, MALAYA, EVACUATED; JAPS ADVANCE ON MAINLAND. ● RUSSIANS TAKE THREE MORE TOWNS (FRONT, THREATEN GERMAN FLANK A ● BRITISH IN LIBYA TAKE DERNA AIRFIEL AXIS FORCES IN PORT OF DER

HONGKONG GARRISON FIGHT TO THE LAST

'Final stand' at picnic mountain turned into a Gibraltar

HONGKONG, FIGHTING TO THE DEATH WITH SWARMS OF JAPANESE WHO LANDED YESTERDAY AT MANY POINTS ON THE ISLAND, REJECTED WITH SCORN A THIRD OFFER OF SURRENDER TERMS, AND THEN CAME SILENCE.

Late last night it was officially announced in London:—

"The report from Japanese sources that Hongkong has been in Japanese hands since this morning cannot be confirmed or denied, as no communication has been received from the colony since early this morning."

Berlin, quoting Tokyo reports, said the Japanese flag had been hoisted in the port of Hongkong, and that points of final British resistance were being broken.

Tokyo announced last night that the remaining defenders of the colony had withdrawn to Victoria Peak, the 1,800 ft. "picnic mountain" at the western end of the island. where they were putting up a last stand.

PENANG EVACUATED

From Malaya came news that Penang, the island oil and rubber port on the west coast, had been completely evacuated.

British forces battling on the mainland south of Penang have withdrawn to a new defence line south of the River Krian.

The main battle of the peninsula is now in Perak State, where a bold stand is possible

JAPS CLAIM A CAPITAL CITY

In messages from Kowloon, the Japanese claim to have "occupied Victoria, the capital of Hongkong, intact" . . . The city extends along the coast for about 5 miles . . . The harbour of Hongkong (Hongkong Roads) covers an area of 10 square miles.

21-22 Dec 1941

I went to Confession at French Mission building at top of Battery Path – a young Irish priest stopped me (and others passing) and asked if I was RC and would I like to go to Confession. Inside on ground floor a priest was hearing confessions. Because Holy Communion would not be given immediately, I left without receiving it. Olive and I had exchanged tin helmets on account of size difficulties. I now felt horribly conspicuous in a red steel one.

Marjorie Cook and I had one big row over water. There was none in the taps (Japs had turned reservoirs off). One day she ushered a coolie into our room carrying two kerosene tins full of water; she announced she was going to use it all herself. I called her a selfish bitch *((the first time I ever used that noun.))*

In the tunnel Peggy was always getting presents of chocolates etc. I was very jealous. Then one morning Mr Manning of ARP staff brought me one dozen 4 oz packets of Cadbury's milk chocolate – he said he had heaps in his firm's godown *((warehouse))*. I ate one on the spot, gave one each to Mrs Bebbington and Mrs Pryde in Dina House, put six aside to send to Mum. Got the six bars sent to Mum via Olive, who wouldn't have any of it herself.

23 Dec 1941

Sid phoned me at Dina House, saying he was on the first floor of Hong Kong Hotel (now a convalescent hospital); he had lost the tips of two fingers on left hand. I already knew that, as had had a note from Mabel telling me. I careered down to hotel and found Sid lying on a 'biscuit' *((a folding cushion bed))* on the floor *((with dozens of others))*. He looked a bit wild and woolly. He had seen Mabel that morning at the Military Hospital where he had been first taken. They had become engaged! Sid talked of marriage too, but I didn't seriously think anything could be done then. Over the past few months they had paid off some $50 at Windsor's Jewellers for an engagement ring. His finger stumps were paining him a lot, he lost them at Wanchai Gap.

I put my name down to help at hotel hospital after 3pm each day but the sister in charge said they had enough help so far. I felt superfluous at Sid's side, knowing he wanted Mabel all the time.

24 Dec 1941

Went to see Sid again. Olive and Topper came to see him just as I left.

25 Dec 1941

((Diary doesn't say anything about my working part of this day... an anxious time as we knew Japanese troops were advancing towards Central where we

were, and heard that our AA guns were to be set up outside the tunnel we were working in.))

Mr Bendall took photos outside the tunnel in morning of Mr Garton, Mr Skinner and me. *((These photos were developed and printed post-war, and one is on this book's cover.))*

Left work at 3pm. Spent Christmas Day with Sid at the hospital, sitting beside him on the floor. No question of going to Mass, duties sacrosanct now. While I was sitting there, Mrs Johnson, a friend who was helping the wounded, came over to us and said 'I have bad news for you – we've surrendered.' She was half-crying, and wouldn't look at us.

Sid shouted to his neighbour, 'Did you hear that? We've surrendered!' The news passed about quickly, and from the biscuits everywhere up popped bearded faces, because everyone naturally queried it, especially as shelling was still going on and planes overhead; and a news bulletin was circulating, giving heartening news about our defences. But then we heard confirmation of surrender, and still could hardly believe it. We'd all laughed so much at the Peace Mission that had come a few days earlier and been rejected.

Olive phoned me at the hotel hospital and told me to go back to Dina House, so I did, but not before going first to the P. Grill for a meal... had turkey but no dessert.

Back at Dina House, we all wondered what was going to happen to us. Mr Bevan said there was talk that we might be sent to barracks in Tsingtao.

In evening Mr C. Bailey came into our girls' room wearing a paper hat and asked me to go along to the men's room for a party. But the other girls weren't feeling like celebrating *((most of them were married women who didn't know where their fighting husbands were, or even if they were alive))* and I didn't want to spoil their mood, so said no thanks. But Mr Bailey came back again, paper hat askew, and gave me a bottle of eau de cologne from him and Tony Cole, so I went. Mrs Vi Evans was there, Mr Hyde Lay, Lillian Hope, Janet Broadbridge and Tony Cole. We had Xmas pudding *((heated on a kerosene stove))*, absolutely delicious, and chocolate and sweets; and played games.

((Mrs. Evans died during an operation in Stanley Camp. Mr Hyde Lay and his wife Betty were both killed in Stanley during an air raid by the Allies on 16th January 1945.))

26/27 Dec 1941

We weren't allowed out of Dina House. We had some tinned food and pooled it. Japanese officers moved peaceably into Dina House.

28/29 Dec 1941

Japs said we must move out. Someone among us suggested we move to some offices within their knowledge in Shell House. So all we ARP folk immediately did so, only a short walk from Dina House. We swept the floor and cleaned up, and saw some of the wounded soldiers on Hong Kong Hotel verandah on the opposite side of the road.

Jap planes were showing off against a blue sky, dropping leaflets. Some sort of Jap parade *((probably the Japanese forces' ceremonial entry into the city, some officers on horses.))*

After half an hour in Shell House, someone in authority came and we were told we had to go back to Dina House, and then go where we were sent. Did so. Soon after, we ladies were given a lift to Tai Koon Hotel, Des Voeux Road, next to Central Market. Men followed on foot. Separate cubicles, ladies on 2nd floor, men on fourth floor. More a brothel than a hotel.

((Cubicles were all in a line, along which ran a wide verandah looking out on to Des Voeux Road; wooden and glass partitions in between. Each cubicle had a large bed which took up most of the width, then a wash basin. Another line of cubicles backed on to the front row, so you could talk through the flimsy partitions to five immediate neighbours. Someone said the hotel was a brothel. I couldn't bring myself to undress, fearing some kind of contamination, so slept in my day clothes.))

A Japanese propaganda leaflet dropped on Hong Kong

We all pooled whatever tinned food we had, and clubbed together any money and bought vegetables, there was a kitchen on our floor. Desperately cold. We were allowed out, Tony escorted me to Hong Kong Hotel where I saw Olive who was billeted there, and Sid in hospital.

Mr Himsworth reported he had seen Mum at the Queen Mary Hospital and that she was OK. *((At that time I knew nothing of Mum's horrific experiences at the Jockey Club Hospital in which Japanese soldiers entered and raped some of the young nurses; this is told on the following pages, and in more detail in my mother's memoir 'It Was Like This...'))*

30th Dec 1941

Ah Ding *((our family amah))* appeared at the guarded front door of Tai Koon and asked for me. We were allowed to talk at the door.

She was very upset because our flat had been entered by the Japs who had taken mattresses and blankets, and my new red coat material (bought 7th Dec.) as a blanket. She had orders to leave our flat. She had found out that I was in Dina House by going to the ARP HQ in Happy Valley, and asking the Chinese ARP messengers who were still there.

31st Dec 1941 - 2nd Jan 1942

Amah came again and brought me a few of my clothes crammed into a rattan Hong Kong basket. She had ruffled her hair to make herself look like a peasant instead of an amah who was helping the defeated British.

Being New Year's Eve, we were not allowed out lest celebrations be made. Hill fires (charcoal) were wonderful over at Taimoshan *((across the harbour, beyond Kowloon))*.

((Charcoal fires were a common sight on the Kowloon hills. Without knowing much about them, I understood it was a thriving industry; they were deliberate fires to produce charcoal, which was used for cooking – I suppose on Chinese chatties, where you fed bits of fuel into the space beneath the earthenware containers. We had chatties, some makeshift, in camp and had to use twigs, grass etc., whatever we could find, to feed them.))

My mother's experiences at the Jockey Club wartime hospital

December 1941 – January 1942

by Mabel Winifred Redwood (my mother)

'Well, who's going to hang up their stockings tonight?' whispered my friend Connie as we crawled into our cold camp beds in the darkness in the war-time civilian casualty clearing hospital set up in the Hong Kong Jockey Club, in Happy Valley. Most of us were still wearing our grey Auxiliary Nursing Service uniforms, the niceties of washing and undressing at bedtime being things of the past in Hong Kong this Christmas Eve 1941.

The Japanese had attacked the colony three weeks earlier and were now swarming all over the island. Intermittent shellfire had become a familiar sound, together with that of planes roaring overhead and the thud of bombs. Bullets from nearby snipers' rifles made you think twice before you ventured to the lavatories which were across the open yard.

Connie's joke helped, for we felt the situation could hardly have been grimmer. We were a group of about 24 European women and Connie, an irrepressible Australian, auxiliary nurses. Our patients were Chinese and few of them spoke English. The military situation made it impossible for us to return to our homes after ward duty so we were compelled to live on the job. The water supply had failed; we were unable to wash either ourselves or the patients. Bedpans could not be emptied or cleaned.

Both the original kitchen and the makeshift one were out of action through shelling. The only way to cook was on native Chinese chatties.

The military post adjoining our hospital had been abandoned. We appeared to be cut off from our own people; our last visitor – a Methodist minister – had told us that there was heavy fighting some miles from us, but that our forces were holding the enemy. The oil installations about a mile beyond our position were in flames, as was a row of houses on a rise just opposite the Jockey Club. There was no telephone communication, so I was no longer in touch with my three daughters who were serving in other parts of the colony.

Earlier in the day trench mortars had been fired into our hospital, though by a miracle no one was hit. The patients were accommodated in beds in the betting hall which had no doors, only large entrances open to the weather (and the war). These entrances had been partially sandbagged, but some of the mortars cleared the sandbags and exploded on the concrete floor within.

Lack of manpower for removal and burial of bodies of dead patients meant they had to be piled up in the outside garages, spreading putrefaction. Hungry, dirty, weary, frightened and apprehensive, when we came off day duty we tried to settle for the night.

It was only when Connie spoke that we remembered it was Christmas Eve. For a few minutes there was an exchange of banter on the subject, then out of sheer exhaustion, we slept. Our camp beds had been crammed side by side in the betting booth, separated from the patients by a half-swing door.

Machine-gun fire woke us up suddenly. It was alarmingly near. Everyone sat up. The firing continued and seemed to be getting nearer. We began to see the reflection of the flashes in the high windows which faced the road; there were bursts of firing on the other side of us and we realised with horror that fighting was going on all around us. Then came a change in the tempo of the firing, and it dawned on us that the Japanese were fighting their way toward us, and our men were being driven back towards the city, so here we were, helpless, between the lines, right in the path of the advancing enemy. We tensed in our beds in the darkness, expecting a sudden onslaught on ourselves and the patients. We could hardly hope for survival now.

Gradually, we realised that the firing was receding in the direction of the city. We had been by-passed. All we could think of now was how our dear ones would fare with full-scale battle raging in the crowded streets. That night dragged interminably. I thought of last Christmas when we entertained the girls' boyfriends and several lonely husbands of evacuated wives to dinner. Although there was no chance of sleep, there was no desire for conversation. I think we were all afraid to talk for fear of triggering the emotions of the more nervous (not that any of us felt very brave).

Morning came at last, and we rose with grim set faces, knowing without doubt that this Christmas Day was going to be as none other had ever been. Those of us on morning duty walked to the sandbagged entrance to take a few breaths of fresh air. A mist hung over the racecourse, adding an air of unreality to this period of waiting to see what happened next.

Dr J. Selby, a Scottish doctor who had joined us from an evacuated post the previous day, appeared from the yard. 'Well, that's that,' he said. He had persuaded some of the Chinese ward boys to help him dig shallow graves on the racecourse to dispose of the bodies in the garage. It was a great comfort to us nurses to have a European man around – the only other was Tom, a soldier casualty who had never been collected by the Royal Army Medical Corps. Our thought now was that the Japanese would take over the hospital before long. Realising that things might go badly for Tom and ourselves if the Japanese came and found a soldier in a civilian hospital, we hurriedly pulled his uniform from beneath his bed and stuffed it down behind a huge stack of wooden chairs at one end of the building. Luckily, his rifle and hand grenades had been handed over to the military post which had still been functioning next door when Tom was brought in to us.

With the doctor, we considered our water problem. He suggested we collect some in cans from the water in the base of a large fountain in the cemetery across the road, as this water could at least be used for washing. Before we could do this, an Anglo-Indian doctor, well known in the colony, came into the ward. His hands were tied behind his back and he was propelled forward by several Japanese soldiers who held a rope attached to his hands. The party advanced towards us. The soldiers were draped in netting with greenery stuck in the mesh as camouflage. With bayonets and rifles at the ready, they halted. One, holding a revolver, stepped forward.

Dr Selby placed himself in front of us and faced the soldier, who gazed around at the patients and said 'Oh, hospital? You doctor?'

'Yes.'

Motioning to him to put his hands up, the Japanese went through all Dr Selby's pockets, scanning letters and papers then throwing everything to the floor. Next, he directed the doctor over to the table in the centre of the ward where the hospital records were kept – although we had long since given up writing them. He scrutinised each sheet in turn, casting them to the floor as he finished with them. He then carried on a subdued conversation with the doctor in stilted English.

Meanwhile, we nurses just stood where we were, the soldiers regarding us with curious toothy grins. A more unprepossessing lot one could not imagine – dirty, unkempt and unshaven. I suppose their condition was excusable as they had been fighting for days; no doubt we ourselves didn't look any too spruce by normal standards.

Dr Selby, still covered by the officer's revolver, related to us what he had been told: we were now prisoners of the Japanese and must not try to leave the building; we must remain here and look after the sick people, and do as we were told.

'I'm not able to stay with you,' he ended, 'but have courage and carry on with your duties.'

Matron reminded him of the water difficulty before he was led away, so he asked the Japanese for permission for us to go to the cemetery to get some. Permission was given, so gathering up every available pail and jug, several of us hurried through the main entrance. Here we encountered two Japanese sentries who lunged at us with fixed bayonets and halted us.

One brave nurse dangled her bucket aloft and said 'We want to get water – plenty sick people.' The bucket did not impress the soldier, but her rings did: making her drop the bucket, one relieved her of her rings and a gold wristwatch. Both then systematically inspected us all and demanded our valuables, chanting 'Gold for Japan.' Girls with platinum rings were lucky as the sentries did not want them, nor did they want my chromium watch, but I had to hand over my wedding ring; they also demanded Will's ring which I had worn ever since his death. I pretended it was too tight to get off, but a bayonet pointed uncomfortably near my stomach quickly made me change my mind. Pocketing their spoils, the men motioned us to go and get the water.

We crossed the road to the cemetery gate. It was locked, so the younger nurses started to climb over it. Immediately bullets began to fly from the direction of the cemetery, zipping against the wall of the hospital behind us. Evidently there were snipers among the tombstones up in the terraces in the cemetery. We all dashed back to the hospital entrance for shelter, greeted with great hilarity by the sentries who had been watching. Possibly whoever was doing the shooting only meant to scare us, as had they wanted they could have picked us all off very easily. Anyway, we decided that water would have to remain a problem a little longer.

Back in the hospital the atmosphere was very tense now that Dr Selby had been taken away. Every so often little groups of Japanese soldiers would come and just gape at us. At Matron's direction, we sat or stood around the table in the centre of the ward and busied ourselves tearing up sheets and mattress covers into bandage lengths and rolling them. Any idea of getting together a meal for ourselves or the patients seemed out of the question. We hardly dared speak to each other for fear of giving way.

Presently in trooped a large party of very scruffy soldiers, armed to the teeth and looking very pleased with themselves. They stood around and surveyed us all, conversing animatedly. The strain for us was horrible. At last they moved off through the building. Some time later, one of the few remaining Chinese ward boys came running in to say that soldiers were raping the young Chinese girls belonging to the St John Ambulance Brigade who had sought refuge with us several days earlier. There was nothing we could do except to try and comfort the poor girls when they came in to us, crying their hearts out and badly shocked.

So Christmas Day wore on, with intermittent visits from small groups of soldiers who watched us curiously. Excepting for occasional attention to some pain-racked patient, there was little we could do but continue the bandage-rolling. The materials to hand were almost all used up so we had to go slow on the job in order to keep ourselves and our minds occupied. Soft conversation gradually resumed among us. Connie was making a stock of swabs with the only remaining roll of cotton wool. When the roll was finished, she painstakingly re-rolled the swabs over and over again.

'They'll make good hand grenades if I roll these things much more,' she muttered.

When a heavily-armed party of soldiers drifted in, she whispered, 'Just look at them! They've got everything on but the kitchen sink.'

One of this new mob appeared to be drunk and was waving his revolver in an alarming manner. He leaned over the table between two nurses and jabbered Japanese to them in maudlin tones. Some of his companions tried to coax him away from us, but this seemed to anger him. Just then, Dr Selby re-appeared, escorted by an armed guard. He was allowed to speak to us for a moment.

'Keep your chins up,' he said, looking drawn and anxious.

The drunken soldier rushed over to him, still brandishing the revolver; then, taking the doctor's hand and resting his other hand with the gun on the doctor's shoulder, he proceeded to dance with him, grinning the while. Dr Selby carefully waltzed him away from us up to the far end of the ward. Here stood a trolley with the usual hospital paraphernalia. This seemed to interest the soldier, who stopped to investigate. He then made signs on his wrist with his forefinger to indicate that he wanted an injection. To satisfy him, Dr Selby quickly took a syringe and gave him an injection of what, we did not know, but he seemed well pleased with himself and went off quietly with his companions. Our doctor was led away again.

We had noticed that the Japanese were very friendly towards two of our Chinese patients – shell victims who were only slightly injured. The soldiers brought them cigarettes and biscuits, and presented them with khaki drill caps such as they themselves wore. These two patients proudly donned them, and though in bed, wore them from then on. We considered them to be fifth columnists.

We were very wary of another patient from the moment he was first brought in to the hospital. He looked more Japanese than Chinese, and lay on his bed, smoking continuously, assuring us in perfect English that he had influential friends who would get him taken elsewhere for medical attention. He refused to put on hospital clothing and insisted on wearing his excellent quality overcoat all the time. Immediately the Japanese walked into the hospital, he was on very good terms with them, and conversed freely with them in Japanese.

Our soldier Tom had been admitted before all three of these suspect fifth columnists, so we hoped they did not know he was a British soldier. So fearful were we that he would be discovered that we smothered him with blankets and warned him not to show his face. Luckily he was very dark-haired, but we felt very nervous on his behalf every time soldiers sauntered into the ward.

Reluctant as we were to move about unnecessarily in the presence of our captors, in the early afternoon hunger drove us to rustle up some kind of a meal – our first that day. A few tins of meat and beans were opened and shared around. A handful of food was passed under the blankets to Tom, and some water in a feeding cup. No one's hunger was satisfied as the portions were meagre.

The afternoon dragged on. We resumed bandage re-rolling, feeling a compulsion to appear busy whenever soldiers passed through, so kept dropping the bandages to have the excuse to re-roll them. The heavy shelling had stopped, although planes were still around. There was a sense of the whole world standing, waiting, for we knew not what.

In the middle of the afternoon there sounded what we thought was a long-drawn roll of thunder, followed by other rumbles. This seemed as strange as everything else that was happening to us, for the bright sunshiny weather was anything but thundery. What a good thing for our taut nerves that we never dreamed the truth: our own guns were being destroyed before surrender to the enemy.

Came the evening, and although no thoughts were voiced, the strained looks on our faces spoke of the dread of the night hours. We made the patients as comfortable as possible, and when the night staff took over, the rest of us retired into the unlit sleeping booth.

Many of the younger girls, nervous of the way the soldiers had eyed them during the day, made up beds for themselves by spreading blankets underneath the counters. Some even crawled beneath the low-slung camp beds with blankets, prepared to spend the night there, despite the concrete floor beneath. Presently we heard ribald singing from the next enclosure – our captors were making merry. We lay listening and wondering, but never guessing that the Japanese were celebrating the surrender of our forces. Suddenly the beam of a powerful torch appeared at the ward entrance. We could see it from where we lay because our booth had only half-swing doors. A group of soldiers shone their way to the beds where the two coolie fifth columnists lay. There was much jocular conversation among them all, then the torch flashed around our booth, and we huddled beneath our blankets.

'Get up, all,' commanded one of the soldiers. Two carried bayonets and rifles, the others were unarmed. We scrambled up as best we could – getting out from a camp bed by way of the foot is not something one can do with dignity – and stood in a line there. The girls on the floor kept perfectly still, hoping not to be noticed. The Japanese pushed their way along the narrow gap between us and the tables, scrutinising each of us in turn as they shone the light in our faces. It was a terrible ordeal. One of my near neighbours was an attractive continental widow; her eyes flashed defiance, she looked like a wild animal at bay, and I prayed she would do nothing to anger these uncouth men, as I felt sure she would claw at them if they made any advances to her, but they passed her by – she was probably not young enough for them.

Four of the younger nurses were selected to accompany the soldiers back to their quarters, with the threat: 'Go Jap – no come, kill all!' They went off with the terrified, sobbing girls, commanding the rest of us 'Sleep!' We got miserably back into our beds, not daring to talk, stunned as we realised how completely we were at our captors' mercy.

At length the poor girls came running back in great distress. Before we could try to comfort them, the soldiers returned. This time they did not make us all get up, but just went from bed to bed shining the torch on each occupant. Then they flashed the torches under the counters and saw the girls huddled there and ordered them out. Again they made a selection, and with the same threat as before, forced them to go off with them; none dared refuse lest we should all be slaughtered.

Presently I felt a movement under my bed, and a voice whispered, 'Can I get in with you? I'm so cold.' There was really no room but the owner of the voice was very small and thin and managed to squeeze in beside me. She said her name was Pat; she was a school teacher who had joined us halfway through the battle when her post was evacuated. I only knew her by sight.

'Don't let them get me,' she pleaded.

How I could stop them, I could not think. I said if the soldiers came again, she must wriggle right down in the bed and keep very close to me; perhaps with my 170 pounds bulk she might not be noticeable, especially as I had my heavy coat on top of the blankets. Pat did not wait for the next visitation, she dived down right away and I was afraid she would suffocate. She was not discovered when the soldiers returned for more victims, nor were any of the girls hiding beneath the beds discovered – the beds being so low and so tightly jammed together that there was not even space for the soldiers to get down and look.

A young married woman became hysterical as she was taken away, and fainted in the ward. The soldier dragged her back to her bed. One stalwart nurse bravely snatched the torch from the soldier to search the medical trolley for something to revive her, and motioned to the soldier to bring a large bottle of boracic lotion; he obediently did so, and using this in lieu of water we managed to bring the girl round. The soldier seemed rather worried by this turn of events, and as soon as he got his torch back, departed alone.

Again we waited for the return of the latest victims. It was harrowing for us older women. We could only witness their distress without being able to lift a finger to help them; those like me who had daughters elsewhere in the colony could only hope and pray they were not being treated in the same way. The night seemed endless, but at last things quietened down, the singing ceased and, we dared to hope, the visitations.

'Do you think they'll come again?' whispered Pat.

'No, I should think they've settled down for the night,' I said hopefully.

Pat began to get up, saying 'I can't stay here.' Thinking she meant to crawl back beneath my bed, I tried to persuade her to spend what was left of the night in the warm with me, but she insisted on clambering out and disappeared in the darkness.

Morning came, but glad as we were to see daylight once more, we faced it with terrible misgivings, knowing now what to expect from the enemy. Several soldiers walked through the ward, all seeming very jubilant. Through the gaps in the sandbags at the entrance facing the racecourse, we could see numbers of small ponies lined up on the grass, so we realised the Japanese had landed quite freely in large numbers; the fact that they could transport not only themselves, but also their ponies, seemed ominous, yet although we could hear no gunfire, it still did not dawn on us that they were now in complete possession of the colony.

Hollow-eyed and drawn, we went our rounds as usual, doling out sips of precious water and giving what ease we could to the patients. Connie had some surprising news about Pat, my bedfellow: it seemed she had borrowed a spare Chinese suit from Connie's amah who had joined us for safety a few days earlier; wearing this, she had escaped from the hospital during the night.

It was another trying morning, each of us trying to keep occupied doing nothing in particular; the only job we could do was to take the used bedpans out to the lavatories to empty (without flushing as there was no water) without fear of being shelled as heretofore.

Towards mid-day, for the sake of something to do, several of us went into the booth where the remains of the bed linen was stored, and began – quite unnecessarily – to re-stack it. In rushed one of our girls who had been raped during the night, crying, 'Hide me, quickly!'

Before we could do so, a dishevelled soldier ran in and grabbed her, saying 'Go Jap.' She tried to cling to me, crying piteously. I motioned to the soldier to release her, saying, 'No can, plenty work to do.' But he dragged her away, and they were halfway down the ward when there was a sudden shout from the entrance. He let go of the girl and dashed away, and she ran back to us. Then we saw why – a group of officials were coming into the ward. We recognised, with overwhelming relief, our Director of Medical Services, Dr Selwyn-Clarke, with another European and two Japanese officers. They went over to our Matron to whom the DMS introduced the Japanese who bowed politely. One of them then announced that the war was over; we were all friends now, etc. etc.

Matron was not interested in flowery speeches. Calmly addressing herself to the DMS, she asked that we be removed from the hospital forthwith. The DMS said there had been fantastic tales of the happenings here from some hysterical woman, and they had come to investigate. Matron told him there was no fantasy about what had happened: the behaviour of the soldiers towards the nurses had been appalling and we must not be allowed to spend another night in the place. The DMS said he had already acted on the girl's report, having called on the Japanese commandant who had said if we could identify the men who had robbed us of rings and watches they would be duly punished. (What a hope – all the soldiers looked alike to us.)

By now, we realised that Pat's brave escape to report our plight to officialdom was the reason for our deliverance from more horrors. How relieved we were to know that she herself had come to no harm. The officials agreed that the whole post should be evacuated: we nurses to the Queen Mary Hospital, the patients to be distributed among two other hospitals. We were to accompany the patients and see them into their new places on our way to the Queen Mary.

The DMS took away as many of the shocked rape victims as he could cram into his car, and the rest of us prepared ourselves and the patients for evacuation. Tom, the soldier patient, was still on our minds. Even though the war was now over, the Japanese were the victors and we could not be sure how they would react if he were to be discovered in a civilian hospital. Matron had the brilliant idea of disguising him as a European female patient who could therefore come with us to the Queen Mary. She bandaged his head, then over the bandage tied a piece of sheet that looked like a mob cap.

Around three in the afternoon, lorries arrived and off we went. The route out of Happy Valley ran past our flat in Gap Road. There were Japanese soldiers on our verandah. We could not hold back the tears at the sight of the devastation of so many familiar places. Detachments of Japanese soldiers were everywhere; it was with great relief that we saw the Queen Mary Hospital towering ahead, and knew we would soon be among our own people.

Stale and unwashed for days, we were dying for a bath, or even a wash, but gratefully sat down first for some tea that awaited us. The water supply had been restored here, so we all had a glorious bath. We were accommodated, four to a room, in the Sisters' Quarters adjacent to the hospital, and tumbled thankfully into bed, to drop into our first real sleep for weeks.

We were given the next day off to recuperate and, surprisingly, were told that since hostilities were over, any of us who were able to do so could return to our homes and connect up with our families. Since few of us knew if our homes still existed, nor the whereabouts of our families, and in any case had no transport, the last thing we wanted to do was leave the security of the hospital after all we had been through, so we all stayed to continue nursing.

We spent the free day roaming about the quarters, asking everyone we met for news of relatives and friends. There was no way of finding out anything definite, but I did meet people who had seen both Olive and Barbara recently with their respective units. Mabel, as far as I knew, was still at the Military Hospital – I prayed so, as there was talk that during the war some of the VADs had been sent to augment staff in a hospital at Stanley where there had been terrible happenings – many soldier patients and three VADs murdered.

We found out how Pat had fared after she left us on Christmas night. Almost invisible in the amah's black jacket and trousers, she had dodged across the road to the cemetery, the terraces of which extend up the hillside to the main road. Using the tombstones as cover, she safely reached the road, then walked nearly two miles to the Military Hospital which she reached, exhausted, in the early hours of the morning. She managed to convince the British sentry at the entrance that despite her disguise she was English; she was taken to the medical official there to whom she poured out the story of our plight. He took immediate steps to get the information to the DMS who contacted the Japanese commandant, with the result that we were saved from another harrowing night.

Once back on duty in wards full of war casualties as well as civilians, our days were well filled, as many members of the Chinese staff had left to fend for their families in this difficult situation. Tom, no longer disguised as a female, was in a ward with some of his buddies at last.

In addition to anxiety about relatives and friends, there was the ever-present question – what will the Japanese do with us now? Our soldiers seemed resigned to being shipped off to Japan as prisoners of war, but we knew of no precedent for the treatment of several hundreds of civilian prisoners. The Japanese were in and out of the hospital all day long making inspections, the officers clanking around in huge brown leather boots and trailing swords, some of which were fitted with a small wheel for ease of progress.

I fell ill and had a few days as a patient myself. When I returned to duty, many of the badly wounded were greatly improved. Many of the casualties were Canadians, pathetically young, some having lied about their ages in order to join up. They had had little training before arriving in Hong Kong, only three weeks before the Japanese attacked. The brief war had taken a terrible toll on their ranks.

As transport began moving a little, news began to trickle in of relatives and friends. The driver of a lorry from the Military Hospital brought me first-hand news of Mabel: she was safe and well. Her fiance Sidney was at that hospital, having lost the tops of two fingers. From another visitor I learned that Olive and Barbara were housed separately in small Chinese hotels in the city with their units.

Rumours about our future came and went, but one gained ground: all civilian and service personnel were to be interned, civilians in Stanley, and combatants to barracks in Kowloon, though we had no idea when this would take place. In the event the Japanese gave us in the hospital one day's notice. On January 19th 1942 they told us nurses to have all naval and military patients ready for removal – the bedfast to the Military Hospital, the convalescent to Shamshuipo Barracks, Kowloon; we civilians were to go to Stanley the day after.

Most of the servicemen had no clothes other than hospital pyjamas. Their uniforms were still where they had been piled when taken off them. No one had had the chance to wash and cleanse them during the fighting, and now they were only fit for burning. We managed to rig the convalescent out with dressing-gowns, but there were not enough slippers to go round, so many men had to go barefoot.

The sick patients were moved on stretchers handled by coolies under Japanese supervision. One young sailor had a terrible arm injury on which he had an aeroplane splint, and we always had to handle him very gently. 'Don't let them touch me,' he begged. When his turn came, I tried to support the splinted arm as the coolies went to lift him from bed to stretcher. The Japanese officer in attendance motioned the coolies aside, then by signs indicated that he and I would help to lift him. Never will I forget how tenderly he handled that patient.

The patients away, we could now think of our own departure. Internment was an unknown state to us all, and we could not imagine what our living conditions would be like, but instinct told us to take with us everything we could possibly carry. The regular staff who lived in adjacent quarters were able to select their wardrobes and chattels, but we auxiliaries had only the clothes we stood up in and a small suitcase apiece. We were delighted then when, once they had finished their packing, the Sisters told us to help ourselves to anything we fancied that was left in their rooms.

After living in dingy grey uniforms for so long, it was a real joy to handle nice clothes. In no time the Sisters' quarters resembled a dress store during a bargain sale, all of us clutching our newly acquired possessions and searching for more – and all free! It was wonderful for morale. We were also allowed to raid the baggage room and take any of the remaining cases and baskets in which to carry off our spoils.

Matron decided we should take with us some spare mattresses from the storeroom, in case there were not enough beds to go round in Stanley. Since the store room was on the seventh floor and the lift out of action, the only way to get the mattresses downstairs was to slide them one by one down the stairs from floor to floor; two girls were stationed on every landing (lit only by hurricane lamps) to turn the mattresses around and start them down the next flight. It was a back-breaking job, but we felt well pleased when a goodly number were piled on the ground floor ready for internment with us. Alas, Matron had overlooked the fact that she was no longer in sole charge of the hospital; next morning, when the Japanese authorities saw what we had done, they refused to allow us to take the mattresses away – thank goodness they did not make us return them to the store room!

We rushed around that morning, carrying baskets of food stocks and medicines intended for the future internment camp hospital, also baskets of fresh vegetables from the hospital gardens, and of course our own belongings. Matron handed us each a few tins of food and some cutlery. How we regretted later that we had not helped ourselves more liberally to the useful things lying around! Looting was not part of our make-up, otherwise we would all have gone into camp better equipped with the little everyday things which we didn't miss until we found ourselves without them. I picked up an alarm clock and a small teapot as I went through the kitchen on my way out of the hospital, and both items proved their worth in due course.

When lorries arrived, we clambered aboard, dragging our luggage on as best we could. There followed the usual long wait associated with official arrangements all over the world. Someone had the excellent idea of using up all the remaining perishable foodstuffs in the kitchen, so while we sat perched on our luggage, we were handed thick cheese sandwiches, the hot mid-day sun (even in January) melting the butter. When and where we would get our next meal was beyond conjecture, so every mouthful was savoured.

After an hour or so the sun on our bare heads became too much for us, so two of the Sisters went back to their quarters and collected all the hats and umbrellas they could find and distributed them amongst us. I got a tricky little number in black velour with a broad satin bow.

At 2.30pm some Japanese officers arrived and ordered us all off the lorries while our baggage was inspected. A couple of soldiers mounted each lorry, and to our exasperation tumbled everything out of the cases and rummaged through our belongings. Containers that were roped or secured in any way soon yielded to a strong knife. They threw off such articles as rattan and other pieces of furniture which some Sisters had hopefully loaded, then directed us on to the lorries again to bundle our things back in the cases as best we could.

At last we were off, round the familiar coastal roads, but the picture postcard scenery was ignored, for the Japanese driver occupied all our attention with his erratic driving. At times we feared we might be swept off the lorry by overhanging branches of trees at the roadside. My velour hat blew off, and the last I saw of it, it was being fought over by a couple of small Chinese urchins.

The Japanese flag was well in evidence at most of the wayside stalls and dwellings we passed – more a matter of expediency than disloyalty, we thought, beginning to recognise that our lives would no longer be our own, but regulated to whatever pattern our captors dictated. There was little conversation among us on the five-mile journey, owing to the presence of a Japanese guard who might have understood a little English. Now, as we passed the grim gates of Stanley Gaol (and how thankful we felt that we were not taken through them as we had feared), one of the girls whispered, 'What now?'

Connie whispered back: 'Cheer up, girls! Whatever happens, it's only for three months. Remember Winston said so.'

Three months did not sound so bad, but if at that moment we had been given the power to see not three months, but more than three years stretching before us, we just could not have borne it.

P.S. The nurse called 'Pat' was actually Marie Paterson. I don't know if she ever received official recognition of her bravery. She certainly deserved it.

My sister's VAD days

December 1941 – June 1942

by Mabel Redwood (my sister)

I was a young 18 when the Japs attacked Hong Kong, living with my mother and two elder sisters Olive and Barbara in a flat in Gap Road, Happy Valley.

I was working as a shorthand typist at Army HQ, though my real ambition was to train as a nurse. My mother had made enquiries about this training two years earlier, but it seemed that no facilities were available in Hong Kong for girls of my age to start this. I had a boyfriend, Sid Hale, who was the pianist and clarinettist in the Royal Scots Band.

Sid and I had gone to lunch at the Dairy Farm shop in Central on Sunday 7th December 1941, and we had just about finished eating when somebody came in, called for silence, and said that any Army or Navy personnel should return to units immediately. Sid went to find a phone; when he came back he said, 'I've got to go to Lowu' (in the New Territories, where the Royal Scots were camping), 'so I must get to Lai Chi Kok where there will be transport.' I went off with him.

We crossed to Kowloon on the ferry, where Sid met up with quite a lot of Army people, but no one seemed to know what was going on. Neither did we. We took a bus to Lai Chi Kok, Sid got on some Army transport, and I came back home.

The following morning, Barbs, who worked at ARP HQ very near our flat, was called to the office by messenger at 7.30am, and Mum and Olive and I were having breakfast when we heard planes come over. We went and stood on the verandah and saw what looked like planes dropping bombs. We still thought it was a practice!

I decided I had better go to work, took my purse and went to the bus stop opposite the Jockey Club where I always caught the bus, and waited. A couple of other people who normally got that bus with me every morning were also waiting, including Captain Ebbage who lived in the same block of flats as we did and also worked at Army HQ. No bus came.

Captain Ebbage said he was going to walk to work, so he and I and one other person set off together, walking right through Wanchai, past all the coffin shops. I can't remember there being any talk of actual war on the way, but when planes came over we rushed for the first building we could find – inside the Army gate guarded by a sentry.

Captain Ebbage was in uniform, and I had my army pass so we were allowed in and waited in the nearest building. By this time, from the conversations going on around us and the general excitement, we realised this really was an air attack. Also we saw that our shelter was an ammunition store, so we shot out as soon as the All Clear sounded.

As I passed the barracks there were all sorts and signs of war activity – troops all over the place waiting for transport. When I got to Army HQ I was told I could not go in. All the bigwigs had gone down to Battle HQ and females were not allowed there. We'd known this beforehand – us four girls who worked at Army HQ – Peggie Scotcher, Joan Sanh, Virginia Beaumont and me – but no plans had been made for what we should do instead. Here I met Joan and Virginia, and we decided to go to the nearby Colonial Secretary's Office and offer our services there, which we did, and we were given some typing to do.

When it came time to go home, with the bombing that had been going on I was wondering what to do with no buses running, as I didn't fancy walking through Wanchai on my own. Virginia suggested I go to the International Club in Central with her as she lodged there with other unattached females, so I marched off with her, although I had no overnight kit with me and never did get back to our flat.

Bowen Road Military Hospital

On the Wednesday morning before I left the Club for the C.S.O., I had a phone call from Mum to tell me Sid had been wounded and was in the Military Hospital (BMH) on Bowen Road. I simply decided I wasn't going to work, I was just going to see Sid. Off I went, no transport. The previous day I had met Jimmy Bendall, a family friend, and he asked me if I had any money. 'Not much,' I said, so he gave me $15, saying, 'You can pay me back later.' I never did!

I'd never before been to the Bowen Road Hospital, but I knew the Peak Tram Station, so I walked up Garden Road to the lower terminus – but no trams seemed to be running. A series of steps went up beside the tram lines, so I ran up these, scrambled across the rails and started along the road to the hospital.

The Japanese were shelling, and it seemed to me that they were concentrating on me! I couldn't see where the shells were landing; as soon as I heard one crashing, I would run along the road a bit, then hide behind something, then run a bit further. I was absolutely petrified until I realised they were shelling very much higher than Bowen Road.

At the hospital I finally located Sid, the only patient in a multi-bedded ward; he must have been one of the very first casualties. I stayed and talked to him all day. He'd got a bullet through his shoulder and was heavily bandaged, though didn't seem too bad; he was more shocked than anything, and worried because he wasn't out fighting and all his friends were.

I become a nurse

I decided I'd better get back to the Club before it got dark. On the way downstairs I met the Matron, who called out, 'Girl, what are you doing? Go and get your uniform on at once!'

'I'm not one of your nurses,' I said, 'but I'd like to be.'

She said, 'We can use every pair of hands we can get,' so I decided I'd be a nurse right on the spot.

Incidentally, after the evacuation in 1940, one of the stipulations made so I could remain in the colony was that I must join one of the voluntary nursing units, starting by learning First Aid. Well, I did that course, took the exam., and failed, not being the exam. type. I didn't tell anyone at the hospital this!

I walked back to the Club, stayed the night there, then went off with my $15 to try to buy a couple of aprons, but couldn't find any; then to a chemist to get toothpaste, tooth brush, soap etc. and off I went to Bowen Road Hospital to be a nurse. I didn't see anything of my mother (who was an Auxiliary Nurse in the wartime hospital in the Jockey Club building in Happy Valley) or of my sisters Olive, working with Food Control, and Barbs with ARP.

We VADs were billeted in a big old house across the road from the BMH. We worked from dark in the early morning until dark at night, there was so much to do. I was in my element – a nurse at last!

The most junior VAD, with no training, I was put on the ward with the most injured patients; it was on the ground floor, the only ward that had been gas-protected and completely blacked out. Because these men could not be moved to safety during air raids, there was an extra mattress beneath every bed. During raids, we lifted these and propped them over the patients – the head of the bed kept the mattress off their faces; then we went under the beds. It was terrifying at first, then we realised that the Japs weren't using very large bombs.

Sid was soon discharged from hospital and went off to rejoin the Royal Scots.

One evening a couple of bombs went through the roof of the third (top) floor but the wards on the two upper floors were empty then, as at night those patients slept beneath the hospital (in space mainly used as a store). This underground part wasn't very high – you couldn't stand up there. You bent your head to go along; in some places you had to crouch down, in others you had to go on your hands and knees.

When bombing was particularly heavy late one night, Matron decided to move us nurses then and there from our house into these underground cellars; lying down to sleep, our faces were only about 18 inches beneath the concrete ceiling – not very comfortable. A few days later, we were given better accommodation in a building linked to the hospital by a small bridge, although this had been bombed and was useless.

I remember that fellow Norman Leith (mentioned in 'The Lasting Honour' by Oliver Lindsay). He came into the hospital in such a bad way – he had this gash from ear to ear, I've never seen such a wound as that in all my life. Then there was a young Canadian who came in with worms in his face; he looked about 15 years old, but must have been a bit older than that.

Dear old Mrs Groundwater looked after us VADs, she didn't work in the wards, but generally mothered us.

Another VAD was Mrs Simon White, whose husband was a colonel in the Army. Apart from uniforms, I had no clothing of my own except what I was wearing when I went to work the day the war started. Nan Grady and I used to share her clothes. A lot of the nurses used to wear slacks when off duty. As I had none, one day Mrs White kindly presented me with a beautiful pair of pale blue slacks. I can't remember what I wore on top – something else someone gave me, no doubt.

I acquired a pair of much-prized scissors from the orderly in the hospital store where I used to be sent to collect dressings etc. He was married and was always showing me pictures of his wife and children. I tied a piece of bandage on my belt and hung the scissors on it. When I was taking temperatures, I would shake the thermometer – and the number of times I hit it against the scissors and broke it… I had to confess to Sister the first few times and was sent to get another; then I reached the stage where I didn't dare tell Sister I'd broken yet another, but the store man kept me supplied whenever necessary.

One day he gave me a bit of material, the stuff you line curtains with. In the store room there was also a sewing machine which he used to mend sheets etc., so with the material I made myself another pair of slacks. They weren't very professional – I didn't have pattern, just used my blue ones as a guide. When Mrs White saw the finished product she said I no longer needed hers and asked for them back, alas!

In our busy life no one had time for such a luxury as a bath, and there were so many of us nurses that we just tried to give ourselves a lick and a promise, but one afternoon a few days before Christmas I was given time off so decided to take a bath. The water wasn't very hot but just as I was about to step into it, a VAD called to me, saying, 'Mabel, your boy-friend's back.'

I immediately abandoned the bath, dressed swiftly and rushed along to the casualty ward, and there was poor old Sid again, lying on a stretcher, the tops of two fingers shot off, in an awful mess, blood everywhere. Everything was so chaotic that it didn't matter at all that I wasn't a trained casualty nurse – I joined the other nurses in cleaning him up before he was taken to the operating theatre. A few days later, he was sent to the convalescent ward opened in the Hong Kong Hotel.

We were now told not to wear our uniforms because the Japs were on the island and there were snipers in the hills around us, and going from one ward to another via the outside verandahs we were vulnerable targets in our white clothes.

The British surrender

On Christmas Day I was preparing a patient to go to the operating theatre, wearing my ordinary clothes. While he was having his operation, the capitulation was announced; right after, a plane came over and dropped leaflets all around – we went running out and got some of them. Then we were immediately told to put on uniforms again so that when the Japanese came in, they would know we were nurses. Thus, when this poor patient came round from his operation, there we girls were, all arrayed in our whites and little cap things. He looked at me and said, 'Have I come to heaven?' – he thought he had woken up with the angels!

Even after the fighting stopped, there were quite a number of injured people coming in; then things began to ease up a little. Just as well, else

I think we would all have died from sheer exhaustion. I suppose that was the time when my thyroid problem started bothering me. One day Sid turned up at the hospital to see me – he'd wangled the trip in a lorry, and was about to be sent to Shamshuipo Camp.

The Japanese arrive

Nothing much changed after the surrender except that the Japanese took over one of the offices, and a couple of their soldiers used to clump around with their swords. Japanese soldiers occupied the house opposite the hospital where we had originally been billeted. One night there was such hilarity and noisy singing coming from that house that Matron decided to move us girls to accommodation further from it; so, again in the middle of the night, we were led to a damaged top-floor ward. There was a large hole in the roof; although it was covered with tarpaulin, when it rained on the tarpaulin, the water found its way over the edges and on to us. Fortunately, a few days later, some repair work was done and the tarpaulin was no longer needed.

I was always happy at BMH. We girls had a wonderful time when we weren't working (though we enjoyed the work – I did, anyway). I was on a ward with 44 men, whose beds we had to make every morning and they had to be absolutely exact, with hospital corners... poor patients, they looked as if they were in strait-jackets.

I had to wash all the sheets and pyjamas for them, and all the bandages which had to be re-used. First these were soaked in lysol: once I obviously put too much lysol in the water and all my fingers shrivelled, dried, then peeled. I had a few days off work with my hands enveloped in bandages as I got an infection in them.

I discovered a short cut to deal with the bandages – I used to cut out all the nasty parts, wash the rest, and just make rolls of short bandages rolled together. I didn't think at the time what would happen when people came to use the washed bandages and found short lengths instead of one long bandage.

With not much hot water and very little soap, I didn't do a very good job of washing the sheets and pyjamas: I put them in the bath, took off my shoes and socks and stamped on them – doesn't sound very hygienic for a hospital, does it? At a later date, some RAMC orderlies formed a laundry to do all this washing. I got on good terms with one of them, he used to wash my uniform for me too, although unis were never ironed.

Major Boxer

I remember Major Boxer was a patient at the hospital. He came to my rescue one day after the surrender. I had been standing on a step at the end of the ground floor building, talking to Bob Bickley, a blind patient, whom I had taken for a walk out in the sun; we were just standing there, he was facing outwards and I was facing inwards, so I didn't see a Japanese soldier coming along behind me – and of course, Bob, being blind, didn't see him either.

Bob had a pair of dark glasses on and was facing where the Japanese soldier was coming. We were both talking and laughing. The soldier came up and grunted at us very angrily – obviously he thought we were laughing at him. Of course we couldn't answer him, I was just petrified. Major Boxer was sitting nearby, his arm in one of those aeroplane splints, the arm jacked right up high in the air (very difficult to dress such a patient, one poor man had two.) Boxer spoke fluent Japanese. He called out to me, 'Don't say anything, don't say anything!' (I was too frightened to say anything anyway.) He came up to me asking, 'What's the matter?' I said, 'I don't know, this soldier is shouting at me… I think he thinks we were laughing at him.'

Boxer straightened the problem out – a very nice fellow. Emily Hahn used to come to visit him. The Japanese would let her in. She used to bring her baby with her in a pram. They lived nearby in Bowen Road, near where my mum used to work looking after Baby Jean Martin just before the war. I remember going to see Mum there once and seeing the gibbons Emily Hahn kept. I knew Boxer too at Army HQ because he was in the office above me.

Concerts at the hospital

With more time off now, someone started organising concerts. Peggie Scotcher – a gifted dancer herself – decided to teach several of us to do a hula dance which we rehearsed in the bakery. I rather fancied myself in the skirts we made out of sacking which we frayed out, and tops out of scarves. We were very decently clad, and decided to give the dress rehearsal to the patients in the ward who couldn't be moved so wouldn't be able to attend the concert itself. Some Japanese officers turned up for the dress rehearsal: they took one look at our hula skirts and said NO to our act.

There were some really good turns at these concerts. An Irish soldier with his leg in plaster sang 'The Mountains of Morne', and Bickley the blind fellow had a very nice singing voice. Tamara Jex, Rhexie Stalker and Alison Black (whose doctor father was killed at St Stephen's) and I did a singing act. I wore a borrowed dress and sat on the piano. We sang 'Ferry Boat Serenade' which went down so well the audience wanted us to sing more, but we hadn't rehearsed anything else!

The move to Stanley Camp

About April, I got a bit of a fright when I was called to go to the Japanese Officer's office. Major Boxer appeared again because he was used as an interpreter. The Japs wanted all sorts of details about me: it was a mystery to me, I didn't know whether I was going to be beheaded or what.

It was some months later that I was told to see Shackleton, the big boss at the hospital, with three other VADs. A Japanese was present. Shackleton told us we were going to be sent to Stanley that very day. Then I learned that Mum had been asking the Japs to have me brought into the camp – that earlier interview with the Jap officer had been because they had decided to have a look at me first. We four were told to go and collect our things right away. I didn't want to go at all! I was extremely annoyed, as I was having the time of my life at the hospital.

Later that day a lorry appeared and we were put on the back of it, an open lorry. I didn't have many bits and pieces. I purloined a sheet and brought it into camp where we Redwoods divided it into four so each had a little piece to put across our tummies.

The lorry went along Bowen Road and down Garden Road to the HK & Shanghai Bank, and there we sat in the back for about an hour, not allowed to get off. It was hot then – June. After a while the Japs told us to go inside the bank, and there we met a whole lot of other British. Some of them were nurses from St Teresa's Hospital in Kowloon.

It was lovely and cool in the bank, with the air-conditioning so pleasant after sitting out in the boiling sun with no hats or anything. We all finally got on the lorry and came via Deep Water Bay... I remember we went all round the road we took when we used to go to Repulse Bay to Jimmy Bendall's matshed.

Passing the matsheds down on the beach, I thought about all our swim suits we had left there; and how when we came home from swimming we used to drive via Aberdeen and call in at the Dairy Farm cafe and have milk shakes and ice cream sundaes... we went that way in this lorry, and I remember looking at all these places and wondering if we would ever live that sort of life again.

When the lorry came into camp, I saw my sisters first, then Mum, but I barely recognised her because she had lost about 60 lbs. in weight through malnutrition and a hysterectomy two months earlier; and there I was, back with my family again – and rather bad-tempered, I think, especially when I found that initially my bed was just suitcases on top of each other!

1942

3rd & 4th Jan 1942

Pauline's birthday (she was Tony's fiance in Australia) so Tony & I celebrated by going to Prince's Cafe and having coffee and 3 hotcakes each – wonderful!

Queen's Road was made into a kind of market. Shops weren't open, but stalls lined the road and you could buy almost anything *((if you had money))*.

Amah came twice, with some of our best clothes, and Olive's trousseau finery, which I took to her in Gloucester Hotel. Tommy Maycock and Mr Himsworth took clothes to Mum at Queen Mary Hospital.

5th Jan 1942

Most of us in Tai Koon were sent to Murray Parade Ground by the Japs to register internees under instructions of Japs. The idea seemed to be to compile some sort of register under such headings as women, children, men, ages, nationality, occupation etc. We were sat out in the open at trestle tables and chairs, and each given a different category to record on printed forms. We hadn't been there very long when we were told to stop, as the job would take too long.

A stencilled edict was passed round giving plans for internees ('internists' the Japs called us), how much food (in ounces) we would be given, what we would be allowed to do, etc. etc. It dismayed us at first.

Returned to Tai Koon, and from then on we weren't allowed out. *((We ARP people seemed to be the first group to be interned in these little Chinese hotels. In due course, most of the rest of British civilians were sent to similar hotels.))*

6th/7th Jan 1942

Watching over the verandah – our normal occupation – we saw the Food Control lot passing by on foot, among them Olive (my elder sister) prominent in her scarlet jacket the same as mine, and her fair long hair. We all waved and called, and everyone seemed to be taking everything as a huge joke. They were put into the Nanking Hotel, not far away from us but on the other side of the road.

We spent a lot of time during the day on the flat roof where it was sunny and much warmer than down in the cubicles and on verandah; but from 7th Jan. we weren't supposed to look over the roof.

Amah came again, she was an absolute brick. I told her where Olive was so she visited her as well and took her some clothes. (I would get a verbal message to say Ah Ding was at the hotel door, and went downstairs hoping the guard would let us talk, and let her pass on to me whatever she had brought in her rattan basket... and hoping the guard wouldn't help himself to the things instead of letting me have them – that never happened though.)

On one visit Ah Ding brought my Collins A5 diaries, 1939, 1940 and 1941, all with a page to a day. (So happy to get them, especially as I was able to use spaces in the pages during internment years.)

8th/11th Jan 1942

Bad cold. 300 more internees sent in to our hotel. The ARP men on 4th floor doubled up, and we ARP ladies left the 2nd floor for new arrivals and moved in with our men. While this was happening, the 300 newcomers were squashed on the staircases waiting to get in to a billet. I now shared a cubicle (and the bed) with Marjorie Cook. We got on quite well, considering.

Because of toothache, my teeth were examined in hotel by one Dr Mullett who couldn't see much wrong.

We took it in turns helping with cooking chores, peeling onions and carrots, etc. The days seemed so long, it was one long wait from meal to meal. Eric Himsworth and Tony (Cole) used to buy bread somehow, and invited me to share it with them at 4pm, plus either jam or butter – it was wonderful. (They must have had contacts outside to get this bread, maybe one of their Chinese clerks).

Mr Bailey suddenly presented me with a half-pound block of 'Star' chocolate which I haven't yet opened – hope it doesn't go musty. It is the Iron Ration. So kind of him, I don't know why he did it.

12 Jan 1942

Medical Dept (?) have started to send bread daily – one slice each at about 2pm, with butter or jam *((this was in addition to our simple basic rations)).*

Finished reading 'Human Being' *((a birthday present a week before Jap attack))* and passed it to Jack Fancey as he had nothing to read. *((Jack – about my age – had TB which had prevented him from going fighting with the others. His mother (also in Tai Koon) told me he might as well have gone to war with his colleagues and risk being killed, as he was obviously going to die soon.))*

We are due for Stanley within the next week. Very cold.

Wrote to Mum. (She was still at Queen Mary Hospital, there were occasional opportunities of contact through someone in the Tai Koon Hotel getting permission to go to the hospital for some medical reason.)

13 Jan 1942

Mum's 47th birthday. Had note from her.

Saw Amah, she said she had seen Olive in Nanking Hotel.

We have been having ration bread these last 3 days.

15 Jan 1942

Stanley looms again, chance of family getting together. Washed hair.

16 Jan 1942

No bread supplied today, but Tony had some and shared it. Lecture about Stars tonight on roof, by Mr Evans *((B.D. Evans, Director of Royal Observatory.))*

Bought plate and cup and writing pad, then will be broke. *((Chinese messenger in hotel must have shopped for me.))*

17 Jan 1942

Cold again but lovely porridge in morning, and much later, much bread. We are supposed to be bound for Stanley tomorrow.

18 Jan 1942

Stanley postponed, thanks to D.M.S. (Dr P.S. Selwyn-Clarke). Froggish throat.

Really grand filling meal tonight – liver; then jam sauce pudding.

Arthur's birthday, therefore bread and jam from Tony.

Letter from Mum – she has been ill, but better now. *((This was probably a reaction to the ordeal at the Jockey Club Hospital.))*

19 Jan 1942

Bad throat. Very cold.

Fire opposite us in the night – very near thing. There were just sooty sparks at first *((from the tenements on other side of the road))*, but later the fire really got going. All the gongs in the neighbourhood were beating as alarms, several huge tongues of fire blew over in our direction. *((Discussions among us at what to do if the wind blew the flames across the road to our hotel.))*

21 Jan 1942

In morning, we were given a quarter of an hour to pack and get out of the hotel, then marched down Des Voeux Road. *((I wore most of my clothes, with blanket strapped bandolier-wise across me. Passed Nanking Hotel and saw Olive and colleagues hanging over the verandah watching.))*

Then boarded top-heavy Macau steamer and set out for Stanley. It could have been lovely – such a beautiful day. *((We sat on top deck and enjoyed the trip and the freshness after being so long cooped up in hotels; not only ARP personnel, also other groups. How envious I was of ginger-haired Bridget Armstrong and brother John, aged about 10 and 8, because their mother was always handing them thin little biscuits with marmite on during the journey.))*

Our boat was too big to go right up to the jetty at Stanley, so we had to clamber over the side of the ferry on to the side of the junk – then jump into the body of the junk. Poor Mrs Grant, who weighed over 15 stone, cried from the side of the ferry that she just couldn't make the transfer, but somehow she did. *((Mrs Kathleen Grant was the mother of one of my Govt. colleagues Rosaleen Millar. Rosaleen had married shortly before the Jap attack; she was a VAD at Bowen Road Hospital.))*

From the jetty a path across a beach led to a steep bank near St Stephen's Preparatory School. Dorothy Holloway, a fellow Govt. stenographer, was at the top of the bank extending a helping hand to everyone as we made the last leap up to flat ground. When she saw Bonnie Penny, who was just in front of me, she told her that her mother Mrs Robinson was already in Stanley. I deliberately avoided asking Dorothy if she knew if my mother was also here, so as not to be disappointed too soon if she wasn't.

Our ARP leaders thought we should try to find accommodation in the Prep School, and took us in there, but someone appeared and said we couldn't stay there so out we marched, and followed crowds making for a group of buildings up on a plateau... when suddenly I heard a familiar voice – and there was Mum! Called out to her, and went stumbling over old tins and rubbish heaps, so wonderful to see her again.

She and I tried to tell each other all our experiences... Mum started a dozen different stories, and I didn't hear the ends of any of them for weeks afterwards.

((She had been brought into camp on a lorry the previous day with nurses and civilian patients from Queen Mary Hospital. She had spent the previous night in a temporary billet in a room in the pre-war Prison Officers' Quarters. There were four blocks forming a quadrangle in the middle. We were thrilled to be sent to live in these good-looking, cream-coloured buildings, having dreaded much worse after the Chinese hotels... we were all so happy to have somewhere clean and fresh, and so marvellous to be near the sea; it didn't seem to matter that there was practically no furniture.))

Mum's billet was only temporary as the other occupants were keeping spaces for friends and relatives expected any day... these actually arrived on the same ferry as I did, so now the room was grossly overcrowded, but as Mum and I couldn't find any spaces in any other rooms, we spent my first night there anyhow, me in a wicker chair, but in the early morning I crept into Mum's camp bed with her until it gave an ominous crack, so I got out and curled up in the chair again. I couldn't get used to the peace and quiet after the noises of the environs of the Tai Koon Hotel. There was just the sound of the sea like the rustling of tinsel. From the window I could see the superb sunrise – exactly like Billie Burke when she materialised as a fairy in The Wizard of Oz. Mum has had a bad time and has lost a lot of weight.

The regular nurses (as distinct from members of the Auxiliary Nursing Service like Mum) were given billets on the top floor of Tweed Bay Hospital within the camp, a small emergency hospital which had been used during the battle; here the nurses' beds were jam-packed together, incredibly overcrowded.

These nurses had pre-war lived in accommodation beside Queen Mary Hospital, so were able to bring in many of their own possessions. When they had packed, they told Mum and the other auxiliaries to help themselves to anything left in their flats. So Mum acquired some extra clothes.

Tweed Bay Hospital was a stone's throw from the sea, about 100 yards from the Married Quarters. The office and the kitchens and operating theatre were on the ground floor, and also a men's ward. On the first floor there were women's wards and another male ward.

22 Jan 1942

Mum and I ate something from our frugal supplies then went room-hunting again around the blocks with Connie Hawkett, an ANS friend of Mum's. (Absolutely no one was in charge.) Once we found an empty room with some furniture, but hastily withdrew when a Chinese who seemed to be an authority came in and said this room was reserved for Japanese administrators. A complete stranger in ANS uniform hailed Mum and said she'd found an empty room and would we like to share it... would we!! – a small room in Block 3 overlooking the courtyard, on first floor. It was a feeling of indescribable security to be in a place where we could remain, some furniture – a spare camp bed (now mine), small chest of drawers & a glass-fronted cabinet, a small table and a fireplace. We shared out shelves and drawers between us. There was also a large wooden doll's house – we were lucky, as most of the rooms were empty of furniture. Our room-mate was Mrs G. Kopeczky, Hungarian.

Later that day we were able to collect some cooked rice.

There was no way of knowing who had got into the camp except by wandering around and trying to find friends. The Japs were simply bringing people in as and when they found them, and by whatever transport was available. Everything was haphazard. How much luggage you were allowed to bring in with you depended on what space there was on the transport, and on the personal opinions of the Japs superintending your transfer. The main difficulty for most of us was that by the time we were captured, we weren't anywhere near our homes and had only a small suitcase or overnight bag, and didn't get the chance to go back to our homes to collect any possessions.

We Redwoods were particularly lucky because of Ah Ding's many journeys on foot from our flat to the Chinese hotels, bringing each time a few clothes in her little wicker basket. *((We found her after the war when we returned to Hong Kong after recuperation in UK. She had a good job with an army family living on the Peak, earning far more than we could afford to pay her. We always kept in touch though.))*

As more and more internees poured into the camp, the red-brick three-storeyed blocks used pre-war as Indian prison warders' quarters were used as billets. They were in a valley just below the Married Quarters and had very small rooms with stone floors and Asian toilets (you squatted over a small drain, your feet planted in huge cemented footprints). These blocks were ranged round a grassed area which ran down to the barbed-wired rocky sea's edge. Other buildings in use as billets were up a steep incline to St Stephen's College, a pre-war boarding school; also used was the nearby Science Block and some bungalows which had been occupied by senior prison officers.

Two of our soldiers had been temporarily buried at the top of the path up to St Stephen's. One victim was the husband of a woman with a small child in camp. Other soldier victims were buried in the old Stanley cemetery; some of the Tweed Bay Hospital staff who had been killed were buried at the side of the hospital.

Some internees settled themselves in two of the bungalows when they had to move as the Japanese decided to use them as their Camp Headquarters.

23 Jan 1942

My kitbag arrived by sea. I happened to be near the bungalows when the Japs evicted internees from them. An unknown young woman who was among them came over to me, distraught because she had a six-month-old baby and couldn't carry away the child and luggage. She asked me if I would take the baby Dorothy and keep her until she had found another billet. Her name was Mrs Evelyn Kilbee, I told her my block and room number, and gathered up the child. Never having held a baby in my life, I felt very nervous carrying her down the hill, over shell holes and stony ground. Dorothy didn't cry or fuss at all. On the way I met my boss, Mr. B.H. Puckle, who looked surprised and said 'I didn't know you had a baby, Miss Redwood!' *((Some fifty years later, Evelyn visited me with Dorothy to say thank you. Last year I met Dorothy again at the VJ Celebrations in London.))*

Was given some ARP provisions *((from the kitty kept in Tai Koon Hotel))* – packet of Kelloggs cornflakes and some Oxo.

Eileen Grant was arrested at Stanley Village. *((Eileen was the youngest of three daughters of Mrs Grant, the overweight lady who had such difficulty in jumping from ferry to junk at Stanley; I think Eileen was arrested because she had walked beyond the camp boundary, but she was soon released.))*

Rice and stew... ingredients sent by Japs, cooking arrangements by our people makeshift... waited hours and hours for it, queuing in Married Quarters quadrangle... about 700 of us. There was only water to drink – unless you had private supplies.

24 Jan 1942

The Salmon family arrived, and Baby Jean whom Mum is taking for the time being while her guardian Mrs Irene Braude was organising a room for other mums with babies.

(The Salmons were a Jewish family with daughters Leah, Frieda, Hilda and Dorothy, and sons Sammy and Herbert. We had been neighbours when we Redwoods lived in Kowloon 1927/8.)

25-28 Jan 1942

Olive arrived a couple of days ago with Food Control staff – now five in the room, plus for a few days Baby Jean.

Fish today – smell put me off. Kelloggs is stale. Diet devastating – rice and fish, or stew. When Kelloggs and Oxo run out I shall just have to eat rice *((had always hated it!))* Stew dreadful too. Luckily Mum still has some tea.

Danny Wilson (Peggy's husband) was taken ill with pneumonia the day we left Tai Koon, and he and Peggy went to hospital in town so they haven't arrived yet. I met up with Uncle Sidney, we went for a walk through the old Stanley cemetery. Saw Ronald Egan's grave *((he was an acquaintance in the Volunteers; hanging on the makeshift cross on his grave was his steel helmet with bullet hole through it.))* Also communal grave of the VADs and others murdered at St Stephen's.

Mum and I met Mrs Hogg (who had been at Military Hospital). She said that having Sid there (as a patient) was all that had saved Mabel's reason during the raids.

5 Feb 1942

Feeling so much better in heart today because we had a piece of fried fish this morning with the rice. I felt dreadful for four days, my cold hasn't quite gone. Food had been dreadful – one day the meat would have to be thrown away because it was bad, and the rice is still an effort for me. I have walked into the chocolate which Mr Bailey gave me.

Mrs Hawkett has left us, and we now have Mrs *((Magdalene))* Greenwood, from Stonecutters *((an island in Hong Kong harbour))*. Somehow she managed to bring with her more luggage than about six other people put together, including several folding chairs and a supply of candles. Every night she reads by candlelight when we're all longing for sleep and in fear of getting into trouble by the Japs for having candle on so late.

Mabel not yet arrived *((from Bowen Road Hospital))*.

We have some jam and Oxo and a little cheese, but stocks are decreasing daily and there's no sign of the promised store.

On Sunday we went to Mass in Prison Officers' Club.

Rumours of repatriation, some say we might be sent to Saigon as a clearing centre, some say Australia, others Canada. It was in the local newspaper *((printed by Japs in English and a few copies reached camp))* that repatriation of women and children might be done.

Olive has written to CSO in camp to see if she and Topper can get married *((her Royal Artillery fiance who was in Shamshuipo camp: they had planned to marry in the summer: sadly, he was sent to Japan and died there.))*

Each been given a postcard on which we can say only 'safe and well' to send to England etc.

6 Feb 1942

Repatriation rumours seem to have fizzled out. Mum not too good.

8 Feb 1942

Loathsome food pow-wow in morning *((in quadrangle of Married Quarters))*. I was ashamed of being there because it was all so bald and horrible. Angry and hungry people quarrelling about the rations and kitchen staff, and cooking. We had dumplings last night – delicious. There was fried fish for the lucky ones but I wasn't among them.

To church at 10am (Mass in Prison Officers' Club). This afternoon we battled our way (great wind) up to St Stephen's Hall to Benediction. I didn't know the hymns, but thought sentimentally of Sunday evenings in England, sausage rolls, cheese straws, jam and currant tarts, tinned fruit – then going to Benediction and joining in processions, us children in short white frocks. So homesick. I'm worried about Mum because she doesn't get enough to eat.

Mrs G getting annoyingly and monotonously argumentative, I'm running out of subjects to introduce as red herrings.

9 Feb 1942

Notable for fried fish in a.m., and pasty in evening.

10 Feb 1942

Food terrible today.

Assistance wanted in hospital – office work, and I'm to start tomorrow, feeding there.

Electric lights on.

11 Feb 1942

Started working at hospital. Day seemed long. Four slices thin bread and mincemeat at mid-day. Bitterly cold. (Non-resident staff like me have meals there).

Letter from Charles Pike (RAMC in Shamshuipo Camp) and one from Mabel. *((Now I wonder how those letters got into camp, there was no postal service!))*

12 Feb 1942

Enjoyed bread *((on hospital meals now))* again. We ate half a tin of our sausages tonight – fried in the tin on wood fire in our room.

13 Feb 1942

44° *((7 degrees celsius))*. Not allowed to leave rooms till 4.30pm. Apple & custard – lovely, but it's so cold. Row with Mrs G.

14 Feb 1942

Mincemeat and beans and a large quantity of badly cooked rice today. Am at last getting better at eating rice among other stuff.

Morning off from work, but had to spend it all being searched in the rain at St Stephen's Prep. School grounds by the sea. *((Japs got us all lined up, near where we first landed in Stanley. There were armed soldiers all round us. We wondered if we were to be massacred, or sent off somewhere. In fact, Japs used our absence to search through all the accommodation, presumably looking for wireless sets, weapons etc. The main worry of us Redwoods was, would they come across the opened tin of sausages with the remaining half of contents, and help themselves.... they didn't though))*.

15 Feb 1942

To 10.00am church, then to work. Tiffin wonderful because there was suet roly-poly with apple afterwards.

To concert in P.O. Club in evening – good fun. Community singing. Some good cracks – 'Who is the owner of this pair of shorts marked

'Bindle'? and 'the Americans are certainly good swipers'. Both jokes refer to the likelihood of people appropriating someone else's property.

16 Feb 1942

For almost a week I've been well fed, and if that stops, I shall have at least have had this little building-up.

Not hard work at the hospital, a little shorthand and typing, somewhere comparatively warm to sit – and hospital rations, which I live for. *((Hospital rations were better than at Married Quarters because when nurses and patients left Queen Mary Hospital for Stanley, they managed to bring much of their dry kitchen stock which helped to supplement the rations for some months. Also, being a tiny community the food was better cooked.))*

Two slices of thin bread, one with butter and jam, and tea, at 9am. At 1pm we get the main meal, rice, veg and generally (very little) meat. Curry once. Another day roast pork, true we only each had three pieces, one fat, one crackling, one lean, but the sight of the roast did my heart good. Cup of tea at 4pm. At 6pm soup or stew – and two slices of bread.

I know I'm feeling much better about food because for the past few nights I've not had to have my imaginary meal in bed. Time passes rather slowly at work, that is because my thoughts are so centred on the tiffin meal.

The reason non-resident staff like me are on hospital rations is because mealtimes in the other blocks would have come in the middle of our working shifts.

Today there was a special edition of the Hong Kong paper announcing that Singapore had surrendered unconditionally. We didn't buy it *((quite cheap, but money was short – just what we happened to have on us when captured. Some internees bought it and passed it round to friends. Probably used as toilet paper, as we were only supplied with Chinese rough brown paper.))* I've been sleeping in bed with Mum for past few nights because it's so cold.

I'm still afraid Mum doesn't get enough to eat. Several nights ago we succumbed to the temptation of the tin of sausages Mum brought from our flat. Fried half one night in the tin on wood fire (some of the doll's house). Then fried small pieces of bread in the fat left in the tin. The result was delicious. Next night we finished the remainder of the sausages cold – I ate all the fat scrapings neat. Our stores now consist of sugar, milk powder, a tin of jam and tin of pineapple, and pork and beans. I think we should save one of these till Mabel comes, but Olive is very hungry and Mabel may not come for ages.

17 Feb 1942

Concert at St Stephen's. Wasn't much. First we had to have a picture show by our hosts. Singapore has apparently surrendered. *((Film show was supposed to be in celebration, mainly a kind of Jap documentary. A few shots of bottles of beer going along the assembly line – there were nostalgic cheers from the men in the audience at the sight.))* Mum got peas in the canteen.

18 Feb 1942

Ash Wednesday, but we were too late waking up to go to the church service.

Lovely pork.

Walk in evening with Mum who gave me verbal cooking lessons – we both enjoyed these meals in our imagination.

((An explanation of the canteen in Stanley:- Limited supplies of prized food were sent into camp, and sold usually twice weekly – if you had money, which was very limited as people hadn't been paid since fighting ended. Each person was only allowed to buy so much of a particular item.

Huge queues at the first canteens – Olive and I took turns keeping a place for hours; when our turn came at last there was little choice, we just got a tin of Instant Postum which turned out to be a delicious drink.

In due course canteen days were well organised so that every person had a shopping turn once in so many sessions, so that the wealthiest couldn't buy up all that was available every time.))

19 Feb 1942

Pork and crackling again. Depressing news. We ate our tin of pineapple.

21 Feb 1942

Fried fish today – lovely.

Glasses gone for re-framing *((hopefully sent in to town – the bridge across the nose broke during the war, and since then the lenses were tied on to the frames of an old pair of sunglasses.))*

22 Feb 1942

Fried ham and spotted dick. Olive and I ate the tin of pork and beans tonight.

23 Feb 1942

Curried fish.

Washed hair *((no hot water and no shampoo))*. Awkward without glasses.

Peaches from canteen in evening.

25 Feb 1942

Lovely rissole today, and one extra slice of bread at hospital. Mum and others got three extra. Colder. I broke Mrs. K's teapot. *((We called Mrs. Kopeczky Mrs. K))*.

Two months since capitulation.

Today a new kitchen staff has taken over, and mum is helping to cut up the vegetables, it means getting up at 7am. We are just about on speaking terms with Mrs G who has temporarily stopped being so difficult since she was sick in the night and Mum looked after her.

The bread ration in camp is up today so Mum and Olive are getting as much as I do at the hospital. Fairly happy working at hospital, so much better to be keeping brain going, and typing and shorthand practice.

Men are voluntarily working, getting food out of the godowns, for Japs, to earn extra food – tins of bully etc. *((Just outside the camp were godowns filled with food etc. – set up by Govt. before the Jap war to provide food stocks in different parts of the colony.))*

Future still most obscure. I like to think about rumours of repatriation to Canada or Argentina, though the journey would be dreadful. Rumours that the regular army men have already left Hong Kong. I'm dying to go back to England and feel so glad I have been self-indulgent last year – boxes of crystallised ginger, many milk shakes at Repulse Bay and the Dairy Farm, peanuts and potato crisps, and went to hundreds of films, before the Japs attacked.

26 Feb 1942

I have fed so well. Today's meals *((at hospital))*: two slices of bread and jam (one with butter) in morning tiffin – rice, soya beans, cabbage, small piece of fatty mutton and lump of fat. Evening – mutton stew, with an enormous bone with meat on (which saved for Mum), slice of cold bully beef and a spoonful of tinned vegetable salad, and piece of tomato, and two slices of bread, one buttered.

Took bread up to room, I had one slice, Mum & Olive shared the other; then cocoa, one fig and one apple ring. Had a fruit drop from Mrs K; a piece of chocolate from Olive; a cup of cocoa, one fig and one apple ring. Mum had dumplings today in rations.

Canteen today, bought porridge, I'm dying to have it tomorrow.

27 Feb 1942

One extra bread, and PORRIDGE in afternoon and evening, and stewed fruit and suspicion of custard after tiffin. Think I'm putting on weight (having lost about 10 lbs since Christmas).

((The porridge, from canteen, was the most fantastic morale builder. For a few precious evenings, the electric cookers in one of the former Married Quarters kitchens were made available to us by our kitchen staff. Inevitable queue of people waiting their turn to go in with their tins to cook up their little bits. Surprising discovery that one internee was hogging a ring to herself

for a long time – actually boiling her sheets because 'she always boiled her sheets'.))

28 Feb 1942

Had quarter of a typhoid injection. Good porridge! Minced meat today.

1 Mar 1942

Spotted dick but other food not so good. Mum had bread ration instead of rice, she isn't too well.

3 Mar 1942

Poor meals.

Cold and blustery.

Porridge lovely.

4 Mar 1942

Meat and bread pudding.

Mrs Hawkett agitating to come back in room. *((She did not come back. Mrs Connie Hawkett was an ANS colleague of Mum's who had originally occupied the room with us, but soon after she found a better billet.))*

Cookers gave out, therefore no porridge... great loss.

5 Mar 1942

Tonight we cooked porridge on chatty in room – not bad. *((Chatty was a makeshift affair in the empty fireplace in our room.))*

6 Mar 1942

Managed to make porridge in evening on chatty *((with more of the doll's house as fuel.))* Lovely meat pie for tiffin – with real pastry.

7 Mar 1942

Very busy in office with Census.

8 Mar 1942

Had last of TAB inoculation, good for 18 months. Morning off. We cooked porridge in evening and had some cold in morning.

9 Mar 1942

Warmer.

Lots of hard work in office – census.

Soon our little stock of firewood (Marina Kingdon's doll's house) will be finished, and that will be the end of the porridge. *((We found that the Kingdon family had pre-war occupied the flat of which our room was part. Mr Kingdon was in camp but family was evacuated to Australia.))* Meantime we are cooking two lots of porridge at night so as not to waste the fire once started, and eat some cold in morning. I still haven't got my glasses back.

Mum has written to Dr Selwyn Clarke (Hong Kong's Director of Medical Services, not yet interned) to try to get Mabel here with us. Over three months since we've seen her. It seems a shame to bring her here to this food if she is getting better food where she is.

Bread ration has slumped – it no longer comes direct to us, but via the Chinese Chief Supervisor. (Bread was sent into camp ready-cooked). Mum has been eating more rice. I still bring her some of any extras we get at hospital in evening.

Olive now a kitchen worker and sometimes gets extra food, though she is generous to Mum with it.

In spare time at work I've been copying out shorthand phrases etc. from Dorothy Holloway's Pitmans book, so that will be something to learn if Dorothy and the book aren't always at hand.

Canteen still functioning, but prices colossal. Sugar $1.50 a pound, 20 toffees for $1 etc, and we have to save some of our little remaining precious money for my glasses' frames.

Often dream of going back to our flat and trying to rescue various things, but the general idea is that there's nothing left in our homes – not even the floorboards. Lately I've been thinking a lot about some lovely

Christmases at Gillingham (where grandmother and aunts lived) – the Christmas tree, and the evening draw for the pink sugar mice etc. on it, and eating nuts and figs and dates all the time.

Today's paper mentions repatriation for the Americans, and that it may be a matter of arrangement for the British. Some think it is out of the question. Others seem to think we will just be released from internment and left to our own devices.

Went to dentist (Shields) but he said he can't find anything wrong (despite aching). *((Mr Shields was a private dentist. There was also a Govt. one, Dr. Lanchester. Both functioned as best they could with what things they'd been able to bring into camp. Their 'surgery' was the only part of the Married Quarters which had been damaged during the fighting – a devastated ground floor room which no one wanted to live in. There were no facilities for major repairs in camp. In 2002 there was a photo in one of the British newspaper literary supplements of Dr Lanchester attending to an internee in that very surgery, with Nursing Sister Mary Rose in attendance. The photo was reproduced because a grandson of Dr Lanchester had just published a novel called 'Fragrant Harbour' set in Hong Kong, both in war days and in the present.))*

13 Mar 1942

Dorothy Deakin & some Colonial Secretary's staff arrived in camp (some were already here).

14 Mar 1942

Talk that Sir Anthony Eden had mentioned conditions here, and said we would have to put up with it but food would be sent.

Didn't sleep well because of Mrs. G's candle.

Mum and I went to Confession.

15 Mar 1942

Mum and I to Holy Communion this morning. *((Most of the RC priests were American – Maryknoll Fathers, and there was one young Canadian priest, Father Murphy. Confessions were heard on Saturdays in the billet of two of the Fathers – an ex-amah's room. During the week Confessions were also heard before a short morning Mass in the Prison Officers' Club where the priest sat sideways on a chair which had a piece of material on its back to give a semblance of privacy, before which one knelt for Confession.))*

16 Mar 1942

New rumour is that we are bound for Shanghai. Nice meat roll today. Colder.

17 Mar 1942

I'm now at the stage where I could eat more rice than I get.

Concert tonight, Irish history, grand: Eileen Grant is very clever. Mum and Olive are staying on to dance.

18 Mar 1942

Dorothy Deakin says meals at Bowen Road Hosp. are porridge, plenty of tea, meat and bread and jam. I had lovely meat roll today.

Mum and I had a grand walk. Saw poor body on rocks. *((It had been there a long time – believed to be a soldier, no one could get to it because there was barbed wire around all the beaches)).*

Gave Miss Hill *((a young nursing sister))* her first shorthand lesson.

19 Mar 1942

Mrs. G. went to hospital at night – gallstones. Still no glasses and no Mabel.

20 Mar 1942

Some people have escaped from camp.

21 Mar 1942

Cholera inoc.

Fried bread in peanut oil in a sardine tin – delicious. Staff in Hospital Office to be increased. A daily report of patients in camp hospital, and of births and deaths, required by Japanese.

Egg ration today – Mum and I boiled ours.

23 Mar 1942

Up early for canteen, but I let family down by not getting up early ENOUGH. *((This means I was at the end of the queue and so little choice of foodstuffs left.))* Heard Military Hospital nurses are doing quite well, food and amenity-wise.

25 Mar 1942

Got weighed. I'm 101 and half lbs. (from 112). Olive has gained 2 lbs. *((rice fat))*. She is to work at hospital office too.

26 Mar 1942

An egg again today, and they say sweet potatoes have come in rations too, and flour.

27-28 Mar 1942

Terrific headache. Meat roll – lovely lot.

29 Mar 1942

Head better but pain in chest – was only mildly thrilled at MEAT PIE. Nasty taste in mouth.

30 Mar 1942

Pain in chest and heart feeling tired.

31 Mar 1942

Feeling bad. Dr Kirk examined me. OK except for digestion, and slow pulse (40). Says I should have a good rest. But Mum is very sick.

Mum very poorly – chill etc.

1 Apr 1942

Mum still ill. Dr came and she had her bread rusked. *((One kitchen on ground floor in Married Quarters was a sort of Diet Kitchen & Baby Clinic, where bread was rusked mainly for babies and toddlers.))*

I'm still very tired and can't taste food, not even meat cake.

2 Apr 1942

Mum still weak and in bed. Mrs Kopeczky suddenly taken to hospital.

3 Apr 1942

Feeling rotten, and Mum still staying in bed.

Over the past weeks food has got much better. Rumour that we would be sent to Shanghai, but the latest is that consuls and journalists are to go, and that is apparently true. A strong feeling in the camp that the troops have been sent to Formosa. If so, we think the actual implication is good, i.e. that the Japs don't expect to hold here.

Feel so tired and weary, keep sighing. Dr Kirk said it is only the diet effects and recommends I take a week's rest. Just now I don't care if I never work at the hospital again. Olive has joined the staff as an extra steno, so that Dorothy and I can have more time off. *((There was of course no pay for any hospital or other work, except that heavy workers got extra rations, and some workers also got some extra food. For Olive and I, it was enough that we were on hospital rations which at that time were so much more varied and interesting than in Married Quarters and other blocks.))*

4 Apr 1942

Married Quarters rations again *((because on sick leave and not working at hospital))*.

5 Apr 1942

Easter Sunday – Mass in open. Mum a little better. The damn kids had eggs. *((Eggs (NOT Easter eggs!) were sent into camp, but given only to the children – two or three each.))* We grown-ups furious.

6 Apr 1942

Mum and I both feeling better. Was able to get fresh milk for Mum from Baby Clinic. *((A small number of little bottles of fresh milk were sent in daily by Japs for children, and a few for the most needy cases in hospital or ill people in blocks.))*

We had fun turning out suitcases *((and enjoying holding Olive's trousseau – lovely silk underwear – which our amah had taken to her in the Chinese hotel.))*

Wet and cold.

7 April 1942

Actually full up tonight, had one and a half pasties, and a piece of Mrs Knox's blancmange (She is a neighbour in our block.) Mrs K back from hospital. My eyes bad.

8 April 1942

Went to see Dr Kirk again, he said take things easy, so I decided I would take a longer holiday, which would mean less queuing for Mum who has gone down so much and isn't at all strong yet.

9 Apr 1942

Some police escaped from camp last night. Lots of good news about – re American planes over Kowloon Docks; Hainan recaptured. I'm very tired again.

SUMMARY OF RECENT DAYS. Mrs G was in hospital and since her return she's been very sweet and kind to us, particularly in bringing extra soup for Mum (Mrs G worked in the kitchen), and for Mrs. K too who has just come back from hospital.

During the past fortnight a kind of diarrhoea and dysentery has swept through the camp. The hospital has had to discharge patients on stretchers.

There is enough porridge left for one more meal.

Stopped shorthand lessons to Miss Hill because of my weakness. On 20th March we learned that some people had escaped from the camp – along them Elsie Cholmondeley, the girl in National Stabilization Board of China where I might have had a job; also Van Ess, and others. Since then Roll Calls twice daily have been instituted.

I don't think there's much chance of Mabel coming in from Bowen Road Hosp.

Mum has lost 27 lbs, she's only 161 lbs.

More flour (but less bread) and sweet potatoes have been coming in regularly for the past fortnight.

Rumours too good to be true: Russians around Danzig; Germans and Japan have not much longer to go; various buildings in town have been sabotaged.

11 Apr 1942

Selwyn-Clarke came in, and money for my glasses money went *((via him into town for new frames)).*

12 Apr 1942

Still weakish. Mum better. Dorothy Deakin and Eric Kennard getting married on 1st May.

13 April 1942

No flour therefore no more pasties.

16 Apr 1942

Newspaper says we are to have $100 each. Now I don't return to (work at) hospital till Monday.

Good extra soup tonight.

17 Apr 1942

Very little to eat. Enjoyed fried rice and sugar in evening. No pasty.

ELEPHANT IS EMPLOYED BY YOU
AND ENGLISHMAN EMPLOYS YOU
ELEPHANT IS GIVEN FOOD BY YO
AND YOU ARE GIVEN WHIP BY
ENGLISHMAN
ELEPHANT OBEYS YOU
AND YOU ARE AT THE MERC
OF ENGLISHMAN

A Japanese propaganda leaflet

18 Apr 1942

Less to eat than ever: cooking (Married Q) dreadful; more kitchen squabbles there. Everyone fed up and starving. One foot seems going to sleep. Wet and blowy.

20 Apr 1942

Back at hospital office again. Good: feel tiredish but more energetic and ate quite an amount of rice, as also did Mum.

Jack Fancey died early this morning. *((He had spent his last days, cheerfully, on a bed near the verandah on first floor ward of the hospital, overlooking the sea.))*

21 Apr 1942

Feeling grand, but Mum in pain and to see Dr Kirk tomorrow. Spring offensive reported starting. Duck egg again.

22 Apr 1942

Mum to go to hospital tomorrow – bleeding womb.

Selwyn-Clarke came, and MY GLASSES!

25 Apr 1942

Mum to have op on Monday. Olive and I tried to get egg for Mum tonight, but kitchen wouldn't. Saw Tony Cole in evening.

26 Apr 1942

Today Mum has had three eggs, hot cake, scone and ordinary food. Tony Cole will give us some apricot rings for her.

Outside news is good – English landings in various French coast towns, destructive bombing raids on specific German towns etc., and bombing of Tokyo.

27 Apr 1942

Mum had her womb removed. It took two and a quarter hours. At 5pm we went up to ward and saw her just for a moment. She was just round from the anaesthetic, and said 'it's so sore' and 'don't worry', but her poor head was so heavy. Her legs were lashed up. She looked dreadfully pale, her hands so thin. We have to get hold of all the food we can for her. Dr Kirk and Prof. Digby did the operation.

I've been back working at the hospital. They made lovely scones yesterday.

When Mum is out of hospital, either Olive or I will have to give up working at hosp. because Mum won't be strong enough to queue or do things for herself. Selwyn-Clarke was in today – there's apparently no hope of getting Mabel into camp, she counts as a prisoner of war.

Japs have offered us HK$75 each, and we have made out lists of what we want to buy and it's hoped they will let someone in to town to buy it soon.

Heaps of flour has been coming in.

28 Apr 1942

Mum frightens me – but there's nothing we can do but pray.

29 Apr 1942

Mum so very much better today, thank God. Got porridge from Welfare for her.

30 Apr 1942

Mum better still. She had custard today. We had lovely pastry at tiffin and sweet potato in evening.

1 May 1942

Mum better, she had Bengers Food and milk and soup. Eric Kennard and Dorothy Deakin married. Baby Jean Addis Martin's 1st[st] birthday.

2 May 1942

Mum still improving. To dance in evening with Tony and Olive.

4 May 1942

Mum had big stitches taken out. Got sugar and choc. via Mrs McGowan *((who was the mother by a former marriage of Betty McGowan and Jackie who were also in camp. Betty and Jackie, then teenagers, were repatriated with Americans in September 1943. Presumably their father was American-Chinese. Mrs McGowan died of cancer soon after the children left camp. Mr*

McGowan worked for the Hong Kong Government. He was killed in a car accident in Kowloon in 1947/8. After the war, Betty became famous on the London stage under her Chinese name Chin Yu; she married her leading man, and they had twins – a boy and a girl.))

5-8 May 1942

Tried to make bread *((by growing yeast from rice, and wrapping it up when mixed with flour to keep it warm. Mrs G cooked it in Married Quarters kitchen where she worked)).* Turned out fine.

Mum had all stitches taken out.

9 May 1942

Sent our $50 note into town via Miss Jeffery *((a young nursing sister with T.B., one of a few selected for x-ray in town as there were no x-ray facilities in camp. All 'lucky' patients were plied with money and lists from camp friends; they usually stayed overnight under Jap. supervision at the French Hospital; they got friendly staff there to shop frantically for them, and returned to camp loaded with goods.*

I never heard of any restrictions on bringing cash into Stanley, but I didn't have much with me anyway! I forget where Olive got her $50 note from... her war billet was nearer the Bank than mine so maybe she got some out during the fighting.

We didn't need much money then, as our meals were all paid for at the cafe where we were registered, so would only need a few dollars to get drinks of coke etc. to go with the meals.

In my experience at least, there was nothing to spend our money on in the war! I can't remember any searches when we were sent to Stanley.))

11 May 1942

News of Churchill's speech 'on the up and up'. Sea battle with Japs ensuing.

12 May 1942

I weigh 108 lbs (was 101 and a half on 25th March).

13-15 May 1942

Some syrup and fruits and seven sweets came in, the rest of our $50 of goods will come later. Olive not well.

Mum not getting up yet, but OK.

17-19 May 1942

Rest of our goods arrived – lovely: cocoa, vitacup, muscatels, prunes, treacle, jam, and cream of wheat. Bill was in Yen – 25. We won't have to give up working at hosp. when Mum comes home after all, because now we only work half-days instead of full days. On 18th May, Mum got up for the first time, very shaky on her legs. On the second day of her op, Olive and I thought she wouldn't get over it. I've felt much better since being back at work in the hospital. Olive is getting fat, but she isn't well – bad cold, throat etc.

All sorts of news coming in – about Italy caving in, peace terms etc., about gas in England: victories in Coral Sea; speeches by Churchill that victory is in sight; that Russians have broken through Germany's spring offensive, and vice versa. All liable to be discounted the next day, as all the news seems to be.

We have a little garden now – Olive, Dorothy (Holloway) and I. Sweet potatoes planted so far. *((That garden was only about 6 ft x 4 ft, a piece of rough ground among the rocks behind the hospital. It didn't do very well. Much later when the rations grew worse, someone (either the Japs or our own camp officials) decided to convert the pre-war football ground near the Married Quarters into garden plots, and our family had one there which actually provided us with some crops.))*

Now I have so much to do in spare time – am reading World Geography, and Florence Nightingale; teaching Miss Hill and Tony (Cole) shorthand; plus gardening and bread making – chiefly sifting flour because of weevils. Much more contented now.

23 May 1942

Forgot to do diary lately. We have suddenly been presented with $17.40 each via the Japs, and will send ours via Mrs G on Monday when she goes into town for x-ray. Always feel rather wary of parting with so much money with period of waiting. Mum doing fine.

Mr Mezger gave us jam – so kind of him. *((He was one of three middle-aged men who lived in the amahs' rooms of our flat. I think they were Australian:- William J. Mezger, appraiser; Henry Harold Fantham, appraiser, and Charles Henry Fuller, appraiser. I have seen mention of Mr. Fantham's diary I think in Australia. These three men were always ready to help us females when we asked them.))*

25 May 1942

Whit Monday. Finished writing 'School Magazine' poem. Mum now slouches about in the hospital ward. She has gone much thinner and has no tummy.

The $17.40 *((see previous entry))* is the balance of the $105 which wasn't spent on kitchen requirement. *((The earlier mentioned prospective gift of $75 each had it seems originally been $100 which was then reduced to $75 so that the communal kitchens could buy basics for all with $25 from everyone.))* Most of our family's money is going into town via Mrs G, she goes in for x-ray today but is inundated with orders like ours, and I'm a bit worried at the outcome. We're also trying to get a hot plate.

The hospital office smells of apricots – there are crates of dried fruit here for the 'Welfare' (a sort of camp charity for the most needy cases – don't know where the funds come from). Somehow it is comforting to see the food, though healthy folk like me probably won't have any of it.

26 May 1942

Rumours that some of regular army are at the Fort (Stanley) to do some work.

Mum came downstairs from ward for the first time, groggy at the knees. We got salt, raisins, cornflakes at canteen today; and an enamel mug, basin, hanks and toilet paper from Welfare!

Mrs G had to shed most of her orders before she went yesterday – most probably ours was amongst them.

27 May 1942

Mrs G back from x-ray today, and bought us food and a hotplate *((a tiny plate like a hob which plugged into the socket in our room: very primitive but very efficient except when, as often happened, the wires broke and had to be continually re-connected with a bit of tin pressed together.))*

We are so rich in food – so wonderful to have all that food, 'choko' (21 oz), 1 lb Vitacup, 3 tins of cream and wheat, 1 lb porridge, pkt prunes, pkt muscatels, pkt table salt, raisins, 2 lbs wong tong (Chinese block sugar), half a lb white sugar, 1 jar syrup, small tin treacle, l lb 'Mother's cocoa', and 6 small tins jam; three 12 oz tins of butter, and a bunch of bananas. Most of that was bought with Olive's $50 note, and we have a 5 lb tin of jam to come, and a tin of salmon to celebrate Mum's homecoming tomorrow.

These last two evenings Mum, Olive and I have been sitting outside hospital on the grass, eating our supper – Mum sitting enthroned in the rocky wooden invalid's chair. Almost everyone who passed commented that it looked as if Mum was the Queen holding court and we girls the handmaidens draped around.

28 May 1942

Mum came home yesterday.

Frightfully hot.

29 May 1942

Despite having my glasses, am beginning to have trouble with eyes – no sunglasses. Went with Mum to Welfare, she got milk powder and apricots.

Mrs. Grant has lost 70 lbs. *((This is the neighbour and friend who, when we were shipped to Stanley, cried that she couldn't jump from our ship into the junk to take us ashore. Mum too had lost a tremendous amount of weight. She weighed 133 lbs. when she came out of hospital, having been about 170 pre-Jap attack.))*

We may be swimming next month!

30 May 1942

Talk of tiger, that one has been shot.

31 May 1942

Mum getting stronger day by day.

Photo in newspaper of tiger caught in Stanley; yesterday there were rumours about tigers being loose and being seen – they must have been true. There are said to be another, and cubs, and a leopard loose – I think from circus.

1 Jun 1942

Some trunks arrived today from Repulse Bay Hotel. Mrs. Longworth *((in neighbouring room))* got one, and so did the Puckles. Makes me think that perhaps some of our trunks at home *((Happy Valley flat))* may be more or less intact. *((They weren't... even the trunks had been taken.))*

Mrs G borrowed a razor and we all shaved under our arms – wonderful after all this time. Rumours of swimming, but not definite yet.

Mum doing fine.

2 Jun 1942

News of DMS wanting nursing sisters for Kowloon. Tongue is sore.

3 Jun 1942

Everyone got two pairs of shorts and two shirts from Welfare today. *((The shorts were a peculiar shape, and unisex but adaptable. The shirts were bright colours which did wonders for our morale, in a sort of cotton ribbing. We girls mainly wore our shirts upside down, cutting off the original v-neck which became the bottom hem; the original bottom hem was then sewn up to go across the shoulders, forming a more circular neck which looked quite stylish – to us.))*

Frightening to remember that now it stays hot like this right through till late October – Mr Fraser's original estimate of our incarceration.

Tiger still at large. Dr Selwyn Clarke came in yesterday and wanted nurses for Kowloon Hospital. Mrs. Greenwood very disappointed – they wouldn't consider her because she has an operation pending. I do wish they would make it an exchange and send Mabel to us. Mum longs so much for her. Some of the Americans have had their $75 parcels in. Mrs K sick.

4 Jun 1942

Tiger still loose.

Mum weighs 150 lbs, Olive 131, me 113 (rice fat).

6 Jun 1942

Rumours are that we will ALL be repatriated. Some of the Americans have had their $75 parcels. Mrs K sick.

7 Jun 1942

No fresh meat in today or yesterday.

9 June 1942

Dr Erooga said Mabel had a goitre – that he saw it when she was in Queen Mary Hospital (just before the war) with dragging foot.

13 Jun 1942

Tonight concert given to the Americans because they are due to leave soon. Costumes grand. Carol Bateman arranged it. Graceful dancing, piano duet by Elizabeth Drown and Mrs Barton. Chorus with good lines about how 'we do like to be beside the sea-side', and 'the joys of Stanley prom, but the lack of to and from.' It was on the Prison Officers' club ground – lovely and cool. At the end Mr Gimson gave a good speech, and said more than one would have expected.

The principal reason for the concert – departure of the Americans for HOME – seems far too good to be true. I know we must all leave here some time (except for those of us who may die in the natural order of things) yet it would be so wonderful to set out for Home – almost a dream.

Electricity went off for a while.

14 Jun 1942

Two nurses here were suddenly informed this evening to be ready to go to Bowen Road Hospital tomorrow at 10 *((I think they had volunteered earlier to go))*, that must mean some must be coming here. Hope that Mabel will be among those to come in.

Tonight Mum and I started brushing up our French with Mrs Cryan.

16 Jun 1942

Up early. Raining, so got into my shorts, borrowed Mrs G's clogs and short mack, and hurried up to admin. bungalow on hill. Heaps of people waiting there – men for the ration lorry; some to collect parcels sent them from people in town, and nurses waiting to go to B. Rd Hosp. After a long wait, Mr Nielson came over and said the rain was stopping the arrival today. The hopes of Mabel coming have almost diminished again, because during the day I've heard of heaps of people who had been agitating to come from the hospital into camp. I waited about a bit longer, then came down. Blister on foot from clogs in the rain on an incline in a hurry.

17 Jun 1942

But Mabel came, after all, about 4.30pm, so wonderful!

While I was working in the hosp. I heard from one of the nurses that a young girl had arrived to join her mother, with a few others from the

Bowen Rd. Hosp., so careered up to the blocks. Outside the Dutch Block a business-like person was directing unloading operations on the lorry – Mabel, wearing unfamiliar clothes: competent, capable, independent *((not like my little sister, five years younger than me)).* She's fatter in the face, and brought messages *((including one for me from Arthur, written in January – this is what he says:-*

'My dear Barbara,

Your very welcome notes eventually reached me – the first one when I was at Wanchai Gap and the second here, both of course brought by Sid. I certainly was relieved to know that you were well and had not been put out too much, though of course I realise how you must feel about the home and losses involved. Never mind, my dear, everything WILL be OK before long. How about those bedsocks right now? Brr. When we first came back from the mainland, after that pitiful effort at holding the enemy, I tried to phone you from Taikoo, seven times in one day. I had no luck; however, one female voice said you were in a tunnel – I didn't think for a moment she was sane, though I heard afterwards you were working under the ground.

The latest news I heard re the Stanley folk, was that they were being treated well, and had no cause to complain of treatment, and trust this correct. We have had many new arrivals from various hospitals nearby, and they were all under the impression that we were living in grand style out here (Shamshuipo Camp) and so on and so on. How the ... do those yarns get around?

We get two issues of rice per day, the morning one without fail naked and ashamed – just plain rice. The evening dish is sometimes accompanied by a cupful of vegetable water, sometimes a cupful of soya beans, and sometimes a cupful of stew, which tastes suspiciously of meat – though visible signs are definitely lacking. However we've been told that the messing

WILL improve and that we will probably get SOMETHING WITH BOTH ISSUES OF RICE.

Before we left Victoria Barracks we got a number of tinned goods, and some tea and sugar. The tinned stuff has long since gone, tho I'm pleased to say the tea is still available. Smokes of course are out of the question, unless one is lucky enough to get an occasional fag-end from these lucky people who get parcels sent in. I wonder how long these will continue. I really think the people outside will have a devil of a job to get food or money in the near future.

Well, enough of the moans. Except for a continuous emptiness in all regions, I feel quite well and have been told that I look VERY WELL. There are a few instruments here and a band of sorts functions occasionally. I take a turn in conducting and blowing a saxophone. A few weeks ago I woke at 4am and thought about a phrase 'How's your morale?' – and before daylight I had outlined a verse and chorus and a tune. The thing is on paper, but I really don't think the time is ripe to put it before the troops.

I am lucky to have borrowed a Pitman's shorthand book and have started to scratch at angles and circles. I find it very fascinating, though the paper question is rather acute.

Sid doing well as a cropper of heads – pardon me, hairdresser. Topper looks well on rice diet, he even appears to be putting on weight. I hesitate to predict my weight after many more months over here.

No doubt you hear many rumours as to the rest of the war. I am keeping a Propaganda Book and so far it is full of contradictions. I hope you are keeping very fit and managing to find enough to do, to make the days pass quickly by. This cold weather is just too bracing for words. I've been sleeping with as much clothing on as I can get on, but I rarely sleep for more than 4 hours at a stretch – it is just too, too cold.

Please give my very kindest wishes to your Mother and to Olive. I trust it won't be long ere we all may meet once more. What a lot of yarns will be swapped across the room. Keep cheery. Sid has just said 'I bet she doesn't get chips with her meals' – what a hard neck! The favourite pastime here is making up menus for future reference. Hope you get this before Christmas.

My love to you,

Arthur.'

((There was no date on this letter, but it was obviously written months before I received it.))

18 Jun 1942

I'm beginning to feel sorry we brought Mabel away, and that I didn't stick out the nursing lectures and have been with her.

19 Jun 1942

Farewell dance for the Americans; we waited outside hall, too crowded to stay inside.

Mabel missing the companionship of the girls at the hospital, she was having the time of her life there, where she was the youngest. There was always the chance to hear from Sid (long since discharged from the Military Hospital, now in Shamshuipo Camp, but lorries from there sometimes brought sick soldiers.) I have been hearing about soldier Bickley who was so brave though blinded, and how she wept buckets when she fed him; how she was always breaking thermometers.

Volunteers are being asked for Military Hospital, how Mabel's face lit up when I told her about it. She said, 'Let's you and I go there.' I would love to but the name Redwood would hardly get past HQ after the fuss we had to get her here. I hope Nan and the other VADs will come here soon.

Selwyn-Clarke came in to office today and gave me, Olive and Dorothy some lovely milk chocolate.

We had a feast tonight – bully beef.

((Mabel was also missing her bed at the hospital: the only bed we had for her was made by piling one suitcase on top of another.))

21 Jun 1942

We only have one tin of bully left, and are counting on our $75 parcels coming in.

Mabel is to start piano lessons which should help out with her boredom. *((Several pianos had been left in the camp, some relics of personal furniture in the flats pre-war.))*

Went to Mr Shields (dentist, known as Sammy), at last he has found the reason for my ache – a large cavity half the size of the tooth. It was horribly painful.

Americans were to have gone tomorrow, but now postponed till Saturday.

23 Jun 1942

Mum said please yourself (about Mabel volunteering to go to Military Hospital) but I know she was hurt that we should want to take steps from her. As it turned out they are trying to get 3 from Military Hosp. without exchange, but have names ready in case there has to be an exchange. Volunteers for Military Hosp haven't come forward in any numbers. Mum says Mabel can put her name down to go back if she wants to – tho I blush to think what Selwyn-Clarke will think about it. Mabel says, why don't I try to come back with her? I would like to go with Mabel, but feel afraid lest I couldn't do all the jobs there. Mum would be happier if I went with Mabel than if she went alone.

Americans were to have gone tomorrow, but now postponed till Saturday.

Today some women (including Mrs G and Mrs Macklin) got an allotment from their husbands *((in Kowloon camps. Although these money allotments were very small, the wonderful part was that these ladies saw their husbands' handwriting sanctioning the allotment so knew they were still alive.))*

News isn't good. Tobruk has surrendered, it's said we have lost 25,000 prisoners there; also glum news of attack on a convoy in the Med.

We have heard guns these past few days, it was suggested that the Japs are re-enacting the capture of Hong Kong.

25 Jun 1942

Today's reported rumour is that Eden is again talking repatriation for us.

Mabel much brighter today. Military Hospital question has arisen again, but I don't think I should go, even if I had the chance, but I mean to read up Home Nursing and First Aid just in case. Mabel agrees that we wait and see who arrives *((from the Hosp., in case her friends come to Stanley on transfer)).*

Canteen – we've restocked the larder on Mabel's $17.40.

28 Jun 1942

Looks as if the Americans are really going away tomorrow.

Rumours that rations cut by 10% – and we will be repatriated next.

Highbrow concert tonight, Arthur Lay at the piano. Tim Fortescue was good in a play.

Started writing new story 'Balancing Jean' – but only put the title and 'Chapter 1'.

29 Jun 1942

Americans are on board the 'Asama Maru' and it's lying off the bay but no lights so far.

Notice on Dutch Q. notice board about 4 relief ships now loading at New York, and that 2 are bound for Europe and 2 for the Far East, and that all civilian foreign nationals will probably be compulsorily evacuated thereon when the ships have unloaded.

Had 3 more teeth stopped today, that makes 5 fillings done since Sunday before last.

3 Jul 1942

The Americans have gone, 30th June.

Went to Dr Kirk today and he has prescribed palm oil for 'K' *((camp medical name for lack of periods, which affected most of us women))*.

Tales that the notice about civilian foreign nationals doesn't apply to us, that Eden is still talking repatriation, and that we are in a very bad way in Egypt. My weight now about 114 lbs, Olive still gaining, Mum losing a little. We haven't got our $75 parcels yet.

No relief in our room though more accommodation is available now American Quarters are vacant.

Started 'Holly' story.

Some $75 parcels are in – not ours.

7 Jul 1942

Sebastopol gone. Thrust on Kharkov by Germans.

Photos (by Japs) were being taken in the food queue today.

8 Jul 1942

I received $15 from A. J. C. Taylor *((pre-war HK Treasury, this must have been a Govt. handout))*. So did Olive – a great help for canteen.

9 Jul 1942

Tony *((Cole))* invited Mabel and I to tea, he had had his $75 parcel. So generous of him, he had saved part of his yesterday's bread ration and we had toast and butter, and tea with sugar. Splendid of people to be so kind in days like these.

Mrs. Barrow's baby Oriana died this morning, of water on the brain. Mrs B *((a Govt. nursing sister))* took it very quietly, though had been expecting the death.

10 Jul 1942

After Oriana's funeral, wrote poem:-

'I have seen the anxious and fearful eyes
Of a wife who knows that her husband lies.
I have heard the hopeless moan of despair
Of a woman whose man is no longer there.
I have stood by the open grave of a child
Whose mother stood by while the earth was piled.

Faithlessness, death – all the risks that attend
Attachments on which we would grow to depend;
I wonder, would this make me hesitate
Though all other voices say 'Marry thy mate' ?

11 Jul 1942

Dance at St Stephen's tonight, Mum, Mabel and I went with Tony. Cabaret too: June Winkelman did a tap dance, a fellow played banjo, and Azalea Reynolds did a dance – very graceful. The band was topping too. R.J. (Dick) Cloake – South China Morning Post reporter – danced with me, and talked about writing.

Got on well with story *((a lot of the paper provided by Dorothy Holloway, who had brought a pack of lined blue foolscap into camp; I wrote originally in shorthand, then typed on the backs of old medical sheets from the records we had to make in the hospital for the Japanese.))*

12 Jul 1942

We *((Dorothy Holloway, Olive and I))* started having one Sunday in 3 entirely free from hosp. office work. Russians not in a good position.

13 Jul 1942

Rumour that 'Conte Verde' with Shanghai Americans aboard struck a mine outside Singapore, and all rescued; another rumour that British stopped the ship because she carried guns, and took off her passengers then torpedoed her. CSO deny it, and nothing in local paper about it.

Egypt news about the same, fierce fighting there. German advances in Russia, camp rumour that Russians have driven Germans out of Sebastapol.

14 Jul 1942

Started teaching Mr Weir shorthand.

Finished first chapter of story.

15 Jul 1942

Mabel and I back from paddling round the blocks with no shoes on. She told me about the shows the VADs gave at the Military Hospital (often known as Bowen Road Hospital); and when she, as the baby of the VADs, was called upon to present a bouquet of flowers to the Matron for some anniversary. And how upset Nanny (Nancy Grady) was when Mabel came away.

News still supposed to be improving – Egypt, and Crimea, but local paper still claiming Germans getting into Russia.

Tony came in evening, we played rummy. His news is that the Japs are jittery – but his news is always on the optimistic side *((what a good thing, he was a great morale raiser.))*

16 Jul 1942

An old man of the sea died today – Anton Munze. He was tattooed almost from head to foot, and was known as 'Canaker Dick.'

Tony came to say Mr Murphy will swap his mattress for our teapot. *((Mum had a real bed, but no mattress so she slept on the springs. There had originally been a mattress but it was alive with bugs so had to be dumped.))*

Mabel's parcel arrived – grand: included 1 lb bacon, 2 lbs biscuits, 5 lb tin jam, 8 oz coffee, 3 lbs raisins, 5 lbs. 7 ozs wong tong and 1 lb butter to come.

We wrote 25-word Red Cross letters (in pencil), stamped Red Cross, Shanghai, 27487.

Mum wrote to Aunt Lillian in Gillingham, Kent:-

> 'Girls and myself all well and together. Future movements uncertain. Will write when able. Probably see Bess and Hilda. Don't worry. Love Mab and Girls.'

((The reference to Mum's sisters Bess and Hilda, who lived in Rhodesia, was to imply that we might get repatriated via Lourenco Marques in Mozambique and could maybe get to them from there. This message reached Aunt Lil safely, her reply was on the back of Mum's and dated 25.2.43:-

> 'Pleased and thankful for your message. All here very fit – weather tempting Alf to garden, me to spring-clean. Love to you and girls, Lillian.'

Post-war we learned that Lillian had been most relieved to get Mum's message that we were all together, as the Red Cross had during war issued a list of internees in Stanley, and my sister Mabel's name was not on it, so Auntie thought Mabel had been killed. She was in the Military Hospital when that list was compiled.))

17 Jul 1942

We have the mattress... hope it's not got bugs in it. How lucky we've been in acquiring things – suitcases *((which Mum was given when at Queen Mary Hospital))*, camp-beds, mattress, hot plate, Mabel (!) and FOOD.

News about Java landings, local bombings, things happening in Burma. We may go swimming on Sunday.

18 Jul 1942

All the rumours are conflicting: we are doing well in Egypt and Russia... we are NOT doing ditto.

At canteen today I bought a Shanghai-produced 'Lacovomalt' for Mum, and someone either swiped it in a split second, or else the correct amount weren't handed out from stock: still, they gave me another tin.

19 Jul 1942

Electricity off in a.m. and hasn't been on since.

Swimming to start on Governor's beach *((in peacetime it was the Governor's))*. Our turn was in the morning, but hitch occurred and we waited in vain *((for permission to go to beach))*.

20 Jul 1942

Electricity still off in some quarters.

Mabel has pain in throat, Dr. Hackett said it might be an incipient quinzy, she has been given gargle.

We have acquired a camp bed for Mabel through one of the young RC priests. *((Up to then, she'd still been sleeping on piled-up suitcases))*.

Shanghai people are supposed to be leaving us for Shanghai if they can get the money for their fare from this end.

Paper today says that ships coming to take 1800 Britishers from Nippon etc., but I don't think it means us.

21 Jul 1942

Elec. off all over until evening.

Shanghai people postponed for a few days.

The papers say that Britishers in Hong Kong will not be repatriated.

22 Jul 1942

News bad in Russia, so-so in Egypt. Pork today – Olive felt bad after it and went home from office, and Dr. Selwyn-Clarke came in and so I was busy as busy. Our flat's electricity still out.

Mabel's throat worse, she can get her food at the Diet Kitchen today – tomato soup and rice pudding.

((To make the rations more palatable for invalids and very young children, some adult invalids qualified to get their meals from the Diet Kitchen (ground floor room in Block 2) where the rice was cooked into a mash.))

23 Jul 1942

Two years today since Dad died.

Nine bombers flew over, and one ship towing another.

Elec. off on our floor. Nothing in the way of meat.

Shanghai people standing by.

In evening Mabel and I walked to St Stephen's in the hope that Elizabeth Drown would be playing, but no. We went to cemetery, and saw body on ricks and bundles on the beach.

24 Jul 1942

The bottom fell out of the HK dollar – now worth only half as much as before.

Madame Le Bon visited camp and was in a great state about it. *((I think she made trusses etc. for hernia cases.))*

Worried lest the value of our $75 parcels drops *((only a few internees had so far received their parcels.))*

People haven't left for Shanghai.

25 Jul 1942

Grand concert on Bowling Green. Good new song – 'We're going to sail away, sail away etc *(('We know internment here will end one day; we want to go; we've got to go, for we're longing to see the land that we love so... There'll be happy hearts and free, when we're going out to sea, Afloat on a boat on the way to Lourenco Marques.' – rumoured to be our destination for exchange if ever we were repatriated.))*

I had a row with a man over my programme (I one of the lucky ones who had one.)

Mrs Drown (piano) in white pierrot dress with black bobbles, white collar coiffe and frills round her wrists. Ian Heath played piano too. June Winkelman and another child did a good acrobatic turn. Eve Gray (a teacher I think) was good, even when forgetting her lines.

Olive met Paddy Gill's wife Billie, she has asked us to go to tea next Friday. *((Paddy Gill was an Army friend of our family up to early 1940 when he was sent to the UK. We knew he married her before his departure, but we had never met her; she had a baby boy later that year.))*

Launches came for the Shanghailanders, but departure postponed again.

In morning we went to cemetery, saw launches come for the Shanghailanders, but they were postponed again.

26 Jul 1942

The Shanghailanders really left this afternoon. I'm still getting fatter, 120 and a half lbs.

28 Jul 1942

Paper says the Americans have arrived at Lourenco Marques, transhipped and are on their way to America.

29 Jul 1942

Part-typhoon, white billows and great foam and spray breaking against the rocks beside the hospital and the little island beyond.

Dr Selwyn-Clarke came in, said No. 9 signal is up.

Miss Hill has stopped shorthand lessons for a while. Swim in morning. I wore Welfare shorts (khaki, unisex, and hanky front.)

30 Jul 1942

Olive's 26th birthday. She made a currant bread loaf, and had 'party' in Joan Walkden's corridor. Ginger (H. Angus, Govt. clerk), also Bill Kerr. Also there Lorraine Money, of 'Courtlands' Kennedy Road, Bicky (B.I. Bickford) and Nielson.

Bill Kerr told how he had milked the cows at Pokfulam during the war, and pinched piglets!

Mrs Ross died and was buried. *((She was a late middle-aged lady, on her own in camp, who lived in a room two doors away from ours. She just gave up trying to live. Felt dreadful for her, when listing her poor little collection of personal effects at the hospital.))*

31 Jul 1942

News bad about Russia.

Row with Olive about buns. I threw one at her. *((At this time there was still a flour ration, and we each had a bread bun every day. Of course they weren't exactly of uniform size, so we used to take it in turns having first choice from our room's supply. On this day, I thought it was my turn to choose, so took the best one; but Olive insisted it was HER turn, so we had a fierce argument, then I threw my bun at her – it hit her on the face... I felt so ashamed afterwards, and we all wept.))*

Baby Elizabeth Mary born to Mrs Dorothy Fyffe.

1 Aug 1942

Little boy McLeod blew himself up – he's all right so far. *((He must have picked up some small explosive lying around; he recovered quickly.))*

Mr Watson (Police) started giving me Cantonese lessons.

Olive and I went to see Mrs Billie Gill and Brian who was 2 years old yesterday, in Bungalow B.

Brian looks mostly like his mother, but he has Paddy's mouth and teeth. Very big and talkative for his age.

Paddy went through Dunkirk.

2 Aug 1942

Olive and I went to tea with Mary and Peggy Taylor and Sheila Bruce. *((Peggy's husband Alex Taylor, Mary's brother, not in Stanley))*. Jim Johnson (Police) there too. He thinks another 2 years of this – he isn't usually wrong about politics etc.

My weight about 122 now. Started having thyroid tablets as well as oil (treatment for K). An old lady, Mrs Mary Williamson, died this afternoon.

Mrs G says she expects to be moving *((from our room))* within a day or two.

3 Aug 1942

Last night we ate our last tin – it was of sausages – and this afternoon, our parcels arrived! Grand, tins of corned beef, salmon; bovril, cod liver oil and malt, chocolate, cheese, crystallised ginger, oats, biscuits, oxo, and toilet paper and soap.

In morning Mrs. K, Olive, Mabel and I went swimming. Dr Loan was there, looking after the kids – he is 'Uncle John' to them, such a grand, earnest man and wonderful with children. My legs are tired, I've been up the slope about 5 times *((between Married Quarters and hospital, and along the catwalk round the boundary of Stanley Gaol to the beach and back.))*

Repatriation rumours have died down and everyone talks about when we will be back in Hong Kong.

Russian news still very grave.

Had my hair cut short today – fed up with it being straggly and hot; so will let it lie fallow for a few months, then turn it under, in preparation for a perm later on *((i.e. when we get out of camp!!))*

4 Aug 1942

Rumours that Kai Tak was bombed and working party of our men killed or wounded (down to the name of the officer in charge! – later discounted.)

5 Aug 1942

News came in today, and discounted, that the troops, and/or folk at St Theresa's Hospital Kowloon had been sent over to Hong Kong. Kowloon said to have been bombed, and that public hadn't been allowed to go to Kowloon on Monday because Japs said there was bombing. First rain for about 2 months.

Paper says Prof. Robertson, who has been working in Bacteriological Institute in city all along, has died.

James Mason died in Indian Quarters this afternoon; according to rumour, he has Chinese family outside and had been trying to get them in here.

6 Aug 1942

Tiger marks opposite hospital path!

This morning a large grey ship came rushing across the sea, and a launch followed it, tooting loudly and continuously; we saw smoke and wondered what it was all about, but no satisfaction.

Mabel and I and Mrs K went swimming in morning. The ginger we got in the parcel is absolutely delicious.

7 Aug 1942

Selwyn-Clarke came in, and brought false teeth, which aren't Mum's. *((Just before the Jap attack, Dr Chawn in town was making a denture for Mum, so in camp she asked if there was any chance of getting it. In retrospect, what a fantastic person Selwyn-Clarke was to take time, under difficult circumstances i.e. the Japs, to try to ferret out someone's denture!))*

Wonderful news – all the VADs are due here on Monday, so glad for Mabel's sake.

8 Aug 1942

'Amateur Nite' concert. Gimson made good speech at the end. Danny Wilson (Peggy's husband) amazingly good in impressions. People lying back on the grass in the darkness, smoking. Lightning sometimes. Hottest day we've had.

Swimming, I wore new yellow bathing costume made this afternoon from Welfare shirt. Olive and Mabel have blue ones. Mum's old Jantzen bathing costume is in camp. *((Mum saw it hanging on the clothes line in the courtyard, and recognised it by its large size and the huge button she had sewn on it as the original one was too small)).* Mrs Fisher has it, she got it from Mrs Greenberg who died early on in camp, who apparently got it from the matshed at Repulse Bay *((where we kept our swimming gear pre-war))*.

Row with Mrs G about space in room.

9 Aug 1942

Mabel and I went for a swim this wonderful morning – Brian and Billie Gill there. Notice that we're not allowed beyond gate tomorrow when VADs come.

10 Aug 1942

Mabel is happy. 'Mara' (Tamara Jex), 'Nanny' (Nan Grady), and 'Jin' (Virginia Beaumont) are here. Mabel and I sat in boiling sun on grass above the Indian Quarters and waited patiently. I had all day off. VADs arrived in 3 buses, their luggage came by sea. Rosaleen (Millar) was hanging out of the first bus. Nan spotted Mabel and called her, and Mabel called 'Nanny' and it made me want to cry. Mabel careered over to them on Bowling Green where luggage was being sorted – much embracing.

Muriel McCaw came as a stretcher case and is in hospital now.

Colossal row over bedspace in room this morning during washing floor operations. *((There were now 6 of us in a very small room.))*

11 Aug 1942

Mum and I to lecture on Philosophy by Rev. Short – on bank by hospital.

Little Brian and Mrs Gill and (friend) Freda came to tea in afternoon. Brian so sweet.

12 Aug 1942

To St Stephen's, heard A.T. Lay playing *((piano))*.

Mrs G moved out today, we have changed beds around.

We stenos at hospital are to have holidays. *((i.e. not just days off))*.

Muriel McCaw has been in hospital (Military) for 2 months, has had all her hair cut off, lost a lot of weight, weak voice.

13 Aug 1942

Received $14 from govt. – only worth 3 and a half yen, but a great help.

Tales that many of the men *((POWs in other camps))* have died of diphtheria.

Miss Hill *((Eve, a Nursing Sister))* re-started at shorthand.

14 Aug 1942

Mr Stott ('Bok') at French Hospital escaped, and now no more folk are allowed to go there from camp for x-ray. *((Stott was married to a Chinese lady.))*

Rumour that 'Eagle' has been sunk, Mrs. G's boy is on her.

Vatican has sent camp $150,000 – it will be about 1 Yen each.

The rumours of 4-point invasion of Europe are said to be false.

In evening Mum and I sat on bank outside the Leprosarium *((as it had pre-war been; now used as quarters for the doctors, as it was fairly near the camp hospital))* and talked to Dr. J. Selby. I looked at 'Southcliffe' (holiday home) across the bay and thought about the time when I almost went there for my leave last year.

15 Aug 1942

Jap paper says Berlin reports that 'Eagle' has been sunk.

Softball match tonight on the Indian Quarters Green, men dressed in various Stanley fashions – one in a hula skirt, one in Mae Westish costume, played against a regular girls' team. Later, community singing there.

Police have made gardens now in front of the block to which they have been moved, and there's a V-shaped piece of land in a corner, a V planted inside it. *(('V' for Victory!))*

16 Aug 1942

We went swimming – including Mum, her first attempt in Stanley, with a roll-on suspender belt underneath costume. So gorgeous, able to wallow in that lovely warm water. *((No hot water to wash ourselves or clothes in the blocks)).*

Talking about writing to Golly Anslow *((Francis Joseph, son of F.P. Anslow who worked in the hospital office. Golly often came to talk to his dad as they weren't billeted together. Little did I think then that he and I would be married six years later)).*

17 Aug 1942

Mrs 'X' wanting the sink removed from our kitchen; committee being asked about it tonight, we sent in a protest – almost all the block.

Miss Ellis *((Leontine))* – from St. Theresa's – died this morning.

So tired and sunburnt, afternoon off, spent it at the beach. Olive started to have a week's holiday, Norah Witchell taking her place for the time being. *((Post war, Norah married Hong Kong policeman Stutchbury. She was murdered in Malaya during the troubles there.))*

18 Aug 1942

Mum and I went to talk by Mr Gilmour. (Boss to Mabel for 2 days when she worked at CSO at the beginning of our war.) Grand, very amusing. He was District Officer of various outposts. *((We saw him in early 1972 in a TV documentary about the Far Eastern war; he was still in Singapore, looking blooming.))*

The kitchen sink *((see yesterday's diary entry))* will NOT be removed.

19 Aug 1942

Am annoyed because the camp voting hours *((for Council))* don't let me vote *((because of my hospital office shift)).*

HK News (paper) rather depressing – about Germans pressing through the Caucasus. Rather ominous that we haven't had any news of the usual good sort lately. Extra potato at dinner.

Mary (Taylor) is in hospital just now, she looks so pale.

20 Aug 1942

Mrs G has moved to Block 2, Married Q. *((She was given a room to herself – an awkward tiny ex-boiler room, where she could snore to her heart's content without annoying anyone.))*

I weigh 119 lbs.

21 Aug 1942

Olive and I went to talk by American Maryknoll priest, Father Donald Hessler, about marriage, in the garage near where ration lorry comes. *((First met Peggy Barton there, and she was to become my dearest friend.))*

I had first Menformon injection today (for K).

22 Aug 1942

Started 5 days' holiday. Swimming in morning with Dorothy (Holloway), and in afternoon with Mabel and the VADs.

Concert in evening: hula dancing; and Mrs Drown (piano); Steve Moring (banjo or similar) sang Camp Down Races with great vim and vigour, and played his own composition called Troubles. Mr Gimson spoke at the end and one of the hula girls presented him with a lei and he kissed her. Then Mr Gimson gave Elizabeth a lei and kissed her.

23 Aug 1942

Rumours of British landings on continent, with rather severe losses.

A policeman, Fred Kelly, for whom I did some church typing recently, has promised to give me some writing paper.

24 Aug 1942

Swimming with Mabel. At last she's got a pair of shoes – a swop with someone, black patent, for white rubber-heeled. I had second injection. Got a little paper from Kelly.

Felt honoured because Elizabeth Drown invited me to sit beside her on a wooden crate in the pantry, and think of ideas for a sketch she and Ian Heath are doing in the next concert!

Re-started *((writing in shorthand))*. To French lesson with Jimmy Ferrier.

25 Aug 1942

Went to a lecture on Tea by Mr P.E. Witham in evening.

26 Aug 1942

Lovely meat cake at tiffin.

Did more writing during the rest hour. *((Camp consensus decided that the hours between noon and 2pm should be kept as far as possible as 'quiet hours', i.e. the time immediately after the 11am meal finished)).*

Went to see Mary (Taylor) in hospital, she's not to come out for about a week.

27 Aug 1942

Dorothy has given me some blue lined paper to make next year's diary. Good walk round after hearing duets at St Stephen's by Elizabeth Drown and Miss Bicheno.

To French lesson. Jimmy didn't come, but Dr Barwell was there.

Swimming late afternoon.

Paper says that Duke of Kent has been killed in a flying accident.

28 Aug 1942

This evening Mr Fred Kelly (Police) visited us, also Father Moore, an American Maryknoll Mission priest, very young and sincere. *((He was one of eight newly-ordained RC priests who had flown into Hong Kong just before the Jap. attack for transfer to Missions in China. They joined enthusiastically in camp sports, but much of their time was taken up in language lessons (Chinese) given by an older priest, Father Bernard Meyer.))*

Fr Moore said he's having the best time here he's had since he was a kid, he gave us lovely new soft-back prayer books, and promises to lend us books from the American library.

((Americans had managed to bring their very good Club library into camp, but it was made available only to the Americans. The much-prized books were housed in a small secured lobby in the Prisoner Officers' Club hall. After the Americans were repatriated, friends of the Americans (and friends of friends) acquired tickets, as did we Redwoods from Fr Moore. There was also a very small makeshift library for us in an ex-boiler room in the Married Quarters, its contents just a few books handed in by internees after an appeal, so very little selection but better than nothing!))

Hong Kong News reports that Hitler has been 'missing' for the last 6 weeks, and attributes it to supposition that he is away planning a new front.

Mabel and Nan slept on the roof last night. I'm going to try it tonight.

29 Aug 1942

Meant to sleep on the roof last night with Mabel and Nan. Glorious moon and wonderfully cool, but hardly slept at all – very hard surface; at 2.30am rain began in real earnest so I came down then, tho the others stayed.

Mary not so well now.

30 Aug 1942

Mabel 19 today. Popped up to ward to say Happy Birthday to Mary, it's her birthday too – 24th. Mara, Nan and friends gave Mabel pretty birthday (home-made) cards, and hankies, and a party this afternoon in the cemetery.

Mrs G cooked the cake! – nominally for Nan's friend Una in Married Q. kitchen. *((Constance Una Brown, whose husband in HKVDC was killed during fighting; their little daughter Annette was also in camp.))*

Mabel and Nan got swamped up on the roof last night, so came down and slept in the bathroom. Nan has two sisters – Eva nearly 17 and Jean nearly 16, both in UK with parents.

To Benediction in afternoon. In evening piano recital. The lovely music upset Mabel, because no Sid here on her birthday.

Later we fried sweet potatoes from Mr J.H. Gelling's garden *((they were a birthday present))*, and had salmon and rice; Nan came along too – a nice little spread.

Duke of Kent was apparently killed on 25th August.

31 Aug 1942

Rain and typhoony. Electricity off for a while. French in a.m., some other girls have now joined. *((These classes were held in the upper gallery of St Stephen's Hall.))*

I should have had 4th injection but electricity off therefore no sterilizing could be done.

Thought I was going to lose my fountain pen this morning *((i.e. I was writing my diary with it beside the Prison Officers Club))*: two Japs came along and had their eyes on it – but nothing happened.

1 Sep 1942

Mary's name is down for x-ray and the threat of chest trouble looms again. She gets 2 bottles of milk a day at hospital and that will help.

Rumour is (a) the Russians are retreating round Stalingrad, and (b) the Russians have counter-attacked on various fronts. Also, that Canada has invited us in the Far East to go to Canada, all our expenses paid.

Mr Bendall gave Mabel a lovely cake of good soap for her birthday – Agafuroffs sent him it in a parcel. *((Pre-war we often played tennis with Jimmy Bendall and the Agafuroff brothers at the Civil Service Club, Happy Valley. The Agafuroff brothers were not interned, I think they were Indian and probably both worked in the HK Government. I never heard anything of them after the war.))*

2 Sep 1942

We may write to Shamshuipo Camp – 50 words, but only 1 card per family, but Mr Fantham says I may use his.

Finished Chapter 2 of story *((written in shorthand))*.

3 Sep 1942

Repat. rumours in the air again.

In evening, to St Stephen's to hear Mrs. Drown play piano with Miss Bicheno – wonderful music.

Baby Ogley (Olivia) born today. Baby Cautherley (George) yesterday.

Olive has bad cold. She despatched $5 to Topper (in Shamshuipo Camp).

4 Sep 1942

We each received HK$5 from the Vatican. Olive has already sent hers to Topper, Mabel and I intend to send ours to the boys tomorrow. *(('The boys' were Arthur Alsey and Harry (Sid) Hale, Royal Scots, also in Shamshuipo Camp.))*

We were all inoculated against cholera.

Got enamel plate from Welfare, and some white material. *((No crockery, cutlery or bed linen was supplied by the Japs – you just used whatever you were able to bring in to camp, or improvised.))*

Olive had one big row with Miss D. Geen (Assistant Matron at hospital), ended with tears and apologies, and Miss Geen saying what a wonderful girl Olive was.

Notice on pros and cons of repatriation came round. The gist was (among other things) that Mr Gimson had laid before the Japs a scheme of repatriating 1,000 women, children, aged and infirm; that any scheme the Japs would consider would embrace the large majority of us. Most people here think it means we won't be going.

5 Sep 1942

Had 4th injection. Joyce Shaw's father died (Joyce was a friend of Mabel's, she was in Australia.)

Further warning about taking too much notice of repatriation prospects came round today.

Optimist's Concert good, especially Vi Evans and Mr Garton. *((Vivian Garton, PWD. Vi Evans had been a neighbour of us Redwoods in Gap Road, Happy Valley. She died later in camp.))*

Played around with 'planchette' gadget this evening by Una's room – I always was incredulous... never believed in it.

6 Sep 1942

Mabel had been saving her bread slice for afternoon when she and friends were going to have a picnic. She said she felt sick and dizzy in church. Later on in morning, she flopped down in the room, it turned my heart over. Dr Tomlinson came and said it was only through not eating things; but now the lids have been taken off the Bovril and Vitamalt *((our iron rations))* just as well to have it inside us, I suppose. How dreadful that Mabel should faint from hunger. Wrote small poem:-

'Give us this day our daily bread
And take from us our daily dread
That we and ours may not be fed,
Nor stumble weakly on the bed
And faint, because of lack of bread.'

No lights in evening – blackout for about a week expected.

8 Sep 1942

Electricity came on again today – we've *((in Married Q))* been off about 4 days, and most of camp about a week.

To French conversation class this afternoon, with Frieda Salmon and Pauline Beck. (Pauline played piano accompaniment to many of our children's plays.)

I can't imagine us being out of here by Christmas.

Tony Cole called and gave me a small empty 1936 diary, and some cumquots *((small Chinese hard fruit which sometimes fruited within camp precincts.))*

9 Sep 1942

Finished Chap 3. Yesterday was Dad's 50th birthday. I had 5th injection.

We stopped having tea to drink at the hospital, supply has run out at last.

Madame le Bon came.

Mum, Mabel and I watched ball game in evening.

10 Sep 1942

French lesson, between American Blocks 2 and 3, with Dorothy and Frieda Salmon and Pauline Beck. Then went to 'chapel' in American Block and said a Rosary for Peace, rosary given me by one of the Sisters. *((The chapel was a curtained-off half of a small room)).*

Too hot to go swimming. *((It was a long walk)).*

11 Sep 1942

Post cards to send to the Troops etc. are materialising at last. We have to pay 8 cents each *((to get a post card to send)).*

Mabel went to Dr Talbot ('Harry') who sent her to hospital. She has got thin again, says she often feels dizzy. It makes me rather frightened to look at her. Dr Yaroogsky-Erooga said he considered the goitre he'd said Mabel had was larger.

Father Moore came over and gave us some cocoa and sugar and milk. He and the other young Maryknoll Fathers are going out tomorrow *((into town, with the hope of eventually being allowed to go to their China missions or USA)).*

12 Sep 1942

So worried about Mabel. Dr Erooga says she will probably be in hospital for about a month; he will try to get extra food for her, but if she doesn't yield to treatment, they may have to operate. So terrible that we haven't anything extra or tempting to give her. Mum is looking so skinny and drawn too.

Fr Moore etc. left today, only Father Meyer and Father Hessler (Maryknollers) remain, plus Canadian Father Murphy and the Sisters of the Immaculate Conception. To Confession.

Tony came in evening. We all went to concert, not bad but I had a heavy heart throughout because of Mabel. 'Pinafore' number arranged by Cheape was good.

13 Sep 1942

Dr Y. Erooga has ordered Mabel to have 2 bottles of milk a day. *((A small number of little bottles of fresh milk were sent in from town daily to the camp for very young children, and some to hospital for patients specially in need)).*

We've got our post cards *((to write and send away via Japs)).*

Bonnie Macklin had on a sweet little tussore dress & lovely red hair.

14 Sep 1942

Sent our postcards today. Mabel to Sid but didn't say anything about being in hospital.

15 Sep 1942

French lesson alone with Sister Mary, the Salmons didn't turn up. Mabel is liking the hospital food, I'm afraid she'll find it a rotten change when she comes back on these.

Olive and I went to see Billie Gill and Brian. Also there, Hugh Goldie *((Police, the first man who saw our tiger))* and Mr Matches (also Police) whom Brian calls the Chinese version 'Foh Chi'.

More repat. rumours in the air.

16 Sep 1942

Cholera and typhoid injections – in one from Dr Selby.

Got 1 lb sugar (Yen 1) for Mum, and one for Mabel from Medical Canteen.

Dug up some of our own sweet potatoes – enormous, but not really sweet. Fried them tonight – we had pork fat for tiffin luckily.

Finished writing Chapter 4.

Played bridge in evening. Mrs Franklin kindly gave me a piece of pastry crust.

17 Sep 1942

Dr. Y-E thinks Mabel is in a pretty bad condition, but so far responding well. He says an operation will be necessary at some time – preferably not in the camp. He would like her to have a private room for rest, that she will need careful watching all her life, but that she MIGHT outgrow it.

Such a surprise – Father Moore sent us a parcel from Bethany House, Pokfulam: a lovely big tin of cocoa, a catty of sugar, and a tin of bully, so kind and thoughtful and generous of him. I'll NEVER forget it.

Fried our sweet potatoes tonight, in oil from Mr F. P. Anslow *((my father-in-law to be, six years later!))* in exchange for some of our potatoes.

19 Sep 1942

Crisped burnt rice is ruining my teeth. I keep meaning not to eat it, but never succeed. *((A lining of burnt rice collected on the rice boilers each day; it was prised off and distributed to a 'burnt rice queue' after the meals.))*

'Gymkhana Water Sports' but I was too tired to go, also it was during hospital visiting hours.

Request Concert in evening. I liked Wilkinson girls (young Joan, Maureen & Marjorie) and Irene Drewery (9) singing, Japs taking flashlights, and everyone crooked their fingers into V's. Japs apparently also photographed the Water Sports and the food queue.

20 Sep 1942

Rumours that bread ration is going down, that money we sent to Shamshuipo has been returned.

Started Patients' Card Index system at office.

Dr says Mabel is progressing all right. Nan Grady was 22 on the 18th.

21 Sep 1942

First day of my 5 days' holiday.

Mabel looks very pale *((still in hospital))*. She vomited all her tiffin today, it was pork. Dr said her blood pressure was better today.

Delightful piano recital at St Stephen's – Mrs Drown and Ian Heath.

22 Sep 1942

Notice says International Red Cross are sponsoring a moving picture to be taken of life in the camp.

It was said that some planes which came over today (I'd heard them) made a 'V' formation, and that they exhaust-piped a 'V' in the sky, and that they dropped pamphlets. *((I hadn't seen any)).*

Spent rest of our money on tomato ketchup and sugar. I got rubber sandals from Welfare.

Mabel snowed under with re-knitting unravelled baby clothes *((for new camp babies.))*

Lecture on Africa by Dr McLeod *((whose little boy had been 'blown-up')).*

23 Sep 1942

My heart is so tired, dragging feeling most of today. Mabel much better. Kind Mrs K took her a little wong tong.

Mr. Bendall in hospital with septic foot, and Mr Skinner (Wally) with dysentery.

Olive and I went to choir practice on Maryknoll Sisters' verandah: Elsie Bidwell, Eileen and Kathleen Grant, 2 Bartons *((there were 11 Barton children in camp with their parents:- Alec, Marie, Peggy, Leo, Terence, John, Audrey, Wendy, Jacqueline, Rosemary and Daniel: another son Bernard was in Shamshuipo Camp.))*

The Sister was so nice. Novena to Little Flower for Peace begins tomorrow.

24 Sep 1942

Delicious frothy dumpling. No more flour ration. Mum and I to church for Novena.

Benediction in evening in grotto, then Catholic Action meeting.

A. Bush (48) died last night of blood poisoning.

Concerts have been stopped until further notice because of our 'V's last Saturday!

((The so-called grotto was a rough and rocky space between the American Block and the (pre-war) Leprosarium. The Catholics used it for open-air meetings and church services. A makeshift altar was made into the rocks at one end and a cross cemented in it. Concrete blocks which had been lying about the camp were humped there to make several rows of low and extremely hard seats. In due course most people made tiny cushions and carried them wherever they went – to concerts, meetings etc.))

25 Sep 1942

Mum received $15 from the Relief Committee on account of herself and Mabel, principally to buy sugar.

Rumour that the troops from Shamshuipo are coming into the Prison; that the Germans on the Stalingrad front are in a chaotic state; that British (or Allies) have got into Caucasus via Iran. We did garden over in morning – Dorothy, her Martin nephew and I. Then washed clothes and hair *((no shampoo or hot water, a sliver of Welfare poor soap))*.

To Benediction in grotto in evening. Finished writing Chapter 6.

26 Sep 1942

Mr Kelly said rumour is that within 4 days we shall hear something favourable about repatriation.

Irish Red Cross has donated money to Irish internees, who have handed it over to be devoted to Hospital deserving cases. Got dates and sugar, boiled same and result was some quite respectable jam.

Olive has an idea that we make bookmarks for all the patients who are in hospital on Christmas Day. Nice idea.

The gallery in St Stephen's Hall. All the wood from the seats had been removed by internees for firewood, so we just sat on the concrete.

27 Sep 1942

Wonderful rumour – that BBC (not BCC which is British Communal Council) announced that all British civilian internees are to be repatriated soon – but the rumour isn't yet very strong. Trouble over notices on Board, not seen by Superintendents. We are still very much in disgrace over the 'V's' at concert.

Mum gave Mabel her 'seconds' in pasties – so pleased she had the chance to give her something. *((Seconds were 'second helpings' which were served at the end of a meal if there was any left over after the regulation rations had been served; strict lists were kept of seconds, every person had their turn of seconds in rotation. Pasties were the best meals in camp, even if the contents weren't always meat: the pastry casing was heaven.))*

Finished writing Chapter 7.

28 Sep 1942

Received $15 from Mr L. Barton *((Treasury))*.

Camp in disgrace for being generally lax, notably not keeping to the Japs' rules of being in the vicinity of our respective blocks after curfew.

Glorious tiffin of dumpling, roast meat (small bit) and a baked sweet potato.

Rumours of repatriation not yet substantiated. Mabel OK.

Lovely recital by Elizabeth and Heath tonight in St Stephen's.

29 Sep 1942

Petition is going round about wanting to be repatriated. First didn't mean to sign it, but then after talking on the bank with Mr Fantham and Mrs Braithwaite, decided to do so. I do want to go out of here, tho I really feel we should have no say, yet it might help as Fantham says, if Gimson really wants to know what we want to do.

Went for a swim after French lesson.

30 Sep 1942

Mabel has to have 5 or 6 teeth out.

We now have a bench at office, room for many on it. *((Up to then, there were only chairs for the 2 stewards and us stenos; with the bench, some of the doctors could have tiffin in the office.))*

Mrs. Braude has sent Mabel a little bit of margarine and a TIN OF JAM – so terribly generous of her. *((Irene Braude, the head of the VADs. She looked after her toddler daughter Patricia, her mother Mrs. Deacon whose husband had died in camp April 1942, and also little Jean Addis Martin whose mother (a VAD officer) had died in 1941. Jean's Dad Mr T. Addis Martin was in camp in a different billet. Mabel used to take Patricia and Jean and little Bill Owen out for walks most mornings, and make clothes for them.))*

1 Oct 1942

Heard that the 'Tatakuma Maru' arrived with parcels on board for prisoners of war. I didn't see her come in, but Mabel did.

Mabel is to have teeth out tomorrow, Sammy Shields officiating.

2 Oct 1942

Typhoon around, great howling gusts all night and day, enormous waves. 2 small ships sheltering in cove.

Mabel had 6 teeth out. Went up to see her at half past two. She was just coming round and asked 'Didn't he come with you?' I said 'Who?' She said 'Sid.' (Her boyfriend in Shamshuipo Camp). It made me want to cry. Then she asked 'Where's Mummy?' and later 'Where's Olive?' They wanted to put her back to sleep but she said she'd wait till Mum had been. Seemed quite chirpy later.

Choir practice this evening, Olive and I.

Rumour that regular troops ARE away *((i.e. they had left Hong Kong.))*

3 Oct 1942

Mabel looked so weary and frail this morning. Olive and I went to receive 'scapula' medals at the Maryknoll chapel. Feast of the Little Flower. *((St Teresa)).*

The wall, cutting policemen off from the hospital office, is complete. *((Several policemen were billeted at the hospital as protectors of the Sisters, since apart from patients, only one other male – the duty doctor – stayed overnight. Until this wall was built, these policemen had occupied a section of the office behind piles of hospital stores)).*

4 Oct 1942

Heard that some of our troops had gone away. Saw the fat 'Tatakuma Maru' going out.

This evening Mrs Drown and Heath played. People humming softly to Schubert's 'Ave Maria', 'Today I feel so happy', 'Cheek to Cheek' and roaring out 'We're going to sail away'; then a quick 'I want to be happy' – and 'Rule Britannia', everyone yelling out that Britons never would be slaves.

5 Oct 1942

Pasties at the hospital, delicious pastry. Mabel looking so much better. Had Welfare issue of lav. paper. Lovely Elizabeth in evening, after Rosary service in the open.

6 Oct 1942

No French lesson because Sister Mary has a fever. So I went to see Mabel and tripped in the gutter en route and made a mess of my knee. No rumours today.

7 Oct 1942

This evening I went to see the Salmon family. I don't know why I don't go oftener, I do enjoy them. Mr Salmon said that we will hear within a day or two that we are to be repatriated; that our troops have not gone away – that that rumour emanated from fact that Eurasian and Chinese internees have been released *((from men's camps))*, and that Canadians sent from North Point to Shamshuipo.

Mabel is to have extra food from Irish Red Cross.

8 Oct 1942

Worrying news that a ship 'Lisbon Maru' carrying British and Australian prisoners of war had left a southern port, and was torpedoed by American subs. Some were able to swim to a nearby island, others were rescued and a few drowned. Every one here worried about their men, but rumour is that Nakazawa has given his word that no soldiers have left Hong Kong yet. *((The Lisbon Maru was torpedoed on 1st of October and sank on the 2nd of October.))*

9 Oct 1942

I am now considered on the Permanent Government Staff, subject to medical exam. *((Having served 3 years)).*

No real news or rumours except that the Volunteers are coming in to the Prison, and Stalingrad still holding.

10 Oct 1942

X-rays can start going in again. *((Patients who needed X-rays were allowed to go again. They had been suspended because Stott escaped from the French Hospital in town where the X-rays took place.))* Rosaleen's first wedding anniversary. *((Her husband, Royal Scots, was in Kowloon camp)).*

11 Oct 1942

Dr. Y-Erooga says Mabel may get up soon and take a walk, and be examined after it. She said she heard something about her tonsils being yanked out.

Lovely fried fritter and baked potato, but everyone is ready to rebel because of no pasty or dumpling since Monday.

Went to Prison Officers Club in evening, so crowded – I had to sit behind the piano.

12 Oct 1942

Dreadful headlines in Jap paper – the 'Lisbon Maru' which went down on 1st October was full of Hong Kong troops; supposedly 1,800 troops on board and 900 saved. Old Horswell (late P.D.O. Dockyard) said a 'Major M. Greenwood' among the missing; the rank could be mixed up, feel so sorry for Mrs G if it's her husband (he isn't a Major). Also a Lieut Wood is missing – I don't know if that's Joanie's husband. *((He was an officer in HK R.N.R. – but it wasn't him)).*

Don't think Topper or Sid or Arthur would be classed as technicians, which we understood these troops were, but it's an awful doubt in everyone's mind. Haven't told Mabel (still in hospital) about the ship but she's bound to know sooner or later – dreadful, because she's doing so well.

X-rays started again.

13 Oct 1942

Not feeling so sure that our men are all right, but no good worrying. Mabel taking it well.

Mrs Blair died (in her fifties).

Dr Selwyn-Clarke came, gave us girls (in office) sweets between us.

Lilian Hope has gone to Shanghai and thence to Canada.

14 Oct 1942

Mabel broke down and cried, so unsettling about the 'Lisbon Maru'. Today's notices are that Mr Yamashita is trying to find who was on board, survivors etc., and will try to find out whereabouts of anyone whose name we give in to C.S.O.

Mabel wants to come out of hospital *((being a stone's throw from the sea, which looked so grey and cruel today, made her anxieties worse.))* I collected her glasses from Welfare. *((She hadn't worn glasses before this, and I hadn't known she had a problem. In much later life it was discovered that she was practically blind in one eye – had been since birth.))*

Maureen Kathleen Seymour born.

Mary went in for X-ray and returned, and thinks there's nothing wrong.

Dr Uttley gave me a medical inspection, for permanent establishment.

16 Oct 1942

Mabel allowed out *((of hospital))* for a walk in evening; she, Olive and I scrambled round path up from hospital by Leprosarium, and sat on a stone while service was going on. After choir practice I walked round with Marie Barton.

17 Oct 1942

Dr says Mabel has filled out nicely since she has been in hospital. She is being allowed to come to Elizabeth's playing tomorrow evening. This evening Olive and I went to see Billie Gill and Brian.

18 Oct 1942

Ploughed through difficult chapter 11. Kind Mrs Seath brought Mabel a blancmange to the hospital. *((Mrs Ernestine Seath whose husband was killed by the Japs when they first landed at North Point. Her daughter Mrs Joan Wood was also in camp. Both mother and daughter were VADs. Joan's husband was a p.o.w. in Kowloon camp.))*

Mabel allowed to come to the music this evening. Mr Kelly brought me a box to sit on. After, I careered back to hospital with her, I'm afraid she's frightfully excited and overwrought.

19 Oct 1942

Norah Witchell's 20th birthday, we made her a card – lettering by Olive, verse by me, drawing by Dorothy. *((Norah had recently joined us 3 girls in the hospital office as a stenographer. Tragically in 1950, as Norah Stutchbury, she was murdered by guerillas in Malaya)).*

20 Oct 1942

Poor Mr. Kershaw *((William, aged 45))* died today, such a shame, as he almost got better and actually went out of hospital for a time.

Pat Cullinan *((Police, he had TB))* came back from X-ray yesterday, said he saw Father Moore who asked to be remembered to us.

Did a bit of 'Catholic Action' in evening, by speaking to Elizabeth (Betty) Aslett about coming to choir practice tomorrow.

21 Oct 1942

Just finished writing Chapter 12.

Prof. Digby had an operation today – suddenly.

Mabel fed up, because she hasn't been put in the ward with babies.

22 Oct 1942

Mrs Denton is in next bed to Mabel. (Ivy Denton, nee Thirlwell – Eurasian). She says a Chinese said the men who went from HK *((on 'Lisbon Maru'))* were mostly Wavy Navy (HKRNVR), and that the regulars are working at Kai Tak with shaved heads.

Mr. Pyke died (Alfred, aged 59).

Catholic Action meeting in evening.

A bulletin gives names of people who have died since internment *((i.e. who died in other camps))*. One is Mr Lacey, husband of Annie Lacey; she is here with twins called Winston and Wavell, aged 1 year.

I'm now considered on Permanent Establishment of Senior Clerical & Accounting Staff of Govt.

23 Oct 1942

Great news – we are to get parcels from Red Cross. Notice says they are 'beautifully packed', each contains 12 tins of assorted food. Also clothes have come – 500 trilby hats; cocoa, tea etc., dried fruits – absolutely wonderful... will help so much with this winter and relieves my mind about Mum and Mabel.

Roast meat and lovely baked potato. We drew 2 canteen tickets.

Notice also says that the prisoners of war *((i.e. men in other camps))* will have twice as much as we are to have – that is making everyone happy. Olive & I received $15 each.

24 Oct 1942

Stye coming on the other eye now. Dr Hargreaves is going to take out my lower lashes.

Visited Frieda Salmon today.

25 Oct 1942

Great excitement, many planes about, very high. Some people saw ack-ack puffs later (Olive did). I thought I heard bangs too – grand if so, though it's probably goodbye to our Red Cross parcels.

Mr G. Buchanan died suddenly, on Bowling Green. I went to Mr Carrie (W.J.) about funeral arrangements. Mr Puckle *((Director of Air Raid Precautions, my boss))* lives there too.

26 Oct 1942

By all accounts, an air raid over Hong Kong last night, and there have been planes around all day.

Mabel fed up and spotty. Pulse better after concert.

Selwyn-Clarke was expected, but didn't turn up, which may mean that raiding is real. I'm afraid for the boys perhaps working at Kai Tak.

27 Oct 1942

Dr Hargreaves tugged out some more of my *((infected))* eyelashes *((he'd had to do that a couple of months earlier))*. Eyes ache and are sore.

Jap. papers admit air raid, they say they shot down 2 planes. No word of our parcels, all fear we may not get them now due to lack of transport etc.

Selwyn-Clarke didn't come in, upsetting all X-ray arrangements.

Mabel getting really fat in the face.

28 Oct 1942

Another air raid today, we distinctly heard bombs, and saw ack-ack fire. Must have been big bombs for us to hear all this way, think they were at Taikoo. Dreadful to think of the poor Chinese casualties there must be at the docks and other places.

Dr Y-Erooga said Mabel's heart beats are showing through her skin, said it's pushing against the chest wall and isn't right.

29 Oct 1942

Blackout last night. Still haven't finished next to last chapter of Louie.

Great losses on Solomon Islands, both for U.S. and Japs.

Nan in hospital.

30 Oct 1942

Had front tooth filled.

31 Oct 1942

Mabel still has to stay in *((hospital))* quite a time. She is to get about 2 or 3 Yen from VADs.

Mr Thomas Nicolas died this morning *((Ship's Officer)).*

Mrs Mitchell had a baby daughter this afternoon – Rosemary. *((The first true Stanley baby, her parents were married at the very start of the camp. Rosemary came to see me in 2010 – we had a wonderful chat. Her father Alec Mitchell was prison staff pre-war; after the war the family had a flat in the Married Quarters in Stanley!))*

I typed story all afternoon.

((N.B. After the war was over, we learned that Sid and Arthur indeed had been on the 'Lisbon Maru' when it was torpedoed and sunk. Both were rescued and ended up as pows in Japan and survived the war. Topper was not on the L. Maru, but was taken on a later ship to Japan, where he died.))

1 Nov 1942

Rumours of more bombing, and of parcels coming in on Tuesday – let's hope so!

Betty Drown *((in room next to ours))* wasn't going to play tonight (she has a temperature) but when Mum told her Mabel was going out of hospital to hear her, she did play. Choir sounded nice at church. Mabel felt dizzy again yesterday, and today before she went to hear music. Meat cake today.

2 Nov 1942

Finished writing story – 'Limelight on the Lower Fifth', not very satisfied with the ending. Very flattered today – Mrs Pryde stopped me and talked about my poems. She likes 'School Magazine' best.

The Red Cross parcels are actually in the camp, brought by boat.

Betty Drown isn't well, she has flu and tonight Ian Heath played alone *((they often played duets))*.

Mrs. F lent me her story the other day. I do hope mine doesn't read as disjointedly as hers does to my critical mind.

3 Nov 1942

Parcel rumours much in the air – that there are only 900 of them, only bully beef and clothes.

We have been ordered to black out tonight. Rumour has it that the Allies will be bombing heavily after today, and Chinese have been warned to keep clear of military objectives. Worried a little for ourselves and the boys at Shamshuipo, as we aren't lit up at night.

Mabel still in hospital, very bored. I don't think she's looking quite so well either. Future uncertain – will we be retaken by Allies, then bombed and interned again?

Played bridge in evening. European news still supposed to be good.

4 Nov 1942

We have to black out again tonight. Lovely rissole for tiffin. Had fried egg last night and tonight, really delicious. *((Duck eggs sometimes for sale))*.

Tale is that of loose Red Cross food *((i.e. not in the small individual parcels))* we will each have 30 tins of bully, 25 lbs sugar, 25 lbs dried fruit, 1 & half lbs. of caramel, and of cocoa. Lovely if true!

We have drawn a canteen ticket for tomorrow. Made a front cover for 'Limelight on the Lower Fifth.'

5 Nov 1942

Dr Y-Erooga is going to tell Mabel tomorrow that she will have tonsils out the next day.

Welfare presented us with tinned fish liable to blow. We had kedgeree at hospital.

Dorothy *((reading my school story))* is most enthusiastic about it.

6 Nov 1942

Amazing edict today – all men of military age whose wives aren't in camp (Police under 40, civilians under 35) have to go and sleep in the Gaol for about 3 weeks. Supposed to be because there might be escapes attempted in the blackout, then the Japs would have to punish all of us. Even the young doctors had to go – Dr Loan, Dr Y-E and Dr Alan Barwell, although C.S.O. staff have been exempted.

Had 'upper left 8' tooth filled temporarily today. If it doesn't ache after 3 days then dentist will fill it properly. Finished typing story.

Mum's block had herring today – lovely big ration, and seconds of them too. We *((at hospital))* had ours in chow fan.

7 Nov 1942

Mabel had tonsils out today, said she hardly felt it, she ate half a pasty at tiffin. She later on looked paler and unhappier.

Lent 'Limelight on the Lower Fifth' to Golly (F.J.) Anslow today.

The gaol birds came out and by all accounts spent quite a good night. Most have cell to themselves, they were let out at half past 7 am.

List of what is in the parcels came today – tea, margarine, bacon, biscuits, choc, cheese.

8 Nov 1942

Rumours that Germans in Libya have collapsed.

The men this morning had orders to assemble outside to bring up parcels, but it was a false alarm – tomorrow instead.

Mum and I went for walk through the cemetery; graves *((war ones))* have been made up beautifully, and poppies – hand painted – placed on graves, especially on the murdered VADs – Mrs. Begg, Mrs. Buxton (whose husband also was killed in the war), Mrs. Smith and others.

Mabel better, she ate a rice pudding in evening because Sister Maureen Carew couldn't eat it.

9 Nov 1942

The parcels were distributed. Contents: apple pudding, beef steak pudding, tinned sugar, cheese, margarine, bacon, creamed rice, syrup, 4 ozs chocolate, soap; some Pascall green drops. The boxes (light brown cardboard) were packed in 'Bermondsey' and 'London', most of them dated between April and June.

Dr Uttley says there are more parcels at Lourenco Marques awaiting shipment. Newspaper mentions our prisoners of war working in factories in Japan.

Saw Baby Mitchell, born 31.10.42, she looks exactly like Mrs Mitchell.

Japanese women went into gaol today.

10 Nov 1942

Standing in the cupboard is an aquarium jar two-thirds full of date and ginger jam – looks lovely. The parcel chocolate, although plain, tastes so milky that it's almost incredible to think there is something better, i.e. milk chocolate.

Had a spoonful of Nestles Milk – absolute heaven!

Washed my hair in cold water, because Mr Allison wouldn't give me any hot water. *((Mr A presided all day long over a couple of household electric water boilers in the Married Q. There was always a queue for hot water for tea or whatever. This morning he told us the water hadn't quite boiled, so I said could I have my ration as I didn't need boiling water for washing my hair, but he said I couldn't have water for hair-washing.))*

Went visiting for choir members. Betty Aslett says she will come if we have Latin classes.

In evening, to Dr. I. Newton's 'Glimpses into Surgical History' about asepsis.

11 Nov 1942

11th Nov – but no official silence.

To choir practice. Edith Batley came.

Peggy Sharpe and Robert Minnitt are engaged. *((Robert was a Cadet Officer in HK Govt, worked with Mr Gimson in camp)).*

Dr Tomlinson's wife suddenly had to have appendix operation. Mabel's bed has been moved again as Mrs. T needed the corner bed. The Woods twins Aileen and Doris, who had been famous singers in their younger days, were visiting a patient in Mabel's ward when they suddenly saw her and whooped 'Oh Bette!' and came over to tell her that she looked so like the film star Bette Davis whom they had met in Hollywood during their singing career.

((Ever after, they called Mabel Bette. Now in their mid-fifties, they had stopped performing after their mother, their accompanist, had died, but I heard later that they had sung in one of the hospitals during the fighting)).

Men don't have to go in the gaol again – suddenly stopped. I went to St Stephen's, heard choir, A.T. Lay playing piano.

News is good, even in Japanese newspaper. Americans have landed in North Africa. Fighting in Libya said to be over.

12 Nov 1942

Today's rumours: Italy is asking for peace at any price; we have declared war on Spain and landed there; Germany has asked Russia and England for a truce but Roosevelt, Stalin and Churchill all say they will fight to the bitter end. The only part people believe is that maybe Italy has capitulated, but we've heard that before.

Another rumour = Tokyo has cabled Japanese to treat internees (British) with every consideration.

Men have been clapped back into gaol again tonight.

Mabel heard air raids in night, so did other people (not me). Major Manners says Taikoo and Kai Tak hit.

News that Shanghai people *((in Stanley))* are going in December.

This evening we opened one tin of creamed rice, it was delicious – rice pudding never tasted like that. We sampled peanut butter this afternoon which someone gave Mabel. *((Peanuts were sometimes for sale in canteen. We ground them in the rice grinder into peanut butter.))*

13 Nov 1942

Headlines that Germans have moved into unoccupied France to forestall Allies, which shows that there is some ground in rumours that we had made landings in Spain and Marseilles.

Tony Sanh has been taken off by Gendarmerie for swearing at one of them who flashed a torch in his face, and hasn't been heard of since. *((But he was OK)).*

The two Macintyre children, Ailsa and Muriel, came into hospital with malaria, arrived on the same stretcher.

Goodwin and Simmonds of Gas Company came into camp. It is said that French Hospital moved to North Point, and Bowen Road Military Hosp to Gun Club Hill. *((False, I think)).*

Choir practice tonight.

14 Nov 1942

Mabel and I are entitled to a tin of Galantine between us – Olive and Mum have opened one tonight but I'm not partaking, I think it's silly to start on iron rations before we have the promised 8 tins of corned beef per month.

Dr Selwyn-Clarke came in, looking very old and ill – his hair badly in need of cutting.

Rumour that we have re-taken Tobruk.

Hill and Mackie came back *((from X-ray in town)).*

Gilbert & Sullivan concert at St Stephen's, voices blending beautifully.

15 Nov 1942

Mabel home just for evening *((from hospital)).* We shared an apple pudding – delicious but not enough of it.

Peggy Barton and I have been delegated to go to find out who can come to the Study Club *((Church))* and choir. Mrs Drown came in our room to play bridge later. Mabel and I went back to hospital under one mackintosh, dark, misty, rainy and blowy.

16 Nov 1942

Mabel's pulse up so Dr. wouldn't let her out this evening.

Mr V. Benwell and (Police) Dixie-Beale came back from X-ray. Mr Benwell gave me two French books the Sisters at St Paul's gave him when he was there.

News that Churchill had church bells rung in England because of victory in Egypt.

Mrs Drown played tonight, started with the 'V' sign, then played church chimes because of victory.

I received a parcel! From 'Informal Welfare' – 1 tin pineapple, 1 tin paste, 1 tin of ginger, 1 tin beans. *((I've no idea what the 'informal welfare' was.))*

Sad to hear that Shamshuipo haven't received any Red Cross parcels yet.

17 Nov 1942

Frieda Salmon has lent me a dictionary of girls' names. I've hurt my eyes starting to copy it. There was a theft yesterday in Block 2 – Mrs E. Tollan and Mrs Simmons lost 25,000 pre-war HK dollars' worth of jewellery. Mum won an egg in a draw. Food came from godowns.

Rosaleen has moved to Mabel's ward. Rosaleen's poorly... other trouble as well as temperature and dysentery. *((The other trouble was TB which kept her out of action for the rest of internment. She didn't stay in hospital long. Instead her mother and sisters looked after her in their flat in Block 2. She eventually recovered.))*

Study club meeting this afternoon, when Peggy Barton and I appointed to tell everyone about the choir and social evening – we wandered everywhere tonight, to visit R.C's – Mrs Jack, the Mejia girls, Cullen girls, Anderson girls, Mrs P. Mace, Rozeskwy *((This was the beginning of the 3 priests left in camp organising the Catholics, forming study groups, a choir, entertainments, helping others.))*

18 Nov 1942

Lots of people had letters from UK/Australia, but none of our family did.

Had hot drink of Nestles Milk and water – delicious.

Choir practice this evening, Father Murphy (Canadian) took it – Adeste Fidelis and Peaceful Night in parts, for Christmas.

Japs have order distribution of food *((presumably bulk Red Cross stuff))* to stop for the time being, but St Stephen's and bungalows have already had theirs.

19 Nov 1942

Mabel finally came home from hospital today. *((Note the word 'home'!))*

We ate half a tin of bacon tonight, half a tin of liver pate, and a small tin of tomatoes – a delicious fry up eaten on Mrs K's tiny table borrowed for the occasion. *((It was Mrs K's table because she was the first occupant of the room where it was.))*

Rumour of big naval victory for us by Solomons – Churchill said 'another Jutland.'

Lots of babies have dysentery.

Gaol birds provided with camp beds.

20 Nov 1942

We tried to work out how much back pay we'll get, if we're let out by end of this year. I would get $3200 (£200), Olive £3800, Mabel £630. Grand if we DO get back pay! *((We did.))*

Rumour that some more letters are in town being censored.

Lots of folk at choir practice in evening. Fr Murphy conducted it. The Woods' twins are going to give me a Roget's Thesaurus.

21 Nov 1942

Vague news that Mr Budden is in Bowen Road Hospital and going blind. *((Mrs M. Budden and daughter Barbara were in Stanley. Mr Budden had been a Naval Dockyard colleague of my Dad's, so p.o.w. in Shamshuipo, with his son Gilbert who was HKVDC. The Buddens were our neighbours when we Redwoods lived in Naval Yard quarters, Naval Terrace, Queen's Road. Tragically, Mr Budden and Gilbert both died in Shamshuipo)).*

Concert at St Stephen's in afternoon, the Viennese chorus was colourful. Azalea Reynolds wonderful dancer, and Bridget Armstrong very sweet. Billie Gill and Brian were there, Brian restless of course, but not too bad, considering whose son he is!

Mabel and I had fried galantine tonight – delicious.

Benediction in evening in 'Maryknoll Chapel' – actually half of a small room in American Block curtained off from the rest of the room.

22 Nov 1942

Golly Anslow says it's a good story *((my book))*, that characters were well-drawn, that conversation was rather more as we would speak than girls of the given age; that there seemed to be too much fainting. *((Now I think, trust him to find something to criticize!))* I saw him going into the gaol this evening and couldn't resist going up and asking what he had to say about it.

Made calendar for Tony Cole, presented it to him in afternoon at birthday tea in Bungalow C *((his billet))*. It is the lowest bungalow, built on the edge of the hill. Tea in garden – delightful setting – smooth grass, blue and silver sea, blue blue sky, hills green in the distance.

Mr and Mrs Hyde Lay ('Betty') and Mr C. T. Bailey were the other guests. *((Both Hyde Lays were later killed when Bungalow C was accidentally bombed by Allies; Mr Bailey was slightly injured; Tony had moved out before this.))*

There was muscatel bread (made by Mr Bailey); scones (also with muscatels) made by Mrs. H.L., a wonderful chocolate cake with thick chocolate icing. Tony gave me a piece of cake to take home. SO full up, could only touch soup in evening, with 2 slices of bread.

Mabel went for a picnic in cemetery with Nan and Phyllis.

23 Nov 1942

Had tooth ('upper left 8') taken out.

We had a letter from Father Moore *((still in Hong Kong))*:-

> Received your card yesterday – probably held up a month. Since in it you mention the beginning of October devotions. Heard our contact was still around, so thought I'd run off this note.
>
> Glad to hear about parcels from England. Should be some help. Hope to send you something before Christmas. May it be a happy day for you all, if not quite so merry. Maybe the usual 'Merry Christmas' is not too far off.
>
> The news has been very good. The second front is going nicely; in Africa, the Germans have been pushed back 150 miles beyond Tobruk. Americans still holding the Solomons (3 of them) and sank 12 transports and 11 warships in latest battle. Five years ago I had a New Year plum pudding with the Rear Admiral Norman Scott, who was killed in the Nov. 12 engagement.
>
> We have received definite word we cannot go to Kwangchowan; so we are here for the duration, I guess. However, I've sent a letter via Chungking air mail home, and asked the folks to send your message to Mrs Hall in Australia. Studying Chinese full tilt now. Health generally good – flu or ?? once. Prices terrific, but some things reasonable. Japs expect more bombings. Understand 500 *((?))* books to camp. Hope you find some good reading. Take it easy. Good health to you all, and God's blessing, John D. Moore.
>
> Maryknoll now has new missions in many South American countries – and Mexico. We have been ordered home *((USA))*, but repatriation even from Shanghai is now very doubtful.

I took 'Limelight' to Mrs Lewis, Block A1, for her daughters to read. Mabel and I to music at St Stephen's tonight. She was dizzy yesterday.

24 Nov 1942

Bulk stuff was allowed out of Godowns today and is stored in Block 5, but we aren't allowed to have it until BCC have won the Japs over to their way of distribution, i.e. 2 lbs sugar per month instead of 3, and 6 tins per month instead of 8 each.

Olive received a pair of thick black shoes from the Welfare today – they haven't got my size.

Dr Erooga said that 'Sigmund' whom we met at Kay Grant's birthday 2 years ago, was killed here at Stanley *((during the war; I don't remember his surname)).*

25 Nov 1942

We have just opened tin labelled 'stewed steak and rice' and it turned out to be a beef steak pudding – a lovely surprise; Mum kept hiking out more and more lumps of 'fat' to save for frying – then realised it was dumpling.

Pat Cullinan *((Police))* went in to town today for X-ray.

Mabel got an egg from the Welfare.

News is vaguely that there will be fighting in Stanley.

26 Nov 1942

(written on 27th) Forgot to write up last night – partly because too busy eating, because we were issued with loads of food: each got 5oz dried fruit, 1 lb muscatels, 1 lb cocoa, 5 tins of bully, 4 lbs sugar. Such joy in the camp!

Mrs Drown came in to play bridge, and wants me to help with words for her carol.

I fried corned beef with tomatoes and bread – so delicious.

To Benediction in evening, then to Social, but I was the only person there with the Barton girls. Father Hessler came in and talked, Peggy was hurling questions at him.

Someone said they saw a Jap plane come down into the sea in afternoon.

27 Nov 1942

We drew more cocoa, dried fruit and some tea.

Martha Lewis brought my story back today, she thought some of the words 'rather long for schoolgirls.' *((Martha was 12, in camp with parents and younger sister Sarah)).*

News of Hong Kong raids.

28 Nov 1942

St. Andrew's concert grand, a one-act play of 1745 was well done, particularly Peggy Taylor (Mary's sister-in-law) was nice – her red hair looked beautiful; Sheila Bruce and Rhexie Stalker did Highland Fling with 2 men. Kinlock was good, so was someone who played bagpipes. Some lovely kilts. *((However did the owners manage to bring kilts into camp?))*

Chieftain was Mr. Kenneth Morrison, with a moustache and English accent. He spoke of Major H. R. Forsyth who had commanded Scottish Company of HKVDC, and was killed during fighting in Stanley, and of Captain Black (Alison's father) who was murdered near the very hall we were in. *((Mr Morrison died suddenly early in 1943)).* Forsyth was Vice-Chieftain last year at St Andrew's night.

Have started on thyroid pills again. Mabel and I went for a walk with Tony in morning – beautiful scenery round by the bungalows and St Stephen's, and a seaplane came low down.

News of unrest in town and rockets over Shamshuipo.

29 Nov 1942

We're just heating up our first tin of M & V between us – it looks lovely. *((I always assumed it stood for Meat and Veg – though I suppose it might have been Mutton & Veg. We always referred to it as M & V.))*

This afternoon Mabel & I went to Science Block where the Misses Woods live. We had tea under a tree. They have lost all their mementoes of stage work and film photographs, and letters from Bette Davis and Jeanette Macdonald etc. They had the chance of acting with John Bunny and Flora Finch in 'Vitagraph', but were quite happy with cabaret work, thank you – at that time films weren't well established. They had a letter from Mrs Temple (Shirley's mother). They foretell that Shirley will be a flop if she attempts a comeback.

Their billet is part of a narrow room like a corridor, with a stone floor; their bed is half a ping-pong table, kept stood up on the landing. They share a wardrobe and a small dresser and hotplate, and count themselves lucky to have these little blessings. They have their meals on a slope of grass in front of the block, with a small tree as shade against the sun. Hibiscus flaming on bushes across the water gully, and the sea blue beyond, and Chinese putting up barbed wire – the Science Block residents have got to move soon – 38 people to be housed. Dreadful for them because they know no one will want them. But Shanghai folk are expected to leave soon so that should make some space. At tea we had custard and rice and raisins, and sandwiches of lime-and-sugar syrup. Ages came up; when the twins knew of my birthday they immediately said they would bring me some custard and rice and I therefore invited them; Bendall came along and the twins told him about my birthday so now he's invited too – only hope the food will go round all right.

30 Nov 1942

Not a single plane about today – amazing since there's been that droning all day long for weeks past.

Choir practice. To music at St Stephen's in evening... a small child in gym costume started to go on platform to present Mrs Drown with a red nosegay – then changed her mind!

Football match – England v Scotland, with the Pipes and Drums in attendance.

1 Dec 1942

My 24th birthday. Seems such a great age! To Confession and Holy Communion in morning. Mary gave me a little cloth hanging pocket thing for the wall. Mabel made me a pretty little birthday card. Tony

Cole and Jimmy Bendall arrived for tea. Mr Bendall gave me an old varnished piece of wood with my name and the date burnt into it *((I kept it for years but it disappeared in 1996 when we moved from Seaford to Frinton))*. Tony gave me a TIN OF CONDENSED MILK! The Woods twins came.

Dorothy Salmon came down to be hospital messenger while George Davit, the usual one, in hospital.

Before party, I went to Retreat (church) 2.30-3.30pm.

The ground rice pudding worked out all right, served with pineapple; sandwiches and currant loaf.

The twins gave me a tiny piece of Shelley china. Just as they were leaving, they sang a duet 'One Alone' *((from The Desert Song))*, beautiful and deep-throated (fantastic voices).

Benediction and Stations of the Cross tonight.

2 Dec 1942

Each issued with 3 tins M & V and 3 tins of corned beef. So nice to have lots of food.

Went to Retreat Dissertation in am.

3 Dec 1942

Men suddenly excused from going into gaol tonight, and we don't have to blackout.

Each got 1 and half lbs. dried pears, a spoonful of cocoa and of tea, and 2 lbs sugar. Seconds in sweet potatoes at meal!

Went to Retreat Talk in afternoon.

4 Dec 1942

Feeling very full up, having eaten 4 slices of toast *((probably rice bread))* and honey, and 3 oz corned beef, and half a little basinful of ground rice choc pudding, and a cup of cocoa.

News everywhere good.

Japs say we may have lights on until 11 at night, but must put them off if we hear air raid alarm.

In evening, Rosary led by Fr Murphy.

Red Cross clothing given out. The doctors were trying out their hats (trilbys) in the office – great joke, everyone adapted his to a distinctive style. We each, men and women, received two sleeveless khaki tops. I'd like to turn mine into a pair of slacks.

5 Dec 1942

Dreadfully cold.

Concert in evening – best I've seen here. Compered by Danny Wilson. Barton girls and others in colourful Spanish dance, and 4 girls in white, blue-bodiced dresses. H. Mundy gave a good 'Albert' poem *((a Stanley Holloway piece))*, and 'Hong Kong' – words by Alec Kidd *((probably the 'Alexander Kidd' on the Stanley camp list, I didn't know him at all))*. V Garton was good.

Mary (Taylor) came to tea, I took remains of the ground rice pudding to Rosaleen in hospital, she isn't looking well.

Rumours are that Turkey has entered war, and Hong Kong has been declared a free city; and we will be searched.

Had first of vitamin caramels today – taste fishy. *((Caramels by Red Cross, and distributed to us one at a time.))*

Yvonne *((Blackmore, aged 15))* returned story, verdict: 'this story held my interest all the time, I was always loath to put it down.'

Lent Miss Whale (who was a governess to Pamela Stanley, grand-daughter of Melba in Australia) my story.

6 Dec 1942

So cold. We're having M & V tonight – 2 tins between us 4.

Jap newspaper says British have a setback in Africa.

7 Dec 1942

Everyone has been saying 'This time last year, I was...' *((remembering what they did the day before the Jap attack)).* Lovely day, had tiffin outside in the sun on the grass.

On way back from library I heard distant bangs I thought might be gunfire – but it was only someone kicking a box down the steps to the Indian Quarters.

Father Moore sent us another parcel, bless him – cornmeal, a tin of loganberries, and of pineapple and olives, and some wong tong.

Dr Talbot sang tonight with Mrs Drown, playing Schubert: Serenade.

8 Dec 1942

To Mass *((in Prison Officers' Club, aka 'American Club'))* – Feast of the Immaculate Conception.

Japs have asked us what we want for Christmas! And we are to have 1 lb flour per head.

At 5pm to Immaculate Conception Sisters' room *((in Married Q.))* to wait on their feast. Eileen Grant had set table, Christine Corra directing serving. First the Sisters had tomato soup made by Miss S. Cullinan (Govt. nurse) from real tomatoes; then salad dressed by Mrs K. Grant, it looked like potato and boiled egg and sausagey stuff from tins. And sweet potatoes baked to a nicety – but they had actually been baked in sugar. Then the Sisters each had a good plateful of M & V stew, then pear tart – there was a piece left over for each of us helpers; Sisters then had chocolate cake, tea with sugar and bottle milk, then fudge brought by Miss Cullinan.

Sisters then went to Benediction and we washed up and had some cake, and some leftover baked potatoes which we ate with our fingers, thin strings of toffee were sticking to them, and leftover pear tart.

Mabel and I went for a walk in evening, the lights went off everywhere; we went to bed early. Later the lights came on again. We were notified that we have to have a blackout again. A few planes came over but we couldn't hear any bombing.

9 Dec 1942

Remainder of (Red Cross) parcels given today = 3 between 4 persons – just right for us. Our meat tins were mainly curry. Nestles milk is wonderful again; one marmalade pudding and two apple puds. Glorious meat galantine, and choc.

Dorothy Holloway away from work, she said I could have her rations, that meant a nice big piece of roast meat for Mum, and a double dose of gravy and sweet potato for me.

Mr Kelly (Fred) gave Mabel a tin of biscuits.

Played bridge.

In morning, orders for the men to go to gaol, but now order rescinded, and no blackout.

10 Dec 1942

Two more khaki sleeveless garments each issued.

Slept in with Mum last night because my camp bed gave way when Tony sat on it.

Walked with Mabel and the toddlers in morning, dear little Jean Addis Martin, Patricia Braude, Bill Owens, and little devil Christopher Jones trying to put devilry into Bill. The girls looked so sweet in the pixie hats Mum made for them. *((Mabel made looking after toddlers and re-making their clothes her camp job)).*

Concert in evening. The star turn was 'Marie and some of her Boy Friends' – Marie O'Connor has a voice like Deanna Durbin's – sweet and true.

Every one busy sewing *((adapting the sleeveless garments into more suitable wear)).*

11 Dec 1942

Sore place under nose, eyes and forehead aching. More Government money pending, on strength of which we had eggs and bacon tonight. *((Bacon from Red Cross tin, I think – bacon was occasionally available on black market but far too dear for us to buy)).*

12 Dec 1942

Olive and I each received $15 from Govt. source, thank goodness. Feeling better though sore under nose increased.

Mum came down to office and used sewing machine there, working on our khaki things. On way home she fell and made a mess of her leg, so to Outpatients – she had anti-tetanus, and thiamine injections; she must have more thiamine because she had a floppy foot *((which caused the fall))*.

Received 2 vests each and a pair of long socks from Red Cross.

Rumour about an Italian priest in town having been murdered. *((I think this proved to be true.))*

13 Dec 1942

Just had fried galantine and tomato bread.

Mrs Drown says it is going to be official that we can write cards to Shamshuipo men for Christmas and send a parcel. She washed her pears in soapy water!

Mabel made sweet little slippers for Patricia Braude whose birthday is tomorrow.

Rumour that we have lost a new aircraft carrier in the Med.

Bridge.

My bed has been mended, and I have a palliasse made out of the parcel stuffing *((shredded paper: we didn't have mattresses on our beds))*.

Benediction in afternoon. Miss Whale returned my story, she told Mum the story was of the selling sort. She gave me a list of grammatical errors and slang.

14 Dec 1942

We can send small parcels to Shamshuipo for Christmas, and a ten-word greeting.

I weigh 128 lbs *((rice fat))*.

Trouble over money – Mum has applied for some, so has Mabel, but Mabel put that she wanted hers for shoes *((not food as expected))*.

15 Dec 1942

Gorgeous bacon and egg tonight. Mum having her leg dressed, they think it might be malnutrition that made her leg weak.

Have decided to make mittens to send to Arthur *((in Shamshuipo: wool from unravelled garments.))*

Mabel and I to Retreat Conference at Maryknoll room – Father Meyer. To Benediction in evening, and another conference – composed principally of Bartons.

16 Dec 1942

Retreat in morning, and choir practice. Mum and Mabel won eggs in the Welfare.

17 Dec 1942

Mittens rather a botch. *((Of course we didn't know then that Arthur & Sid were no longer in Hong Kong.))*

'Blitz' *((someone's dog))* has to spend the night in the gaol with the Medleys' dog for mating reasons, Japs say.

Retreat finished this evening.

18 Dec 1942

Japs didn't come for Blitz after all. Police concert, I didn't go.

So busy – passage cleaning *((we took turns at this))*, choir practice, washing and packing mittens, sending them in my name; and vest and mending outfit in Mr. Kelly's name.

Margaret Lillian McDermott born today, 8 lbs.

19 Dec 1942

Wearing tartan skirt and green jumper and scarlet jacket *((the winter clothes I was wearing throughout the battle for Hong Kong.))*

Confession in afternoon.

20 Dec 1942

No news about the parcels and cards we sent in yesterday for despatch to Shamshuipo. Visited Pat Cullinan *((Police, TB patient in hospital))* He's now caught malaria. He said how wonderful Dr Y-E had been to him, (and to M. Manning and C. Coull, both also Police in hospital with TB). That either he, or Marcus Manning or C. Coull *((all 3 HK Policemen in hospital with TB))* had some complaint when Mark made his morning rounds. He's fed up at getting malaria, as it's another bother for Dr Y-E.; I don't mind, I can take it.' So brave of him. I didn't stay long, he has loads of visitors and they were lining up. Pat had been having APT treatment every week for about a year before our war, he said there was a time when he thought he was for the next world, but Dr Y-E pulled him through.

Mabel and I went for a tramp this evening to collect a 'Yule log'! Only managed a few twigs. We went to see Billie Gill, Brian already in bed, so sweet.

Elsie Bidwell came in evening to have slacks fitted *((*Mum and Mabel and Mrs K helped people to adapt clothes.*))*

21 Dec 1942

Shanghai people vaccinated this afternoon, but whether or not they will be going soon is in question because now a case of diphtheria is in camp – Mrs. Williams, who was in our room on Friday visiting Mrs. K. Good work for Dr Y-E to diagnose right away. Consternation and panic as soon as the Jap authorities knew. Mrs Drown's concert cancelled, or postponed, and presumably all gatherings will be banned – Nativity plays etc. – another strange Christmas. Such a pity when everyone has been trying to make it as gay as possible under the circumstances. Hospital out of bounds to visitors.

Bridge tonight, I played with Kelly and let him down badly, through ignorance principally. Tony came up and joined in.

Father Hessler asked Mum to be President of the Ladies' Catholic Action Group, which she will. She had a blood count, – OK; she is still having thiamine dosing, her leg much better, bruises OK.

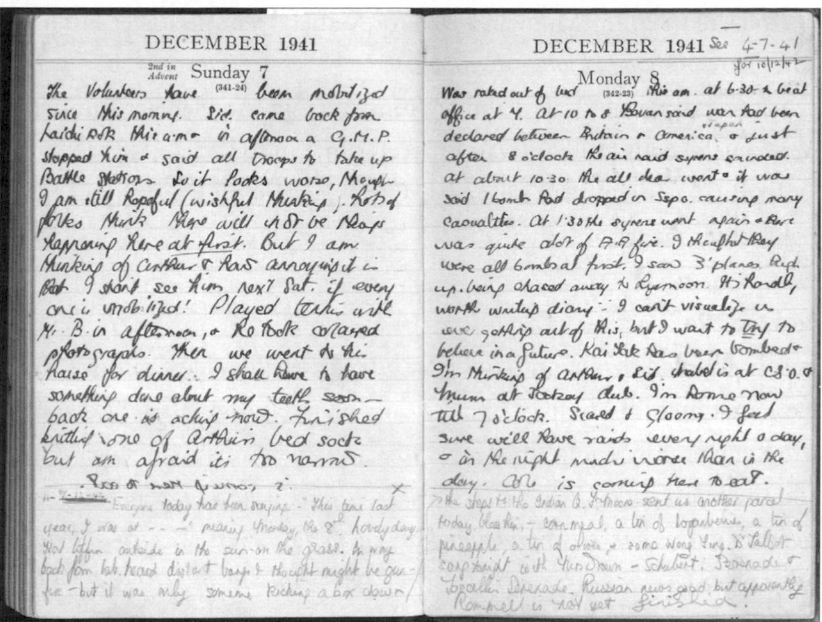

DECEMBER 1941

2nd in Advent Sunday 7 (341-24)

The Volunteers have been mobilized since this morning. Sid. came back from Laichikok this a.m. & in afternoon a G.M.P. stopped him & said all troops to take up Battle Stations so it looks worse, though I am still hopeful (wishful thinking). Lots of folks think there will not be things happening here at first. But I am thinking of Arthur & how annoying it is that I shan't see him next Sat. if every one is mobilized! Played tennis with M. B. in afternoon, & he took coloured photographs. Then we went to his house for dinner. I shall have to have something done about my teeth soon — back one is aching now. Finished knitting one of Arthur's bed socks but am afraid it is too narrow.

8-12-42 Everyone today has been saying — "This time last year, I was at — —" meaning Monday, the 8th. Lovely day. Had tiffin outside in the sun on the grass. On way back from lab. heard distant bang & thought might be gun-fire — but it was only someone kicking a box down/

DECEMBER 1941 See 4-7-41 for 10/12/42

Monday 8 (342-23)

Was rooted out of bed this am. at 6-30 & beat office at 7. At 10 to 8 Bevan said war had been declared between Britain & America & Japan & just after 8 o'clock the air raid sirens sounded. At about 10-30 the all clear went & it was said 1 bomb had dropped in Ssp. causing many casualties. At 1.30 the sirens went again & there was quite a lot of A.A. fire. I thought they were all bombs at first. I saw 3 planes high up being chased away to Lyemoon. It's hardly worth writing diary — I can't visualize us ever getting out of this, but I want to try to believe in a future. Kai Tak has been bombed & I'm thinking of Arthur, Sid. Mabel is at C.S.O. & Mum at Jockey club. I'm home now till 7 o'clock. Scared & gloomy. I feel sure we'll have raids every night & day, & in the night much worse than in the day. [illegible] is coming here to eat.

→ the steps to the Indian Q. [illegible] sent us another parcel today. Bless him, — cornmeal, a tin of loganberries, a tin of pineapple, a tin of olives, & some Wong Fung. Dr Talbot sang tonight with Mrs Drown — Schubert's Serenade & Toselli's Serenade. Russian news good but apparently Rommel is not yet finished.

Pages from the diary.

22 Dec 1942

A Jap doctor visited. Hospital closed to visitors, and Block 13 roped off *((in Indian Quarters where the Williams family lived – Mr. B. (Health Inspector), Mrs. L., Patricia, 4, David, 2; another boy, Raymond, born July 1945))*.

They haven't definitely put off all the festivities as yet.

Shanghailanders now been put off to Thursday.

Mr. S. Lillicrap died this morning – there was never any hope.

Mr Kopeczky had a parcel – clothes. Loads of people had parcels *((from friends in HK))* today.

23 Dec 1942

All concerts, gatherings etc. off for a week – such a disappointment. Maybe church services can be held out of doors.

The Woods twins brought us jam and grapefruit juice yesterday.

Mum sold hot water bottle for 5 Yen.

Collected $20 for Mum and $20 for Mabel from the Relief Fund. *((I have no recollection of what that was!))*

Some people got cakes today from men in Argyle St. Camp *((in Kowloon))*. Loads more (private) parcels came in today.

To R.C. nativity play rehearsal, Olive *((as Virgin Mary))* looked all right, choir ragged.

24 Dec 1942

Japs have lifted ban about concerts, but the doctors have said we won't have anything till Monday. Spent nearly all afternoon (after Bridge with Mr Kelly etc) in doing up the Ward Christmas trees with silver paper, and the bookmarks. *((The 'Christmas trees' were simply large branches we'd collected. Silver paper was probably from cigarette packets. We girls in hospital office made bookmarks for every patient – just small slips of paper with a little drawing on, which we put on the trees.))*

In evening Mrs Drown's choir sang carols on the bank above the Bowling Green.

I made small calendar-cum-engagement 'book' for Mary T.

Some 30-odd folk left for Shanghai today, including Bill O'Neill of Reuters.

We had a handful of peanuts each today – from the Japs.

To Confession at Maryknoll chapel. Father Meyer appeared dragging a huge prickly tree.

We lit a fire in room! Tony and Mr Kelly and the K's and we 4 all sat round it. *((There was a small fireplace in our room.))*

Mabel made a nice little card for Mrs Drown whose birthday is today.

25 Dec 1942

Slept in with Mum last night – my bed folded up because bookcase removed so fireplace could be used. Went with Mrs K to 7.15am Mass in Maryknoll Chapel *((tiny, so few people so didn't count as a 'gathering.'))* Mum and Mabel to 8am Mass in grotto *((near American Quarters))*.

After, egg, bacon, tomatoes and loganberries.

Mrs F Deacon came with Patricia and Jean who gave us 2 packets of Post Toasties from the Braudes *((Mrs Deacon was Mrs Braude's mother))*, and 8 Yen from Mr Addis Martin *((Jean's father))*.

Tony came, gave us tin of cheese and onions.

I wore my blue sharkskin dress – a tight fit. *((That dress was among some clothes our loyal amah had brought me when I was in the Tai Koon Hotel))*.

To hospital; hung over verandah while Mrs Drown's choir sang outside: Happy Birthdays for the new baby born this morning – Janet Sallis, for Jimmy Barnes (medical staff), for one of the patients, and for Mrs Drown herself tho her birthday was yest. Such a bright sunny morning.

Office transformed into a dining hall, desks pushed together made 2 long tables. Miss Davies (Matron) gave each of us office girls 2 lovely little tablets of soap. Meal not gigantic – roast meat, cabbage, gravy, 1 huge sweet potato, NO RICE. Seconds in sweet potatoes. Christmas pudding – a big share. I sat next to Dr Loan and Dr Pringle; Olive between Dr Uttley and Dr Erooga.

Later I went to Tony's bungalow and had tea with him, Stopani Thomson and Bailey. *((George Stopani Thomson, electrical engineer, killed when Bungalow C was bombed.))*

6.30pm – Our Nativity Play rehearsal at St Stephen's to sing in choir. I was the only alto as Sheila (Haynes) was helping with the angels behind the scenes.

In evening Mum and Olive and Mabel each ate a tin of M & V but I wasn't equal to that.

'Xmas pudding' Mabel made was grand, we had it with custard powder (from Tony who came) mixed with wong tong. I have a stomach ache and deserve it.

Mr and Mrs Tribble dropped in in evening.

26 Dec 1942

Postcards from Shamshuipo – I had one from dear old Harry Chalcroft! *((one of Olive's ex-boyfriends))*. Neither Olive nor Mabel had one. Rosaleen had 4 from friends, but none from Bert, her Royal Scots husband. *((We didn't know then that the Royal Scots had been taken to Japan two months earlier on the 'Lisbon Maru' which was sunk. Bert survived, but his marriage to R didn't after the war.))*

I ate a whole tin of M & V tonight, it was a mistake but I would do it; and we had salmon chow fan.

27 Dec 1942

Bridge with Kelly in afternoon. Walk with Sheila after Benediction, then a walk with Mabel and Tony in evening.

28 Dec 1942

Tojo's telling speech in newspaper.

29 Dec 1942

Pasty today.

Spent afternoon preparing for the doctors' party wearing pink dress *((we office girls had been invited))*, but when time came to go I felt unable to, can never feel at ease at these affairs, so didn't. I heard there would be dancing and was certain I would be one of the unchosen so hadn't the courage to go. After Dorothy and Olive and Norah (Witchell) had gone, Norah was so nice, she came back to try to get me to change my mind. Olive said *((afterwards))* it was mainly mass dances and lots of eats. I don't really regret not going – except for the food.

30 Dec 1942

To Cyril Brown's Nativity Play at St Stephen's; Betty Richards looked very sweet, the shepherds good.

Japs want to turn the doctors out of the Leprosarium to make it into an Isolation Hospital, since Japs say Benwell (V.) has diphtheria, although docs. say no.

31 Dec 1942

To Children's Mime in St. Stephen's. Very sweet, particularly the angel Gillian Millar *((aged seven))* who had rather a strain-making part, with arms outstretched for a long time.

Mrs Drown's concert was good, she sang... a dainty sweet little voice in a (simulated) quarrel, also Dick Cloake.

Clifton Large *((later my brother-in-law))* and Eric McNider did a very good harangue between 2 Chinese cookboys; then Large impersonated Mr Gimson, who came on backstage and listened before appearing before Large – and took him by the ear: all marvellous fun. A hopeful speech. The tiny tots sang 'How far is it to Bethlehem' and 'Away in a Manger'. Choir joined in other carols. Mr Heasman played the fiddle.

We girls have been making little calendars for nursing sisters and doctors nearly all day.

SUMMARY OF 1942

I lost about 15 lbs. in weight, and to date have put on 25! Mum has lost about 40 lbs. and had hysterectomy. Mabel has lost 6 teeth and tonsils; she has acquired glasses.

Olive, Mabel & I have to face possibility that our menfolk perished on the 'Lisbon Maru' or are in Japan.

Have learned to play contract bridge, to make bread, to sing in church choir, and to live in a room with 4 other people fairly amicably. Have written 3 poems, and 'Limelight on the Lower Fifth', about 30,000 words *((first in shorthand, then typing it on pages of old hospital returns after rubbing out their pencilled contents.))*

1943

During 1943 and 1944, my diary became very sketchy, as from late 1942 our Catholic priests were gradually organising a kind of RC parochial life for us, and encouraging us to organise it for ourselves. There was a short daily Mass at 8.15am in the Prison Officers' Club on weekdays; this had to be finished on time as that hall was used in the mornings as a junior school.

Study clubs meeting weekly were started for each age group and sex. I belonged to the one for 'young ladies'; it was here I became friends with Peggy Barton, who was four years younger than me. The meetings were held wherever convenient, sometimes in the Redwood room (Block 3 Room 19) if the rest of the occupants could arrange to be out at that time, sometimes out in the open air in the grotto, sitting on old Mimi Laus (breeze blocks).

Initially Father Hessler was in charge of the groups and attended all the meetings, though later we were encouraged to run things ourselves without Father; we sometimes discussed some religious book or subject, also current affairs and problems in the camp. We Young Ladies sometimes had social meetings with our opposite group, the Young Men, with games and eats to which we all contributed.

We were also affiliated with the younger groups. In due course I became an adviser to the Older Girls' Group and attended their meetings. They were a charming lot between the ages of 13 and 16, of all nationalities. British, Norwegian, Eurasians; I got a lot out of being with them.

I wrote a play for these girls to perform, called *The new girl in the Fourth*; everyone had a part, and rehearsals were usually in the open, due to lack of other facilities. It was produced in July 1943 in the Prison Officers' Club, i.e. it wasn't intended to be one of the main camp entertainments. To my delight, it was considered such a success that Bill Colledge, who was very involved with camp entertainments, and Dick Cloake, a Catholic contact, worked on it professionally, and it was then performed at St Stephen's for three nights, the set designed by Mr. T.A.L. Concannon.

Bill enlarged the part of the Ticket Collector played by Clifton Large, the only male in the cast.

As a result Mabel and I became very friendly with Clifton, and we spent most evenings with him, lounging out on the grass near the casuarina tree in the grounds of the Married Quarters. Before long, though, Mabel and Clifton were an item and I became superfluous.

Fathers Meyer and Hessler also set up small groups dedicated to Catholic Action, which not only involved some aspect of religion, but also practical application to camp matters. We members were given specific assignments to contact some Catholics known to have problems, and to give practical assistance such as helping mothers with young children, and also trying to persuade them to come to church.

Additionally there was a group to study Apologetics. All these church groups made life really busy if you wanted to get involved.

My daily routine was roughly as follows:-

8am Congee. This innovation lessened the gap between the two main meals; some of our rice ration was cooked into a mush and served hot round the rooms; usually eaten without sugar if Red Cross parcel sugar was finished. There was an occasional small issue from the Japs which only lasted for a few days; also no milk unless you had been able to save the tin of milk powder from your Red Cross parcel.

8.15am Mass.

9am to 12.30pm Working in hospital office (or from 1.30-5.00pm).
1pm Lunch at hospital (the other quarters' meal was at 11am).
5pm Supper at hospital (also 5pm in other quarters).
8pm All had to be within their accommodation block area.
9pm All had to be in our rooms.

When off duty at the hospital, I went to church club meetings or choir practice; miscellaneous lectures (some in our room by candlelight). I also went to language classes, French and German, though I didn't last long at the latter. Lots of swimming in warm weather.

I spent a lot of time at rehearsals for the children's plays which I continued to write. We discovered that Mary Rogers, a pretty Eurasian girl of about 12, had a pure sweet singing voice; also a small boy, Philip Murray, captivated us when he sang *Over the hills to Skye*. Another highlight was the singing of the young Wilkinson sisters and Delia Mejia in harmony of *Teddy Bears' Picnic*.

We had our own pianist, 18-year-old Pauline Beck.

Mabel looked after babies and toddlers, and remade clothes for them out of oddments. Mum (and room-mate Mrs K) mended clothes for the men whose wives weren't in camp.

There were rumours that we British might be repatriated – mainly children and poorly women, but there was nothing concrete until one day I heard a buzz of conversation in the courtyard below, so rushed down to investigate. John Stericker, a camp councillor, was in the middle of a large crowd, reading out names from the repatriation list. A friend there congratulated me on being on the list, but I knew this was unlikely as I was in good health, and rightly guessed that the Redwoods named were Mum and Mabel, which was wonderful, though no date was given.

18 Mar 1943

(('Esther' mentioned by Mr Jones in today's diary, was performed as a ballet. It was out of this world to us watching it, just superb dancing, music – and

costumes some of which I believe were made of old bits of dyed mosquito netting. Some Japanese officers who attended the performance were critical about the use of mosquito nets for this purpose, and of certain medicines to dye them. What a great morale-booster these Stanley concerts were!))

6 Apr 1943

Mrs. V. Evans, aged 40, died today. *((She became cyanosed after an operation in the camp hospital and died. She would probably have survived had our supply of oxygen cylinders not run out then. She was such a cheery person, and a great entertainer on the Stanley stage. I wrote a poem in memory of her, what she might have said at her own funeral, viz:*

Well I'll be blowed! What, all these people
Come to see me put away?
Left their queues and chores and cooking?
(And it's such a rainy day -
Not a day you'd do your washing,
Never get it dry for weeks;
Yet what can you do when you have
Just two pairs of flour-bag breeks?
Why've you all got hankies with you,
That's what I should like to know.
Big ones too, that means more washing;
How that Welfare soap does go.)
Look here, don't tell me you're crying,
Weeping for the likes of me!
Goodness gracious, well I never!
I don't call that tragedy.
After all, I'm no spring chicken
Though I'm game for much more fun;
There's younger folk than me been taken,
Fair's fair, when all's said and done.
I've had my youth, and then a husband

(Nicest chap you'd ever meet) -
Yes, we lost our little girl – but
While we had her she was sweet
It's this crowd I can't get over,
Half of Stanley must have come!
Still. I s'pose it makes a change, a
Funeral breaks the old humdrum.
Well, I think it's time you're moving
Back to work, and laugh and chat;
And listen, don't waste time on crying
Over me: I'm gone – that's that.

Sadly, her husband died a POW in Kowloon.))

18 Aug 1943

Birth of Norval Willerton, a brother for George and Anne.

21 Aug 1943

Sir Vandeleur M. Grayburn died in Stanley Prison. His body was given for burial 3 days later.

27 Aug 1943

F.P. Lenfestey died on his 57th birthday,

12 Sep 1943

Kenneth Antony Davis born, a brother for Kathleen and June.

HONG KONG HOLOCAUST

(Written in Stanley 1943)
Let not some vagrant write this history –
No passer-by of journalistic fame
Who happened to be here that strange weekend,
Intent on adding further to his name

By visiting the best hotels, the Peak,
And cabling Home, re-phrased, a much-told tale:
How Hong Kong panorama, viewed at night
Would make the lights of fairyland look pale;
Of Chinese youth fast drifting to the West;
Of off-key music, and quaint curio shops
(Displaying goods specially produced – and priced –
For him and other easily fooled fops.)
Let it be told – if written it must be –
By one to whom these hills are lifelong friends;
Who knew the curve of every cove and bay,
The shape of every tree; one whose heart rends
At each whisper of repatriation;
Who wept that Christmas Day, not at defeat,
But at the hurt perplexity of those
He had let down by undreamed-of defeat.
Let him record the fight, the siege, the end
Who mourns no notes nor diaries left behind,
Who speaks without a written testament
Because the tale is seared into his mind.

19 Sep 1943

Brooke Himsworth born.

5 Oct 1943

Margaret Ruth Cook born (South African).

8 Oct 1943

J. Copland, a little Scotsman, died today.

22 Oct 1943

T. Donaldson died. He was an old Marine Engineer who always talked about sailing a ship again.

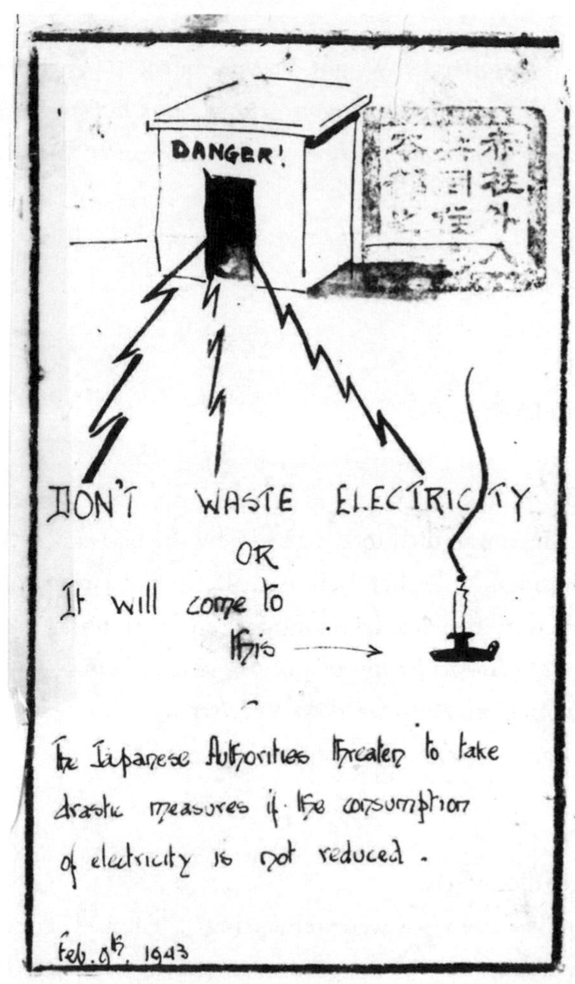

An electricity notice made in camp by M.L. Bevan. His pre-war job was at Air Raid Precautions HQ.

19 Nov 1943

Fiona Kinlock born.

21 Nov 1943

T.V. Harmon died. He might have lived had a proper cystoscope arrived in camp.

27 Nov 1943

Roy Francis Denton (aka Wright-Brown) born. *((His mother Ivy, nee Thirlwell, had given birth the previous year in camp to Camille Tweed, who only survived for two months. There was an older sister, Betty, aged about four.))*

28 Nov 1943

G.S. Rodger died.

1 Dec 1943

My 25th birthday.

5 Dec 1943

Mrs. L. M. McGowan died today. She knew she had cancer, but refused to go into hospital, or let her 2 children Betty and Jackie know she was terminally ill, until they had left camp for repatriation to America. *((They were children of Mrs McGowan's first marriage to a Chinese gentleman with American connections. Post-war, we found that Betty had become famous on the London stage under her Chinese name Chin Yu.))*

7 Dec 1943

C.B. Younger died today.

In December 1943 we were rehearsing a 'farewell' concert by the children *((whom we thought were soon going to be repatriated))* which we put on in the Prison Officers' Club just before Christmas: recitations, choir numbers, and a short play 'The Room in the Tower' which we had adapted from the original (don't know who the author was).

Bill Colledge polished up the play, which went very well, with Anneke Offenberg, Kristine Thoresen, Yvonne Blackmore, Rose and Nita, though there was a last-minute headache because the day before the performance, Anneke forgot to collect her little brother Arnold's milk ration so her parents forbade her to take part. We frantically rehearsed Nita in Anneke's part the next day, when Anneke's exam results came through and were so good that the parents relented. Anneke was even better in the part of Lady Jane Grey awaiting execution, as a result of all the crying she had been doing.

Father Meyer wrote a religious play for Christmas 1943. I had a very small part as the wife of a character played by Hans Lourenz. Mr Concannon was directing, practically from a sick bed.

We burned a fire in our room on Christmas night – there was not much in the way of extra food, though an ounce or so of margarine per head etc. came in.

Children's tableaux in the grotto, with Sally Leighton (4) as Mary.

28 Dec 1943

Jeanette Clark born today.

Her parents had allowed their 2 older daughters, Valerie (3) and Margaret (1) to be adopted in camp by a missionary couple, the Thomases *((more of them in the 1944 diary.))*

1944

6 Jan 1944

Colonel Matthews died.

10 Jan 1944

Daphne Esther Culver born. Her parents were married just before internment.

14 Jan 1944

Mrs Grace Rose Smith (75) died. She was blind.

Mabel and I were digging a garden on our tiny allotment on the ex-football ground when Mabel fell over the edge, 16 feet on to the concrete slope leading to the hospital. She arrived at the feet of Dr. Hackett, and nursing sisters Mrs. M. J. Staple and Miss I. Warbrick *((who were blood sisters))*.

When I got down to Mabel, she was conscious but dazed, half-sitting on one side, being tended to by Dr Hackett etc. I raced to hospital to get a stretcher, then saw her taken to the hospital. She was wearing grey slacks (once Dad's trousers), an old converted shirt of Clifton's, her red, white and blue jumper and Welfare shoes; also her best mosquito net camp-made pants which (and she was most disgusted) they cut off her. Then I ran to find Clifton – her new boyfriend – and my mum, who was playing bridge with the Tribbles. Olive heard about it while in the water queue.

There was a blackout that night, but somehow Professor Digby and the others worked like Trojans to see to Mabel.

15 Jan 1944

Went to hosp. early – Mabel in cock-eyed bed with wooden poles across the top, and her left leg extended and held taut with a dangling flat-iron. That day Dr Myasaka visited the hospital, but though requests were made, nothing was done about x-ray then. *((Her spine was broken but we didn't know it then.))* She had fractured heel, rib probably cracked, and fractured left wrist.

I started to learn German from Mr R. Lederhofer.

31 Jan 1944

Dennis Anthony Clarke was born (the 2nd baby to that family in camp, the first died.)

((Other births around this time: Eunice Jean Nance (American); Christine Stevens; Barry Clarke Tanner.))

3 Feb 1944

Mrs Doris Groves died during childbirth, also the baby Arthur, leaving a husband and 3-year-old Joyce in camp. In 1942 Mrs Groves had also had a son who died at birth. *((In the 1990s Joyce phoned me out of the blue to ask about Stanley memories.))*

5 Feb 1944

Dr. Myasaka took over the medical side of the camp and introduced a clinic system. *((This resulted in much more paperwork in hospital office. Japs supplied forms for the decentralised clinics through the camp, and each patient became the subject of a form. Records of these were made in the hospital office, and we also card-indexed and cross-referenced all hospital patients.))*

6 Feb 1944

Edward Reading died.

11 Feb 1944

Edwin Starling died, leaving wife in camp.

12 Feb 1944

Mabel discharged from hospital. Clifton brought her home on a stretcher.

28 Feb 1944

I suddenly developed mild dysentery, through fish poisoning, and was taken to hospital by Clifton. I was followed by more hospital staff victims – Dr. Barwell, Dr. Yaroogsky-Erooga, Mr. E. Hopkinson, Bill Ream.

((Bread and meat had stopped during January, but a little loaf (more like a roll) was made and the sick and convalescing had one now and again. I had several of these while getting better. Mabel hobbled down on crutches to visit me. While convalescing, I planned the idea of putting on 'Peter Pan.'))

I left hospital on 4th March.

1-31 Mar 1944

Mabel going about on crutches with heel in plaster. Once heel was out of plaster, they put wrist in plaster.

'A Bill of Divorcement' put on by Bill Colledge, very well done, with Norah Witchell, Nina Valentine (Dr's wife), R. Hughes.

Father Meyer busy with Easter play – hectic rehearsals. I had a walking-on part. Hans Lourenz had chief part of Dismus, the good thief, but he was taken ill at last minute so Father Meyer himself took the part.

Catholic Action for youth groups and adults now under way.

At last Mabel (and many others) taken into town for x-ray, it was discovered that her spine really was fractured; in camp, it was decided to make a truss, or put her in plaster.

Alexander Ramsey born.

Nobody in camp died in March.

After Easter I dramatised 'Peter Pan' in 4 scenes from 'Peter Pan Retold for Little People' (lent by Eileen Hill). Pam Pritchard, Harold Bidwell,

Sheila Haynes, Jacquie Anderson and I met to discuss the project, but the first two dropped out for various reasons after the first or second reading – mainly because I wanted my own way about the casting.

10 Apr 1944

J. Stevenson died.

16 Apr 1944

Mrs Henson died peacefully in hospital in the night.

30 Apr 1944

No births during April. Tony Cole moved from Bungalow C to St Stephen's.

Mabel had a truss fitted for back injury but it wouldn't work, so in hospital again, to be put in a plaster jacket. *((This plaster wouldn't set though, so the workshop started to make her a steel jacket out of old ceiling fan blades. She wore this very patiently for about six months and it helped)).*

Still getting no meat and no bread – and not very much of anything.

2 May 1944

Robert Mitchell born. Parents married at start of camp, daughter Rosemary born Oct. 1942.

Mrs R. G. Rose (Chinese) died, leaving British husband in Kowloon camp, and Dawn (12) and Gerald (8) in Stanley. *((Both children were cared for by Mrs H. Aitken, mother of Eddie, until the end of internment.))*

3 May 1944

Clifton in hospital with colic.

9 May 1944

Little Brian Gill drowned at the beach. Saw his pathetic little body brought to the hospital on a stretcher. His mother, Billie Gill, was playing bridge with friends while another friend took Brian for an afternoon at the beach to give mum a break.

10 May 1944

To Brian's funeral. Father Meyer made him a coffin out of the drawer from a chest-of-drawers, lining it with bunched-up white satin. Children sang 'Heaven is the Prize' – unforgettable.

11 May 1944

C. C. Shilton died.

18 May 1944

Alan G.J. Weir born.

22 May 1944

Mrs E.K. Wilmer died.

1 Jun 1944

G. F. Byrne died while rice-grinding.

5 Jun 1944

E. C. Oates died of typhus.

Invasion of Europe started.

10 Jun 1944

((Date is approximate. I don't like to identify Mr A and Mrs B here, as some of the family may still be alive.))

I got to a tribunal, held in a little room in the Married Quarters which was the office of the British Community Council, to settle differences between neighbours Mr A and Mrs B, the latter having alleged that Mr A had threatened 'to knock her block off'.

Mr Evans *((not sure which one))* presided. This was over a clothes line which Mrs B had tied up in a communal area & on which she had hung

Expéditeur SENDER Absender

Name WALLACE,
Nom
Christian name MRS. A.
Vorname Prènom
Address
Adresse

MESSAGE Mitteilung
(Not more than 25 words) (25 mots au maximum) (Nicht über 25 Worte)

HOPE YOU AND GIRLS ARE WELL. HEARD FROM BESS. SHE RECEIVED NEWS OF YOU AND HAS WRITTEN. HAVING LOVELY SPRING WEATHER. ALL WELL. LOVE.
LILIAN.

CROIX ROUGE

Date Datum 18th MARCH, 1943.

PASSED
P 241

Destinataire ADDRESSEE Empfänger

Name REDWOOD,
Nom
Christian name MRS. M. W.
Vorname Prènom
Address "BRITISH CIVILIAN INTERNEE",
Adresse ROOM 19, BLOCK 3, MARRIED QUARTERS,
STANLEY INTERNMENT CAMP, HONG KONG.

Reply overleaf (not more than 25 words)
Réponse au verso (25 mots au maximum)
Antwort umseitig (nicht über 25 Worte)

(N.B. Back used for Church notes)

002792 8 AVR 1943

Red Cross letter to my mother from her sister in the UK.

wet garments. Mr A objected because of the drips and in her absence pulled the line down. When Mrs B found her much-prized sharkskin suit on the floor she was furious, and wanted to put the clothes line and the clothes back. Mr A said why couldn't she put her wet clothes on the clothes lines in the courtyard, like everyone else? I guess Mrs B preferred to keep an eye on her prized garment. When Mrs B went to restore her private clothes line, Mr A threatened to 'knock her block off' so more acrimony followed.

During the proceedings Mrs B's daughter aged 20 butted in once, unable to contain herself, and Mrs B had to be restrained by her husband when her indignation threatened to run away with her. Mr A for a long time refused to take back his words, though Mr Evans pointed out that he had threatened physical violence, and apparently still intended this on his own telling. It ended with both parties agreeing not to disturb each other, provided the other behaved.

There was quite a lot of garden produce stealing at this time.

22 Jun 1944

Mr M Flaherty, an R.C., died of Hodgkin's disease. Much fuss over his coffin, apparently made from a questionable source in camp (all furniture now being strictly communal – there was a Tribunal case over it, against L. Nielson). Mrs Flaherty is Chinese, she spent some time in gaol but is out now.

No births during June. Still rehearsing 'Peter Pan.'

26 Jun 1944

C. H. Goodwin (HK Police) died.

A typed Red Cross message dated 18th March 1943 arrived from Aunt Lily in Gillingham, Kent, stamped la Croix Rouge, Geneve, with a Japanese chop on it, saying:

> 'Hope you and girls are well... Having lovely spring weather. All well. Love, Lilian'.

((At some unrecorded time, another plain typed postcard arrived, dated 28.1.44 and stamped by British Censor, saying:

> 'All well, Home and Rhodesia. Hope you and girls are too. Having mild winter, bulbs up, trees sprouting. All send our love, Lilian.'

The reference to Rhodesia is re Aunt Bess and family, and Aunt Hilda and family, who lived there.))

2 Jul 1944

Rosaleen Frances McDermott born, the second child born to that family in Stanley.

8 Jul 1944

G. B. Foster died (typhus).

12 Jul 1944

W. E. Kirby died.

15 Jul 1944

I. Chalmers died.

16 Jul 1944

H. C. MacNamara died.

20 Jul 1944

Mum in hospital with acute gastroenteritis.

Olive sold her engagement ring.

23 Jul 1944

W. Faid fell off roof at Indian Quarters, and died.

24 Jul 1944

Mr A. L. Shields died; his wife had been repatriated with the Canadians.

25 Jul 1944

Mrs. A. M. Gunningham died.

1 Aug 1944
J. Ross died.

9 Aug 1944
Olive in hospital with tonsilo-pharyngitis.

PETER PAN

((Peter Pan was performed at St Stephen's during August 1944, probably the 9th-11th.))

Sheila Haynes, Jacquie Anderson and myself produced this play. Norah Witchell also helped. Eileen Grant put the show's songs to music. Pauline Beck played piano accompaniments to the dances which were arranged by Peggy Barton and my sister Mabel.

The cast:
PETER – Mavis Thirlwell (aged 13)
WENDY – Ruth Sewell (11)
JOHN – Malcolm Kerr (11)
MICHAEL – Gloria Mejia (7) alternating with Anne de Broekert (7 – Dutch)
NANA – Ingeborg Warild (14 – Norwegian)
MRS DARLING – Anneke Offenberg (15 – Dutch) & Kristine Thoresen (14 – Norwegian)
MR DARLING – George Cullen (18)
TINKERBELL – Eileen Hill (10)
TIGER LILY – Dawn Rose (12 – her mother died in camp, leaving Dawn and younger brother Gerald on their own, as their father was a POW in Kowloon camp. Mrs. H. Aitken thereafter looked after Dawn and Gerald until the end of the war.)
CAPTAIN HOOK – Georges de Vleeschouwer (13 – Belgian)
CROCODILE – Pauline Hill (13)

LOST BOYS:
SLIGHTLY – Pauline Pemble (12)
TWIN 1 – Dolores Bonner (11)
TWIN 2 – Delia Mejia (12)
CURLY – Moira Cameron (11 – whose mother died in camp)
NIBS – Joan Eager (9)
TOOTLES – Tinneke Offenberg (11 – Dutch).

PIRATES:
Brian Clark (11 – Australian)
Pat Corrigan (12)
Billy Bethell (15)
Eddie Aitken (13) *((Eddie Aitken is the son of Mrs Aitken who mothered the Rose children))*
plus some others.

REDSKINS:
Billy Seraphina (11)
Denis Roe (9)
and others.

FAIRIES:
Jacqueline Barton (10)
Rosemary Barton (9)
Sally Leighton (5)
Mavis Hamson (8)
Cynthia Eager (8)
Terry Simpson (6)
Rose Twidale (7)
Daisy Cullen (8)
Flossie James (7)
Matilda Hardoon (8).

The production assistants:
R. E. Butler (lighting; an engineer who did the lights for most Stanley shows)
Richard Cloake (Dick); T. A. Concannon.
Harold Bidwell, Clifton Large, George Anderson, Quentin MacFayden. (These trained the Redskins and the Pirates.)

The biggest hit of Peter Pan was the crocodile (Pauline Hill) who slithered across the stage in an amazingly realistic garment made by one Teddy Harris.

((I was so pleased to meet up with Ruth Sewell (Wendy), Pauline Pemble, Flossie James and Tinneke Offenberg (all three Lost Boys) at the Stanley Reunion in the UK in 1997; Eddie Aitken has visited me several times in recent years. I have also met up with Dawn Rose (Tiger Lily), and Rosemary Barton, one of the fairies. At the VJ Celebration in London in 2015 quite by chance I bumped into another fairy, Daisy Cullen – now known as Barbara – who remembered dancing in 'Peter Pan', and we had a wonderful chat. Another fairy was Mavis Hamson, whose daughter Allana Corbin has written a most interesting and forthright book about the life in Stanley of her mother, uncle, grandparents, great-grandmother and aunt – 'Prisoners of the East', published by Pan Macmillan Australia.))

10 Aug 1944

T. Pritchard died.

15 Aug 1944

((Date is approximate))

Sudden news that we were going to get Canadian parcels.

We all had to give up our private little gardens on the ex-football pitch to become communal gardens as food getting shorter, so our sweet potatoes which were coming on so well had to be hurriedly dug up.

Electricity went off for good (we were told).

Diet Kitchen had to close down.

29 Aug 1944

D.C. Edmonston died. A bank official, he was imprisoned in the gaol; his wife and daughter Mary (in camp) were notified that he was dying and were allowed to go and see him, but he didn't know them, and died. *((Mrs. Edmonston had in January bought Olive's gold manicure set for Mary's birthday. The Japanese allowed Mr Edmonston's body to be buried in the camp cemetery.))*

30 Aug 1944

Mabel's 21st birthday. She and I locked the door and ate a plateful each of fried sweet potatoes and rice bread with some paste I'd saved. We were real gluttons.

7 Sep 1944

Mrs F. E. Hyde died (cancer) leaving Michael aged 6. Her husband was among those executed in October 1943. Lady M. Grayburn is looking after Michael, her husband having died in Stanley Gaol in May 1943.

Veronica Ann Reddish born.

12-13 Sep 1944

Canadian parcels etc. arrived in camp.

All night long and in early hours of morning we heard lorries groaning backwards and forward from the quay. When they were distributed, we got 4 parcels each!

((A neighbour, Mr. W. Pryde (Public Works Department), died suddenly on the 12th so was not included in the distribution. We felt that his widow should have been given his share as well as her own, as he was alive when the parcels actually arrived in camp (though dead before distribution) and she had to cope with the loss of her husband – she was such a selfless person and had lost so much weight. She served in ARP during war. The Prydes' boys were in Australia. Post-war, one of the boys who was married with children died very young, and Mrs Pryde brought them up.))

4 Oct 1944

Olive in hospital with gastroenteritis.

12 Oct 1944

Mr M. A. Johnson died.

13 Oct 1944

Mrs M. A. Duncan died.

15 Oct 1944

Mrs B. R. Humphreys died.

16 Oct 1944

Lights came on again. Started a Retreat, with daily talks, and private readings in evenings.

Terrific air raid, planes like great silver birds.

22 Oct 1944

'One-armed Sutton' died (Francis Arthur). I went to funeral.

Sheila Haynes and I busy helping Mr. Dimond (A.K.) to put on 'The Other Wise Man'. Doreen (Leonard), Nita (Olivier), Anneke (Offenberg) in leading parts.

'Call It A Day' put on by the professionals (Bill Colledge etc.) Kathleen Davis made a big hit. Anneke and Kris (Kristine Thoresen) in it too.

Played bridge with Diana Hardoon and Marie O'Connor.

25 Oct 1944

Mum to hospital with dysentery.

30 Oct 1944

Olive to hospital with dysentery.

So for a few days Mabel and I had the room to ourselves *((Mrs K had by now moved out as she and her husband had got a billet together))*.

One night we had gramophone (always on loan around the camp by its generous owners); Fortescues came in for recital, and we had a candle. Adrian looked so nice by candle-light. *((The Fortescues lived in the kitchen next to our room, basin and draining board having been removed. Even then it was tiny for two adults and a small child, but they valued their privacy more than space.))*

7 Nov 1944

Olive home again.

We were warned that the water was going to be turned off.

9 Nov 1944

Mum came out of hospital.

11 Nov 1944

Water turned off 'indefinitely', but after, we were told it would be on every 3 days.

13 Nov 1944

News of Manila raids.

14 Nov 1944

Night raid here.

Full up with rehearsals, meetings, etc.

Weather very cold.

22 Nov 1944

Mr E. T. Ward died in his room in the night – in next flat to us.

Mr. E. M. Hazeland died.

1 Dec 1944

My 26th birthday.

In the middle of the night there was a BIG BANG, which the camp decided was a raider blasting a gun emplacement on the hillside on the other side of the bay.

Outside roll call therefore no Mass.

4 Dec 1944

J. Channing (Police) arrested, but afterwards released, for alleged selling of rice outside barbed wire.

7 Dec 1944

Mr A. G. Dann, an RC, died.

8 Dec 1944

Went to Mr Dann's funeral during which there was an air raid alarm. *((As soon as the funeral was over, we mourners flew from the cemetery to Block 10, the nearest building; we were pursued by a Formosan or Jap soldier, who objected because we had been out during a raid. He caught us up outside Block 10, and hit Father Donald Hessler across the back with the wooden end of his rifle, and slapped his face. I was next to Father, and expected to get it too, and trembled for my glasses, but he just glared at me.))*

After the raid was over, went to the end of Annie Van Der Lely's engagement party to R. N. Rennie (Police) in Dutch Block.

13 Dec 1944

T. Knox died suddenly, leaving his little wife (who used to live in room adjacent to ours for the first year), and sons in other camps.

Mr A. E. Carey died; he'd hung on for a long time – got over the typhus, but developed gangrene of arm.

18 Dec 1944

We (RC young ladies) gave Marie Barton a shower in honour of her engagement to Vincent Marcus Morrison (HK Police, who, with Randall,

Bidmead and Fay had escaped from Stanley in 1942, but were caught and put in Stanley Gaol; released back into camp this June.)

((Marie and Vincent eventually had a very large family; when in 1963 my eldest son went to Winslade School, Clyst St. Mary in Exeter as a weekly boarder, we found that one of the Morrison boys, Peter, was also a pupil there. There were many other Morrisons then – Michael, Anthony, Frances, Bernadette, Margaret and Angela. The family lived in Sidmouth.

That night I wrote most of 'A child's Christmas', a nostalgic memory of Christmas as a child in the UK, too long to include here.))

22 Dec 1944

Xmas play 'The Other Wise Man'. Little Fleur Cheape (4) played the small child. Air raid alarms made performance difficult, had to start late; also, half the would-be audience wasn't there because they thought the play would be cancelled because of alarms. Doreen Leonard played her part very seriously and well.

((Doreen, a Eurasian teenager, was one of the girls in the Girls' Study Group. I gave her shorthand lessons. Her English father, and one of her sisters who was married with small children, were in camp. Doreen and I became great friends. After internment, like we Redwoods, she and her father went to England, and we exchanged frequent letters. She wanted to be an air hostess. I returned to Hong Kong in June 1946, and on arrival was shocked to receive news that Doreen had passed away. When her dad returned to Hong Kong a few months later, he sought me out where I was working, and handed me a little brooch of Doreen's, saying he thought she loved me best of all her friends... so touching. She was only 17.))

24 Dec 1944

Draw for two 10 lb. iced cakes made by Father B. Meyer. Won by Mrs. V. Murrell and Mrs. B. Doering. Air raid during proceedings.

(During this week, I got Yen 230 from Ivy Denton – some time ago I'd given her a tin of parcel Cowbell milk powder to sell for us to get canteen money to get extras for Mum when she was in hospital.)

There was a draw for a cockerel – from surplus cockerels owned by an enterprising internee who somehow kept a few chickens. Sheila Haynes won one.

Extension of evening curfew tonight.

Walked round camp with Mabel and Clifton while the United Churches choir sang deep-throated harmonising carols. The Fortescues let us peep in on Adrian after 'Father Christmas' had been and left presents, and he was fast asleep. A lovely night.

25 Dec 1944

Stayed to 2 Masses. Visited Leprosarium *((then our TB wards))*. They had a 'Christmas tree'.

Japs had sent flat duck in rations – hospital kitchen put out a terrific meal of beans, pumpkin, 'ragout of duck', greens, and a pudding with wong tong syrup. Married Quarters had pasties and rissoles.

Mr. Cochrane and son Graham visited us. *((Alexander Cochrane of Hong Kong Police was married to Ena Penney who had been a neighbour of ours in 1929 when we lived at 98 Kennedy Road.))* Graham was born in Stanley.

Gladys Johnson gave me a handkerchief, June Cheape a home-made calendar. Beryl Goldenberg gave me a nice card.

26 Dec 1944

Spent morning with Sheila, Peggy, Audrey etc. at St Stephen's arranging the toys we'd made for RC social and labelling them. Social went off very well, with tableaux, a choir in which Mabel sang; and the great cake, baked by Father Meyer and to which all RCs had contributed tiny amounts of ingredients.

In evening, Mabel, Yvonne Blackmore, George Saunders, Eric MacNider, Clifton and myself had a party in Clifton's room *((he shared an amah's room with another fellow))*. We had too much to eat – a terrific chow-fan, George's special congee, and a pudding with sauce. I couldn't move for ages after the meal.

30 Dec 1944

Mr J.S. Anderson died.

Marie Barton married to Vincent Morrison who is now a RC. They had a very lovely Nuptial Mass. Reception couldn't be in afternoon because a Japanese inspection was planned (which however didn't come off.)

Wrote 'The Last Meeting'.

31 Dec 1944

To Marie & Vincent's reception.

SUMMARY OF 1944

Mabel's accident in January, and 'Peter Pan' were the dominating features of my year.

Other notable events included:

We had cards from Aunt Lily, Topper's sister and mother; Margaret Smith and Mrs. Brown (all in UK).

But no news of Topper, Arthur or Sid *((our Army boyfriends))*.

We were driven to the conclusion that we were NOT going to be repatriated.

Food got worse, not much light, little water, no meat, some fish, mainly whitebait.

Invasion of Europe started in June, and by early autumn we were expecting European war to end, and sweepstakes thereon were rampant.

Wrote 'The Last Meeting' , 'The Princess Who Wasn't' – not performed; poem 'A Child's Christmas', and started to write 'Balancing Jean' which is unfinished.

Come and get it!

The food queues in Stanley

The summons for food is the same as the summons for everything else in the Married Quarters of Stanley Camp – a raucous clanging on a broken shellcase with a thick stick. Each set of accommodation blocks has its own particular arrangement for serving; ours, the Married Quarters, boasts a separate serving table for each of our four blocks; each block has three floors which take turns in being first in the queue; beyond this, the rule of 'first come, first served' applies.

In fine weather the food queues are to be found anywhere in the Married Quarters courtyard, the position depending upon the whereabouts of the sun – the object being to place the servers and as many of the queuers as possible in the shade. In wet weather, the question of site is even more complicated, the only spaces affording shelter being the porchways below the back stairs. Today, however, it is sunny, and the shadiest area is at the end of the yard nearest the distributing kitchen; this means that to the general commotion of serving food is added the noisy business of scrubbing out cooking containers and utensils, followed by the sluicing down of the site of these operations.

There are four queues in this particular spot this morning, so close together that to the uninitiated observer it may seem that there is no queue at all, but only a disorderly crowd. Blocks 3 and 4 are serving here, in addition to the 'specials' queue, in which workers receive extra rations allotted to them for their labour, and the congee queue, which caters for those persons who are certified by a doctor's chit as being unable to assimilate rice in its boiled form. Blocks 2 and 5 have appropriated the only other shady place – between the buildings known as Blocks 4 and 5.

The scene from one of the verandahs overlooking the courtyard is one which brings to mind news films of refugees lining up for their daily bread, one main difference being that our food queue is comparatively cheerful, as rumours and gossip are busily exchanged.

The most important aspect of the food queue, of course, is the food itself. A rough idea of what this constitutes can sometimes be gained in advance by reading the menu on the noticeboard. I say only a 'rough' idea for two reasons, the first being that quite often the kitchen staff forget to change it from day to day; the second that the same kitchen staff sometimes let their imaginations run away with them, and describe, say, a flat, fried rice cake about two and a half inches in diameter as 'Uncle Charlie's Birthday Biscuit.'

The menu this morning reads 'Rice; veg. pasty; melon soup.' As we had that sumptuous meal last night, today's meal will have to remain a surprise until it actually comes across from the galley – a converted garage situated opposite the front corner of Block 4.

A chain of sweating men stagger out from the galley into the courtyard, carrying zinc baths full of boiled rice; then the stew arrives. Today it looks rather more interesting than usual, having a rich brown appearance, reminiscent of the gravy we used to have with our Sunday dinners in days of old. On closer examination, however, it proves to be made of minced 'horse' beans; these large beans, black outside and brownish-yellow within, are believed to be those described in a Readers' Digest we came across as 'eaten only by mules and pit ponies, and only consumed by humans in case of famine or exceptional necessity,' but they taste nutty and are a great improvement on the colourless, tasteless melon soup which usually accompanies the morning rice.

There is no possibility, these days, of drawing a double share of food, for the first official you encounter as you approach the serving table is a 'checker', who has a list of everyone on block rations and how much rice they are due. You receive your share of China's staff of life first – served by a perspiring individual from a medium-sized zinc bath over which he operates in much the same way as the ice-cream vendor fills wafers and cornets. On his or her left is a bowl of hot water in which he dips the copper-coloured ladle (camp-made) from time to time to loosen the rice grains which are inclined to stick. The small quantities of rice which collect in this bowl are the recognised perks of the rice server; such rice as is spilt on the ground is swept up and, together with the grains washed out from the larger kitchen containers, goes to the camp chicken farm.

You then present your plate or other container before an oblong tray containing bean stew, of which each person receives one dipper full; the size of dipper used varies from day to day, according to the quantity of stew available; today's ladle was made in camp from a small tin of Chinese tomatoes. The serving from this end of the table (which incidentally is actually a beige-coloured door to which rough legs have been added), is superintended by some trusted member of the Block who can be relied upon to see that the server does not give her friends or relations an extra ladle of stew. The official Block Representative (there is one for each Block) is also in the vicinity of the serving table, acting as a kind of liaison officer between servers and kitchen workers so that a further supply is available as soon as the first containerful is exhausted.

The queues are constantly breaking up to make way for some dripping member of the kitchen staff to come over to a table with a dish of hot stew, and all those within splashing distance have to stand back while the fresh stew is decanted into the serving container.

It is interesting to observe that some people collect only their own ration, whereas others carry makeshift trays with as many as six persons' food. You can see every single member of one particular room lining up for their food behind each other – this is usually an indication that relations in that room are strained and perhaps completely broken off.

A wider variety of containers than those in which the food is collected could hardly be imagined; there is a large proportion of enamel mugs and plates of different colours donated to the camp some three years ago, but many of these have worn out and are replaced by odd china plates, saucers, little trays from pre-war 'tiffin' carriers, and tins of various sizes, the 'Domo' and 'Cowbell' milk powder variety (from Red Cross parcels two years ago) predominating. There are enamel measuring mugs, oblong medical trays of white enamel rimmed with dark blue, even an inverted lampshade with a makeshift bottom. The experienced severs know where the rice goes and where the stew goes – some people are very fussy on this point, but most of the men have 'everything slapped on together' – to quote their own expression.

A good selection of Stanley fashions are displayed in the food queues; most people are barefoot; the men, almost without exception, wear only a pair of shorts, although there are one or two who still consider it *infra dig* to appear without shirt, socks and shoes, no matter how tattered these articles may be. The majority of the women wear shorts and blouses or suntops, usually revealing a sunburnt strip of midriff. The garments are growing a little jaded this year. The Welfare shorts received in camp in 1942 have washed from a bright khaki to a pale fawn, and the shorts made from dresses droop sadly. Suntops are made from all sorts of odds and ends – from flour bags to small squares of different coloured materials pieced together. A few ladies exhibit the more superior Stanley feminine fashion – an old dress which has worn badly has been cut off at the waist, forming a skirt and a short blouse, leaving an exposed midriff which makes for coolness. This is a very popular fashion for growing girls, when the hems of their dresses have been let down to their utmost limit; a new lease of life is added by cutting the dress in the manner described.

Despite the acute clothes problem, and the exigencies of the camp restricting washing to a minimum for soap and personal calorie economy, there are a few women to whom the food queue is apparently the outing of the day, for they still arrive dressed in their best; one elderly lady never appears without a black felt hat belonging to a past decade.

Difference in dress and containers there may be – but difference in the ration received according to one's entitlement – no! Anyone who considers that his rice is slightly underweight may take it to a gentleman who presides at some scales in the yard, where any deficit is made up, or overage deducted (the latter possibility limits the number of those querying their share). Once served, everyone troops back to their rooms, threading their way through the day's washing which usually flutters from practically every space on the clothes lines which run the whole length of the courtyard.

The last queue is served; any leftovers, or 'seconds', distributed to the rooms next on turn to receive them; the servers and supervisors disperse; the tables are moved out of the way and washed. For a time there is comparative quiet in the Married Quarters as 500-odd mouths make short work of – and some remember to thank God for – their meagre meal.

Barbara Redwood
Stanley
1944 or 1945

1945

1 Jan 1945

Noisy New Year, no one went to sleep between 9pm in-room bell and midnight, and much noisy community singing. Just before 12, some people went out in courtyard and clanged Block 5's bell. Several people knocked on our door and first-footed us and wished us Happy New Year – don't know who they all were! Clifton came along and kissed us (except for Mum who then was asleep in bed). People were noisy for about half an hour after.

Mabel had a meal! Half a rissole etc. We each slept on a crumb of wedding cake from Vincent & Marie's reception yesterday.

This morning to Mass, big crowd there. Brought Annie (Van Der Lely – Dutch) back for hot 'pancakes' and lime juice.

Worked in afternoon.

Supposed to be an air raid in evening.

We opened our last tin of bully.

Talk in our room at night by Mr Gimson on 'Elephant Hunting in Ceylon.'

2 Jan 1945

Went to see Mr Davis *((can't remember his initials))* to get date for our one-act plays. It might have to be after April.

Worked in afternoon. Spent evening with Gladys Johnson in her corridor.

Newspaper says 'Neissei Maru' sails 4th January from Kobe, first instalment (food parcels) for U.S. pows and internees in Japan and China; next shipment to go to Philippines and southern regions. Father Meyer says we will all surely get some.

Paper says Soviets refuse American military aircraft permission to land in Soviet territory.

F. M. von Rundstedt's offensive said to be building up for second phase.

United Press says American forces had pushed back German salient for 14 miles.

I cooked for Dr Hargreaves in morning. Visited Fleur Cheape in hospital.

Kristine said she'd rather help with production of plays than act.

Working in afternoon.

3 Jan 1945

Elsie Bidwell has to have a mastoid operation.

Barbara Fox had a daughter this morning – Maureen Patricia.

Fish cake for tiffin. We fried noodles this evening.

Dr Mark (Erooga) came for coffee.

4 Jan 1945

Redwoods' turn for passage. *((The 26 residents of 'our' flat took turns in cleaning the communal passage and areas. Big problem about a mother and toddler who lived in a curtained-off part of the landing between first and second floors as to which passage she should clean!))*

Bulletin on board says there are no indications that we shall get parcels.

Miss Olive Jeffery died at 4.30pm *((a Govt. nursing sister who was already a TB patient when our war started.))*

Spent lovely afternoon outside Block 2 with Pat Lederhofer, Pat and Kristine Thoresen, Doreen Leonard and Tinneke Offenberg, reading plays with Sheila's help.

Captain Batty-Smith lectured in our room most interestingly on experiences in p.o.w. camp in Germany for almost 4 years in WWI.

Parcel ship supposed to leave Kobe.

5 Jan 1945

Worked in afternoon. Typed for Dr H. Talbot.

Annie came to talk re wedding *((I was to be a bridesmaid))*.

Got potatoes from Mr. Ingram *((A. W. I think))* for cigarettes. We ate them in evening.

Mr Davis visited, we can have Feb 21, 22 and 23 for plays.

Peggy came over later, told us of her appendix operation in Stanley, then I visited Beryl Goldenberg who is in bed with a cold.

6 Jan 1945

Ernst Mejia (4) has chickenpox and is in hospital. *((He was the youngest of a family of nine children in camp with their mother. They lived in a room below us in the Married Quarters))*.

Air raid alarm in afternoon, rehearsal of Her First Dance.

Rumour re German collapse.

Went to see Annie, who's quite philosophical about her postponed wedding.

7 Jan 1945

Day off.

Saw Mr Davis, our plays now set for 15,16 & 17th Feb., a week earlier than planned.

Several people in trouble with guards; one was slapped, some had stones thrown at them (over all-clear signal misunderstanding).

Buddens came and played bridge. *((Mrs. Maggie Budden and daughter Barbara Budden who was a stenographer colleague of mine in HK Government. Maggie's husband died in Shamshuipo pow camp, as did Barbara's brother Gilbert who was my age. As children, Gilbert and I sat at adjoining desks at Garrison School.))*

Visited Pat Cullinan (HK Police), he wants to put on trial scene from Merchant of Venice. *((Throughout internment, Pat was hospitalised with TB.))*

8 Jan 1945

To St. Agnes (older girls) meeting in morning, very few there.

Then confabbed with Pat Cullinan re Merchant of Venice play outside Leprosarium (Pat's billet).

Very lean meals.

Matriculation exams on *((organised by teachers in camp for students of the right age))*.

News of landing of task force in West Luzon; rumours of repatriation; of men being sent to Formosa, and of bread supply at weekend.

Mr. de Martin's lecture on Words in our room very good. I was in bed for it. *((Thus made more room for others attending.))*

9 Jan 1945

Diana Hardoon's and Joan Critchett's 21st birthdays.

Ground some rice.

We had noodles in evening, then to Block 5 stairway and heard Miss E. M. Gibbins' first lecture on European History. *((A teacher by profession, she also taught at St Stephen's throughout camp))*.

Adrian Fortescue (3) has chicken-pox. *((He lived with parents Tim and Margery in kitchen next to our room))*.

10 Jan 1945

Bitterly cold.

Got powdered egg yolk.

To St Stephen's, talked with Concannon (T) re our plays. He suggests leaving one out.

Fish stew at tiffin – I couldn't eat it – saved the rice and fried it with egg yolk tonight.

Yesterday's paper said Philippine situation grave – U.S. attacking Japs there.

Worked in afternoon. Meeting in Grants' room, Millie (Thirlwell) and Audrey (Barton) and Annie came.

11 Jan 1945

Cold again.

Went to German lesson.

Each given quarter pound of wong tong free (ex Red Cross) and soy sauce.

Bulletin news not too good – German breakthrough on Maginot Line.

To lecture – Mr. H. L. Ascough *((of Cable & Wireless))* on 'Behind the scenes at a radio broadcasting station.'

12 Jan 1945

Outside roll call in am. Comment made on clogs – 'Have these people no shoes?'

Rumour – we may get electric current. Went to work 10.30am – late because of roll call.

Mr. H.W. Page, aged 71, died.

Catholic Action Council meeting in quarry/grotto... talked with Pat Cullinan and Beryl re play, the rehearsal in P.O. Club. *((Beryl was to play Jessica in the trial scene of The Merchant of Venice.))*

Rehearsal of plays.

Paper says Philippine battle going on.

13 Jan 1945

Mum's 50th birthday. Mabel gave her a brooch from somewhere. Margery Fortescue gave her some potatoes and carrots, and lard to fry them in.

Eleven or twelve destroyers came in and out of bay.

Rumour that electric current will come on again – tomorrow the day.

To Confession standing by the railings opposite Block A3.

To party with St Agnes girls in quarry/grotto. *((St Agnes was a little club of teenage RC girls I helped with. The quarry or grotto was a rocky piece of waste ground opposite the American Block where sometimes meetings and services were held. A few 'Mimi Lau' bricks provided very hard seating.))*

The girls did very well. Mary Rogers (14) sang and played guitar; the eats were wonderful and plenty. *((Everyone usually brought a little bit of food for these occasions.))* Banging – perhaps blasting – going on.

Fried meal in evening.

Various Christmas and New Year greetings from different countries.

Parcels – NIL. Walked round with Gladys in evening.

14 Jan 1945

Yesterday's paper says that another Maru (ship) left Moji on 8th for Shanghai with U.S. parcels, not yet guaranteed safe passage. No one in camp knows what's happened to the Nissei Maru.

Benediction in afternoon, then Catholic Action Section Meeting; Brother Bonnici (Louis) gave a talk on Malta. *((He was one of two Catholic Brothers in camp.))*

15 Jan 1945

Morning roll call late, and had hardly finished when air raid happened. The longest and noisiest we've had yet. Much ack-ack fire. Some say there were 12-14 planes, I only saw 3, flying very low. They came back again for a short time just after lovely tiffin of potato and beans.

Worked in afternoon, visited Fleur still in hospital, rather listless.

Mum had 2 letters from Auntie dated Dec. 1943.

16 Jan 1945

Heard planes coming over just when I went to get congee, and arrived back in room just before kyushu (air raid alarm) went. A long time after, planes came round our area, and dive-bombed Waglan Island.

Bright and sunny.

I flew down to hospital about 12.15; during tiffin planes came round again. They came in waves. I saw 2 planes crash, one collided with the other; the first one had flames coming out of the tail and fell pretty quickly, fairly high up on this side of the Peak. The other fell very slowly; one pilot bailed out, another airman had his parachute out but couldn't get free of the plane. One piece of wing was slowly turning over and over in the air for a long time.

There was a rumour that leaflets were dropped, but it turned out only to be packing from ack-ack shells. Spent a lot of time up in Ward 4 with Fleur (Cheape, aged 4); she was frightened but kept her self-control very well. *((We crouched together under a small table in the ward. I knew her as she lived with her mother on the landing near us in Block 3, Married Quarters.))*

Apparently the planes were after a machine gun on the end of the gaol. A couple of bombs (or shells) landed on the rocks beside the gaol about 200 yards away from us at the hospital. Pom-pom guns, machine guns, blast – terrifying. Mum says it was like that in the Jockey Club hospital during the battle.

The Operating Theatre windows blew in, and some windows in Ward 6. Someone said they thought Jap HQ (on a knoll in the camp) had been hit, then Watanabe came to the hospital, saying 2 people in Bungalow C had been hurt, one 'on the point of death'; he asked for help. Volunteers went off with stretchers etc., and about ten minutes later, Mr Owen Evans came tearing down and said that nearly everyone in Bungalow C had been killed.

Then 14 were reported dead:

Mr & Mrs A. Hyde Lay

Mr. A. Holland

Mr & Mrs E. Searle

Mrs. A. E. Guerin

Mrs. Davies *((sister of our friend Norman Whitley who was also in Stanley))*

Mr. A. J. Dennis

Mr. G. Stopani-Johnson

Mrs I. Johnson (whose husband died in Stanley last year)

Mr. G. Willoughby

Mr S. F. Bishop

Mr. Oscar Eager

Mr S. F. Balfour *((for a short time pre-war he was my boss at the Secretariat))*.

Didn't get up from hospital till almost 6pm, when Clifton had come down with Mr Blake on a stretcher – who'd got shrapnel in leg while rice-grinding. Clifton raced Olive and I up the slope to the Married Q., and more planes were coming over. Clifton had been up at the bungalow to help dig, and to take Father Hessler. The bomb fell in courtyard between Tony's ex-room and garage. *((Tony Cole of ARP Dept., who had only recently moved out from Bungalow C.))*

We slept in our clothes.

17 Jan 1945

Two alarms but we heard no raids, we've all been very jumpy.

To work in afternoon.

Mr Bailey is all right *((he was in Bungalow C))* but a bit shaken, his face has all little scratches from the blast, and his clothes sort of shaggy. Gave him cigarettes.

Haven't seen newspaper, but it's supposed to say 300 planes were over yesterday and 25 shot down; rumour that 3 pilots who came down by parachute were installed in the prison, and that a guarantee has been given that there'll be no more shooting from the camp. (Doesn't apply to the Prison, though.)

The funerals were at 4pm, only relatives and personal friends allowed to go.

Rice increase to 16 ozs. from 1st Feb. Olive and I will probably have to come off hospital rations.

18 Jan 1945

Several rather long alarms today, but no raids to our knowledge, probably reconnaissance planes.

Rice rissole for tiffin.

To plays rehearsal, we have decided to call off more rehearsals till the air raid situation stabilizes itself.

Got sweet potatoes for cigarettes.

German lesson in afternoon.

19 Jan 1945

Yesterday's paper says (re 16th) that 'over 10 bombs' were released at Stanley and killed 15 internees and wounded 34. (Who are the 34, no one knows!)

Paper also says "there have been painted white crosses, an international symbol representing 'no attack' on the roofs of the buildings." – We are all looking for the white crosses!

Mr. C. F. Livesey died.

Mrs. K. Martin (wife of Rev. Martin) died about tiffin time.

Air raid alarm but no planes, though we heard a heavy one come over in the night.

20 Jan 1945

No alarms today. To Mass in am., and to Confession.

Last night went to Block 4 concert on their stairway, good and spontaneous.

Red Cross letter to Olive from Topper's sister *((Topper was Olive's fiance, a pow in Japan where he died; his sister was in the UK)).*

Children's quiz in our room in evening.

21 Jan 1945

Clifton collapsed in cookhouse this afternoon, now in hospital. Probably will be operated on tomorrow for appendicitis.

Played bridge in Mezger's room, with Betty Drown, Dick Cloake and Mez. *((W.J. Mezger; Richard Cloake – journalist))*. Nice cake.

Air raid this afternoon – heard no bombs, but planes and a.a. fire.

Last night about 9pm alarm sounded, and a large low plane circled around.

22 Jan 1945

On holiday this week.

Margery Fortescue, Victor Cross (6), Stewart Valentine (13), Peter Hall (10) and Kenny Macleod (8) have chickenpox, they're not in hospital.

Clifton says he's dying of hunger – maybe appendicitis, perhaps gall-bladder; they're not sure about operation.

Newspaper says the Japs are eager to meet the enemy in Manila. Parcels rumour afloat again.

Quiz in evening, men v. women; men won 14-12. I only managed 2 out of my 6 questions.

Air raid alarm about 9.15, heard planes but no bombs.

23 Jan 1945

Apologetics class in morning. No raids. Rumour that parcels are in town and will come in with next consignment of rice.

Spoke to Wright-Nooth who was in Clifton's room when I went there to get my old black shoes back; he suddenly became serious when I gave my pessimistic view of the relief of here; he said he agreed, but one didn't talk about it unless someone mentioned it first. *((I was anticipating bloody mayhem if the Allies attacked Stanley Fort just above the camp. Can't now think why my old shoes were in Clifton's room... maybe he had mended them?))*

Walk with Annie Van Der Lely; we looked at Bungalow C which isn't nearly as wrecked as I had imagined. I saw Concannon about the plays.

To History lecture in evening.

24 Jan 1945

Our room's turn to sweep the passage.

Clifton Large (right) grinding rice with one of the Barton boys.

Newspaper supposedly suppressed... rumours of Canton being surrounded.

Water-carrying day; spent a long time at water hydrant, then went down to well. *((Strangely, now I can't remember where that well was!))*. There's a pump now. Got most of my washing done, hair etc. Met Concannon there, he carried water up for me.

Clifton still on fluid diet (at hospital).

Lovely stew – carroty and oniony – for tiffin.

25 Jan 1945

Annie insisted on my going home with her after Mass, and I had coffee with sugar!! *((Annie was Dutch; her parents and brother & sisters also in camp; somehow her family had access to food from outside sources, and were always very generous. Many of the non-British internees had been brought to Stanley some time after the British, so had had more time to prepare for internment.))*

Visited Doreen (Leonard), am going to teach her shorthand.

Went to see Concannon in afternoon, he was most useful, then to rehearsal in club.

Olive not well. Had peas (in rations) today.

Yvonne Blackmore (17), Leo Barton (17) and Billy Dudman (16) all got through Matric.

Sunday's raid was on Wanchai, newspaper claims 4,000 casualties.

Rev. A. Rose gave talk on Dreams in evening.

26 Jan 1945

Clifton came out of hospital.

Outside roll call this morning.

Rehearsal in our room in afternoon, quiz for children in evening.

Canteen in morning – got demerara sugar, rice flour, and noodles.

Men went into town to load rice.

Doreen came, first shorthand lesson.

27 Jan 1945

Some internees arrested for liquor selling, and one found – so rumour says – in Stanley Village at 1am.

Requiem Mass for air raid victims.

Rumour that Russians are 90 miles from Berlin.

Eggs selling at 38 yen each.

28 Jan 1945

Air raid alarm at tiffin-time, but heard no noise. My voice gave out at choir today – hopeless.

Hardly any rations – just beans and greens for both meals.

While I worked in afternoon, gramophone recital in office.

Planted N.Z. spinach given by Mr. A. R. Cox.

29 Jan 1945

Mary Rogers in hospital with appendicitis. Ivy Batley (26) and Mrs Lena Edgar also in hospital.

Went to see Annie, she made rice pancakes with sugar rolled in.

Got hot water for Fortescues. Worked in morning *((boiled hot water was served from 8am, when you queued with your container for your share to make tea if you had any left. The Fortescues and the Redwoods took turns to collect each others'))*.

Catholic Action meeting outside.

Newspaper says Americans pushing forward to Clark Airfield in Philippines; going ahead in Burma.

Water on in taps – first time for ages.

30 Jan 1945

Doreen had shorthand lesson.

Newspaper says Philippines waiting for enemy; also suggests an attempted landing at Bias Bay.

31 Jan 1945

Bulletin (via newspaper) gives Goebbels' speech re if German armies of East give way there will be a world's workers' war. Rumour that German HQ removed to Nuremburg.

Mrs G. Goddard asked me about shorthand, we're going to do it often.

Rumours that Japs have said we will get parcels but they are not here yet; that bulk stuff is in Hong Kong and will be sent in as and when we need it.

1 Feb 1945

After work, to beach with Clifton & Mabel to get salt water, then German lesson, and rehearsal, then shorthand with Mrs. G. Goddard.

My watch went *((for valuation and sale through black market))* – marker received.

To lecture on 'Murder'.

2 Feb 1945

Water day *((i.e. it was turned on in the taps one day in four. In evening of water day we filled the bath in our flat and everyone was honour-bound to take out only a certain amount per day, usually three small tinfuls about the size of a tin of soup, nailed on to a piece of wood. You tipped your allotment into the washbasin, washed yourself and your clothes, then pulled the plug, and the used water drained into an old kerosene tin underneath. When that tin was full, one of the men in the flat stood on the lavatory seat and poured the water from the kerosene tin into the cistern to flush the loo.))*

Doreen came for shorthand lesson.

Dr Talbot had a look at my eyes, they're bad today.

Newspaper says Russians 75 miles from Berlin.

Chinese lesson in evening with Clifton (the teacher!) and Mabel. May start to teach Clifton shorthand.

We may get back issue of rice. Got a tomato each.

3 Feb 1945

'Blessing of the Throats' today after Mass.

Japs are asking for information re safe deposit boxes in HK & Shanghai Bank.

Told Bill Colledge I couldn't prompt for him – too busy, absolutely full up with things.

Connie Van Der Lely *((Annie's elder sister))* and I went to play bridge and monopoly at the Bartons – George Davitt (Police) and Dick Cloake there too; nice, and lots to eat.

Rumour that motor torpedo boats are around.

Russians 50 miles from Berlin.

We're not getting back-rice after all.

5 Feb 1945

Wet and very cold.

Mr. John Owen-Hughes died last night.

Catholic Action meeting in afternoon.

My eyes bad. *((I sometimes got infected eyelashes, and had to have them pulled out.))*

Had card from Evelyn Kemp (school friend in UK) posted 2nd March 1944, saying: "Glad to be writing you again after such a long wait. Will write again. Good luck and health to you all."

Mr. Wells gave lecture on 'old Hong Kong' in evening.

Mr. Davis came, our plays to be a week later.

6 Feb 1945

Doreen shorthand.

We got eggs (40 Yen) and pork (500 Yen a pound) but we didn't buy that much! *((These extras were bought with the proceeds of sale of my watch.))*

Very poor, ordinary meals – greens and peas, and cockles. Worked in afternoon.

Crosses are now being dug out in various places about camp *((i.e. to show Allied planes we are a camp))*.

Newspaper says that a Jap. ship leaves Japan about 17th with parcels for us among others – frantic rumours re contents.

7 Feb 1945

Had egg in evening, fried a pancake.

Shorthand with Ivy Batley and Mrs. Goddard.

2 cards from Auntie Lil, one May 1944.

Very cold.

Leilah came to rehearse in passage at 4pm and is good. *((Leilah Wood, teenager. Her mother was Japanese/German, her father English. He was working in Shanghai when the Japs attacked, and died there during the war (probably killed by Japs). In Stanley with Leilah were her mother, her sister Edith and Edith's husband Arthur, and their children Mavis and Richard*

Hamson. Leilah, now widowed, lives in Canada and we often chat on the phone.))

9 Feb 1945

Ate 2 eggs tonight.

Bishop Valtorta visited camp, blessed us in Prisoner Officers' Club.

H. Stainsfield died.

10 Feb 1945

Paper says Manila internees rescued by the US entering forces.

Miss Mavis Lush married Mr. C. Littler.

Walked round with Beryl in evening.

11 Feb 1945

Lovely stew for tiffin.

Catholic Action meeting in afternoon.

Rehearsal in our room at 2, Doreen didn't come. Visited her after meeting, she has malaria.

In evening to Grants' room for talk 'Towards a Better World' but found it completely over my head. *((The Grant family – Mrs. K, daughters Kathleen, Eileen, and Rosaleen (married) lived in Block 2 of Married Quarters.))*

Rumours: parcels (food) leave today *((i.e. for the camp))*, and Germany has capitulated.

Permanent blackout.

12 Feb 1945

Chinese New Year. Worked in afternoon.

To lecture on 'Insurances' in evening by Dr. Lanchester.

Bombing on D'Aguilar.

Rumour that Hitler is asking Pope for 'no condition' surrender.

2 postcards from Auntie Lily.

Captain S. H. Batty-Smith died (A.D.C. to Governor pre-war).

13 Feb 1945

Slept in slacks and scarlet blazer last night, it was so cold.

Rehearsal at St Stephen's went very well. Concannon seemed reasonably satisfied. Anneke offered to prompt.

To Rosary at Bartons' room, then to History lecture.

14 Feb 1945

Ash Wednesday. Rore-ish throat. Worked in afternoon.

Mr. A. J. Collins Taylor gave talk on 'Lourdes'.

Planes around. Had 2 eggs tonight.

Convoy went out, and a camouflaged launch is lying off Tweed Bay.

15 Feb 1945

Terrific explosion in the night.

Lovely chow fan and baked potato for tiffin.

Have slight cold.

To St Stephen's all afternoon, rehearsals, Concannon most helpful.

Clifton not well.

16 Feb 1945

I have a runny cold. Worked in afternoon.

Saw Pauline Beck re music for shows. Father Meyer's birthday.

Newspaper tells of discussions re peace terms in Europe.

Cold and rainy.

17 Feb 1945

Food ship supposed to leave Japan. My cold still annoying.

Dress rehearsal of plays at St Stephen's. Her First Dance not so bad, but The Last Meeting awful; trial scene seemed too long.

People have heard from families overseas to whom Gladys Collard wrote after she was repatriated to Canada.

Olive in bed with cold.

18 Feb 1945

Worked for Olive in afternoon.

Lovely English potatoes for tiffin.

Went to Benediction, and Stations of the Cross, then for a walk with Annie, then to Catholic Action social, with eats – in honour of Father Meyer's birthday.

To lecture 'Ends & Means'.

19 Feb 1945

Paper says Manila in flames and ruins, and fighting at Mackinley *((where we were billeted when in Manila in July 1940))*.

Much bombing of Japan by a powerful task force. The Japs claim 187 planes shot down.

9,000 planes supposed to be over Dresden.

Rumour that East Prussia has surrendered, and that our oil ration here ceases at the end of March.

Henry puss is getting loads to eat – people bringing him remains of some of the stunned fish. *((We acquired Henry when one of the few camp cats had kittens; we four each gave him about a teaspoonful of our rice & stew each day. Can't remember now how the fish came to be stunned!))*

My week off. Olive back at work.

Catholic Action meeting at 3pm, then Sheila and I went to St Stephen's for rehearsal of Her First Dance which Concannon has brushed up tremendously. We have invited him and others to tea on Sunday.

Joyce Wilkinson is engaged to John Wall.

Yesterday Mrs June Cheape had some food stolen. *((Her billet was on one of our landings – no security there!))*

Had a card from Auntie dated June 1944.

Had a long chat with Ivy Batley who is in hospital again.

20 Feb 1945

Water in taps.

Mrs Christine Robson had appendix op.

Doreen came for shorthand.

Americans landing on Bonins.

Spent nearly an hour at Leprosarium with Pat Cullinan, arranging tea party for Sunday. Also saw Ivy, and Mrs Lena Edgar.

Spent most of afternoon with Van Der Lelys.

21 Feb 1945

Still on holiday. Rainy.

Visited Twidales; Betty (nee Cullen) was sick, so I went with her brother George to bring little sister Rosie home from hospital, then to St Stephen's for last rehearsal of The Last Meeting.

We got more eggs.

22 Feb 1945

Raining cats and dogs.

Just when it was light, a large grey ship with big white cross on either end crept past the Fort – so near that I could see the crosses. It later anchored where the last repatriation ship did, but moved off at quarter to eleven. Everyone thinks it's the food ship... hoping, anyway.

The plays went off quite well. 'The Last Meeting' was the worst, no laughs, and words left out; they all spoke too quickly. The Shakespeare play went off fairly well; 'Her First Dance' was best. Kristine (Thoresen) looked beautiful, wearing Sheila's bridesmaid's dress; Mavis Thirlwell very good too. A small audience, due to the rain I hope. *((I don't remember who the Sheila was who lent the bridesmaid's dress, but that almost certainly was Sheila Haynes who was a great friend of mine. She married policeman Patrick Cullinan in camp.))*

Davies was quite pleased, and Dick Cloake said he was pleasantly surprised at The Last Meeting.

A stye coming on my eye.

Talk by Rev. Sandbach.

23 Feb 1945

Still raining. Dorothy sick so I had to go to work in am.

Saw the 'parcel ship' going out again in a.m. when I got congee.

The plays were better on the whole, again a small audience but weather against it. Doreen Leonard very good.

Americans are well on in the Bonins, and large armies assembling in Kunming.

Eric MacNider *((a neighbour, who often did a double act with Clifton on Stanley stage))* went in to town with others to get building materials for camp.

24 Feb 1945

Fine day until afternoon, when rain set in again.

I have a hole in foot due to nail in shoe yesterday. Worked in morning as Dorothy still sick.

Rumour says men standing by for parcels, but Father Meyer says a Formosan said 2 weeks at latest.

Pat Cullinan (TB patient) not allowed to come to final night of plays which went off very well; not a big audience but most appreciative. Even Dr. H. Talbot said he liked the 'sketches' as he called them. Mum and Father Meyer there.

25 Feb 1945

Visited Marie, Annie, Mrs MacDonald and Betty Twidale. Party re plays in afternoon; everyone came including Johnny Anderson, Jacqueline Matthews, Beryl Goldenberg, Pat Cullinan, Sheila Haynes, Pauline Beck, Joe Lewis, Peggy (Barton), Mr T Concannon and Clifton.

We more or less decided to do Alice in Wonderland in the summer. Pauline Beck and Mr Concannon agreed to help.

26 Feb 1945

Rainy again. Dr Valentine was pleased with plays.

Mum sold Olive's grey coat for 300 Yen to Betty Twidale.

Mr Sandbach gave end of Yunnan talk in evening.

Catholic Action meeting in afternoon.

Jane/Jean Lyon married to F. S. Chisholm.

We opened last tin of bully.

27 Feb 1945

Much banging in night, Clifton said he saw flashes.

Mum's 30th marriage anniversary. I was in poisonous temper re re-typing of extra copies at work.

Saw Pat Cullinan re putting on the plays in Leprosarium on Sunday *((for TB patients.))*

Fish came in for about first time for 3 weeks.

Gorgeous day.

Mr. L. E. Ryan died about 6pm.

750 planes over Tokyo.

Egypt and Turkey declared war on Germany, according to paper.

28 Feb 1945

Went to Mr Ryan's funeral with Mum, only about 2 dozen there.

Meeting in afternoon, washed hair.

Blasting still going on.

Japs fussing re issues of dry rice. *((You could have some of your rice ration uncooked – to do yourself – instead of having all your ration cooked; many people then ground the dry rice on the grinders and made little cakes etc. with it for a change of meals.))*

German lesson in afternoon, only Mr Cautherley and me.

1 Mar 1945

Worked in morning; there was an inspection about 2, so stayed at hospital for a while.

German lesson in afternoon, only Mr George Cautherley and me.

Saw Joan Wilkinson and offered to teach her shorthand, she wants to learn, having started lessons with Martha Lewis (age 14).

Some school children arrested for being on road *((presumably beyond gates))*.

Rumours re parcels from Kowloon Godowns on Monday, but Stericker (John) says no news.

Card from auntie at Gillingham saying 'As soon as I know you are on your way, I will attend to larder – chips and cheese, but taboo rice.'

Eric MacNider lectured.

2 Mar 1945

Rumour that parcels will come tomorrow, with firewood, but nothing official – except committee appointed to decide distribution, and suggestions invited.

There's a petition going round to stop food from going to Welfare, and suggestions invited. *((Apparently a plan proposed that some of the parcel food should be kept for people in poor health to give them extra, instead of all parcels distributed equally among everyone.))*

Doreen came for shorthand.

Yesterday news was that Germans must have 12% food cut, and have only enough to last till end of April.

3 Mar 1945

Went to Joan Wilkinson and arranged to give her shorthand lessons. Mist curling right down on us.

Gladys and I went to Indian quarters to get people to come to social. Our efforts rewarded; Joe Lewis came, it was quite a success. Pauline Beck came as well. Dorothy Wilson won bar of choc donated by Father Hessler. Clifton ran the show and did it well. When Harold and Elsie Bidwell arrived, they announced that a loud toot from the jetty brought everyone out – expecting firewood and parcels.

Later, a notice that there will be parcels tomorrow, some private ones, 600 cases comfort parcels, 2 cases books, toilet articles, men's clothes. No mention of bulk foodstuffs to everyone's disappointment. Bulletin suggests that only 2,500 individual parcels in all *((i.e. 1 each, as camp population was then about 2,460))*. From Canadian Red Cross. The committee announce we're to have 1 parcel each distributed at once, minus 1 tin corned beef which will be taken by Welfare and replaced by reserve tins they have.

4 Mar 1945

Very disappointing news – early this a.m. the Japs woke us up calling for Max Bickerton *((a Japanese-speaking internee who often interpreted))*, and men went off re parcels.

After church, I went to help at hospital shelling cockles which came in rations.

Rumours rife – that there was bulk stuff, that there were Canadian, British and American parcels, but after our 3 plays were put on at Sanatorium *((for TB patients))* this afternoon, we came down to earth with a bang: apparently there may not even be enough parcels for one per person, and they are all 1942 parcels from Lourenco Marques.

5 Mar 1945

Worked in morning.

Catholic Action meeting in afternoon, then Red Cross parcels given out, dated April and June 1942, the sort we had in October 1942. Outside they looked in bad condition (brown cardboard boxes) but not bad otherwise. Two or our chocolates weren't good, but there seem to be no blown tins. We opened tin of lobster paste.

Lecture by Dr. Dean Smith on 'Food.'

The Holloway family and Clifton are getting private parcels, which were meant for Charles and Eileen Medley (Canadians) who had been in camp but were repatriated in 1943.

((I don't know how many 'private parcels' arrived with the general shipment: I guess relatives in UK or USA 'in the know' managed to get them included. The private parcels sent to internees who had already been repatriated were presumably distributed by our council. Clifton Large & his parents were Canadian but chose not to be repatriated in 1943 (because Clifton wouldn't

leave my sister Mabel, and his parents wouldn't leave without him), so their nationality was probably what earned them the Medleys' parcel. The Holloways' daughter Edith was married and lived with her husband in Canada; very probably Edith had sent the parcel the Holloways received.))

6 Mar 1945

Gun emplacements being blasted horribly near to us.

Opened steak and tomato pudding this evening – lovely!

Mr J. S. Gibson, aged 72, died.

Went to see Annie in morning.

Doreen had shorthand lesson. Worked in afternoon.

7 Mar 1945

Joan Wilkinson (16) came for shorthand lesson.

Mrs Adams collected our congee.

No Mass because Red Cross clothing is in Prison Officers' Club.

2 postcards from Mrs Irene Cole *((in Australia; her husband was killed at Aberdeen, Hong Kong, during the war. He was a Naval Dockyard colleague of Dad's.))*

Visited Betty Twidale.

8 Mar 1945

Still no Mass. Had a lay-in.

Visited Offenbergs and Annie. The Dutch Block people still say we'll get bulk stuff. That Shamshuipo have had theirs.

German lesson.

Bridge with Marie, Peggy and ?? in evening.

9 Mar 1945

Draw for odd parcel items: I got biscuits, Olive soap and paste; Mum sugar and cheese; Mabel creamed rice and soap.

Rumour no more parcels, and Americans entering Cologne.

Went to Open Forum at Bartons *((American quarters))*, I had to leave suddenly because supposed to be an air raid.

10 Mar 1945

A sad little message from Uncle Harry *((in Bath, Somerset))* saying that his father (also my Dad's father) had passed away on 16th April 1944.

Postcard from Auntie dated 4th July 1944. To Confession in afternoon Went to see Annie, and Pat Cullinan.

There was an air raid this a.m., seemed to be on shipping, someone said it looked like a super-fortress.

In draw, we won a sewing kit, a portion of Naphtha soap, and tooth powder.

11 Mar 1945

Have started curling hair again, but it doesn't last long. *((No perms in Stanley!))*

Worked in am. Sheila came in afternoon to discuss Easter things, then to Benediction, then C.A. Section Meeting where I read quarterly report: Gladys, H. Crutwell and Reddish came.

Bridge in evening with Alec Barton, Peggy and Marie; then talk with Father Hessler and Gladys and Peggy.

A ship sunk by a large plane in the bay – Clifton saw it.

12 Mar 1945

Went visiting re Easter play – Simpsons, Thirlwell, de Vleeschouwer, Strange, Eager, Leonard, Twidale, Offenberg, Williams and Annie.

13 Mar 1945

A shell whizzed over us in morning, and no one knows quite why but it was said that one of our large planes was round.

Visited Mrs Edgar (Mr E most charming and friendly); Forsters (to have Paddy and Maureen in show), and Annie where I had tea, and

Rennie announced he and Annie are marrying in April, and invited me to be bridesmaid.

14 Mar 1945

Canadian private parcels were given out – mostly soap, clothing and cigarettes.

Saw Charlie Rozeskwy re magazine.

At 12 we had first babies' rehearsal on the Bowling Green. Some of them are worse, but some better than I expected.

Had apple pudding (tin) tonight.

Mrs Joan Witham gave a talk about Convents at girls' club.

W. Spark died, aged 62.

Letter from Uncle Bert *((in USA))* saying 'Can we send you anything?' !!!!!!! Even a safety pin would do!

15 Mar 1945

Boiling hot day. No newspapers for 5 days. German lesson outside.

George Davitt in hospital.

Joan Wilkinson had shorthand lesson.

16 Mar 1945

Mum had card from Mrs Burling, a HK friend now in Australia.

Sang tune of 'There Are Fairies at the Bottom of our Garden' to Pauline and Marion Beck at the piano in A3 *((so they could get the tune on the piano for the coming concert at which the toddlers would be fairies, and Denise de Vleeschouwer the Queen of the Fairies.))*

Bridge in afternoon, with Alec Barton, Marie (Morrison, nee Barton), and her husband Vincent *((Police, who had escaped from camp early on, was caught and imprisoned in Stanley Gaol then returned to camp, after which he and Marie were married.))*

Saw Beryl re formation of Married Quarters Girls' Club *((non-denominational.))*

Rumour that European war is over.

17 Mar 1945

Went to see Mrs Ferguson, and Annie and then Pat Cullinan.

Gave a talk on 'What to do when you're grown up' at St Christine's *((younger girls club))* in Harrises room, then to work.

Gave Davitt a pancake in hospital. *((Father Meyer organised a group of ladies to cook a pancake with ingredients he supplied for convalescing hospital patients.))* Marie and Peggy coming for bridge.

18 Mar 1945

Keith Mackie and Jacquie Anderson's first banns called; and Annie and Rennie's second.

We rehearsed the tots *((for Easter play))* in Annie's room, in front of the Van Der Lely family and 2 onlookers.

Lovely tinned jam pudding in evening. Marie brought eye ointment for me – still having styes.

19 Mar 1945

Sheila Bruce's banns are up.

Am having styes. Rehearsed singers with Peggy at 12.30. Saw Sheila at 1.30 (but no cast appeared).

C.A. Meeting in afternoon. Peggy and Marie for bridge.

20 Mar 1945

Still styes.

Joan Wilkinson came for shorthand.

Fairies' rehearsal in Annie's room.

Bulletin about emergency arrangements: we must conserve what food we have.

Spent afternoon with Mary Taylor, nice tea. George Davitt still in hospital.

Peggy got caught over here (in Married Q) for roll call *((she lived in American Quarters.))*

21 Mar 1945

Jacquie's shower in afternoon; also Aileen Thirlwell's 21st birthday, and Betty Twidale's birthday.

Rehearsal with fairies in morning, eyes bad and headache.

Got peach dress from Mrs. Nan Moodie, which only just fits me *((bridesmaid's dress for me))*.

Sandberg arrested *((Norwegian, probably the elder boy Tony, aged 20))*.

U.S. have taken Iwo-jima.

Meeting in our room in evening. Gladys and I went over to Rosary *((in American Quarters))* but had to leave just as it started because air raid whistle went – only an alarm though.

22 Mar 1945

Air raid alarm in afternoon.

Doreen had shorthand lesson. Went to Annie's with dresses, because Angie *((Annie's younger sister, other bridesmaid))* doesn't want Mrs K's.

Tim and Margery Fortescue gave most interesting talk on Life at Cambridge.

23 Mar 1945

Rumours of parcel for Easter, and that invasion (of HK) on 28th!

Rosary started regularly in Grants' room *((Block 2, Married Quarters))*.

Visited Eileen Grant re rehearsals. Rosaleen lent me dress for Angie, but the Van Der Lelys don't like it much, except for Annie.

Rehearsal in quarry (grotto) with Peggy and children at 1.30, then to Marie's for bridge with her, Vincent and Alec.

24 Mar 1945

Mabel and I went to Grotto to help make palm crosses – Peggy, Sheila, Linda Marvin, Clara Fisher, Dorothy Wilson, we made about 600 between us. Then tea on the Fathers' landing (they provided it). Club meeting.

Doreen didn't come for shorthand.

Dancing rehearsal for fairies in a.m. On Bowling Green, complete with singers. All rather chaotic at present.

25 Mar 1945

Palm Sunday.

Went to see Doreen, Aileen Thirlwell and Pauline Beck.

Worked in afternoon, but there was gramophone music in office so I managed to get away to Way of the Cross. Reading and enjoying 'Now I see.'

Opened creamed rice. A tin of paste was blown.

Spanish lesson with Irma Mejia.

26 Mar 1945

Men went to town for charcoal.

2 air raid alarms.

Rehearsal in P.O. Club in morning – hopeless!

Lecture on Burma Road by Owen Evans, most interesting, over 2,000 miles long; Evans stayed in a house where Gene Stratton Porter lived and wrote 'Freckles'.

27 Mar 1945

Met a Jap on way to get congee. I just bowed and so did he. Rehearsal at 10am on Bowling Green, and 11.30am at St Stephen's, but we couldn't get the hall and had to go to the open kitchen.

Dick Cloake said yesterday that there is a rumour that Block 14 (Indian Quarters) will be taken over as a gun emplacement – or tunnel!

Rehearsal was pretty awful. Worked in afternoon.

Saw Frelford today. He may give me his charity story.

Meeting in evening. Dr Kirk came in evening bringing something he wants me to type.

28 Mar 1945

Doreen didn't come for shorthand. Visited MacDonalds and Annie. Wong tong and beans and peas in canteen today.

Rehearsal at St Stephen's. Worked in afternoon and studied German.

Attempted landing *((reported))* on Lu Chius.

29 Mar 1945

Maundy Thursday.

Worked in morning.

Air raid alarm in early afternoon.

At 3pm rehearsal: Ray Forster brought Maureen (6) and Paddy (5) crying their eyes out as they'd had to leave a concert.

Dr Talbot removed my lower lid lashes which were infected. Got aspirin from him.

Lecture in evening on Proverbs and Aphorisms (Mr G.P. de Martin.)

30 Mar 1945

Good Friday. To service am. Eyes pretty stuck up.

Went to see Doreen and gave her an impromptu shorthand lesson.

Rumours: we will get wong tong; and Japs expect hostilities within 4 hours.

To church service at 1.30pm and to play at 3.15pm, 'Behold Thy Mother'.

Valerie Clark has chicken pox and is in hospital.

Mrs Ashton-Hill has just heard that her husband died in Japan last September.

We had a hot cross bun from hospital.

To Rosary at Grants', then walked round with Marie and Gladys.

Mum and I had remains of Carlton pudding in a fritter. *(('Carlton pudding' was the name on one of the tins in the Red Cross parcels but I can't remember its contents!))*

31 Mar 1945

Air raid alarm last night.

Holy Saturday. An unexpected outside roll call, Japs very bad-tempered during it.

Washed clothes and hair.

Newspaper news very good: Americans loaning or selling battleships to Russia.

Bulletin has the wonderful news that a decision has been reached in Europe – no details yet.

Rehearsal in afternoon, on Bowling Green, then in grotto.

1 Apr 1945

EASTER SUNDAY.

Church in am.

Rissoles and pasty. Opened tin of bacon as well.

Went to see Mrs de Vleeschouwer re dresses for her daughters Andree (8) and Denise (3) for show.

((This family, Dutch, had managed to bring many clothes into camp. Mrs de V also lent dresses to other fairies.)) Mrs gave me some sweets.

Benediction in afternoon, then went to see Mrs Maitland in bungalow to get some flowers, then sat in garden and chatted with her. She told me about Lourdes.

Olive and I had pasty from hospital (as a special concession) and rest of food from Married Quarters, quite a lot of it. Rissoles. We opened tin of bacon as well.

Eileen Grant came in evening and put my hair in curlers *((for Annie and R.N. Rennie's wedding next day.))*

2 Apr 1945

Eileen came in early and did my hair for me. Rather severe but very neat. Then she went over to Annie's with me and helped me dress and made me up. *((Annie Van Der Lely lived in Dutch Block)).* Miss Hill's shoes *((lent to me))* high-heeled and tight, but looked all right.

Annie was very calm and unexpectedly unexcited. Livvy *((Olivia Ogley, born in camp))* walked in front. *((The wedding took place in the Prisoner Officers' Club adjacent to the Dutch Block))*. Crowds of people.

I have terrible styes. I had to sign the Marriage Register as a witness, so did Angie *((Annie's younger sister, also a bridesmaid.))* Mr. W. H. Weare (Police) was Best Man. Then we had Mass, and Miss B. Bicheno played Wedding March. Children showered confetti as we entered the Dutch Block, and from the landings as we went upstairs *((to the Van Der Lely family's room))*.

Father Hessler made a short speech, so did Mr. Weare. Heaps of people came in to reception. A band played as we entered room. The cake was lovely and sweet, they gave me a piece to take home to the family as well. Danced with Jimmy Bendall, Jumbo (Annie's brother), Rennie, Mr Weare, and Ed. Reed. *((The Dutch community had come into camp after the British so had been able to prepare better for internment.))*

Teresa Cullen caught the bride's bouquet. Enjoyed a talk with clever dancer June Winkelman about her studies.

1.20pm – air raid on now, and about 40 minutes ago a few sticks of heavy bombs were dropped.

Air raid alarm lasted till about 3.30pm but only two noisy periods. Concert had to be postponed.

3 Apr 1945

Another raid at almost exactly same time as yesterday.

Rehearsed in P.O. Club.

Clifton said he saw a Jap plane brought down yesterday.

Our concert again postponed.

Mrs McDermott wants to learn shorthand, also Sophie Hardoon and Marie O'Connor.

Had eyelids scrubbed again tonight.

4 Apr 1945

Bombers came again at noon, all clear went just before 3pm so no show possible.

(It's said) two big fires were started – one big explosion South Bay way, and another Taikoo way – an oil fire it's thought. Saw the planes – large and glinting and silver.

Fritters tonight – nice.

Went to see June Cheape re German, and did half an hour for Olive at work while she had hair cut. Went to see Burgess in afternoon, and Pat C.

5 Apr 1945

The daily air raid began at about 1 o'clock, it was clear by 2.30 so we were able to go to the Easter Entertainment in St Stephen's (during which there was another air raid alarm.)

This was a concert given by the R.C.s. The tableaux were awful, the choir and Rag Dolls dance good, and the fairies not too bad though I started the song too soon *(('There are Fairies at the Bottom of our Garden'))*; Denise's veil was almost pulled off. *((Denise de Vleeschouwer, who was Queen of the Fairies.))* Raffle: the Fortescues won the cushion cover Mrs Kopecsky embroidered, Leslie Parkin the table centre, and a cake. Rosaleen Millar sold 9 of the winning tickets.

I managed to get into pale green costume *((made pre-war, almost new, brought to me by our family amah when I was in the Tai Koon Hotel before internment; because of rice fat in camp, it was a tight fit now))*.

6 Apr 1945

To Mass then to work, pretty busy.

Newspaper is full of landings on Lu Chius made on Sunday morning last, and the bombing of the French Hospital in town on 4th April, resulting in death of 'at least 4 Sisters and 100 children and babies in creche'. How much of it is near to military objectives is under much discussion here; some say godowns are near, others say that Japs are living there, etc. *((The modern name for the Lu Chius is the Ryukyu Islands – this diary entry refers to the allied landings on Okinawa)).*

Visited Leprosarium and Connie Van Der Lely, and Mrs de Broekert and Burgess in afternoon.

7 Apr 1945

Jacquie Anderson & Keith Mackie's wedding day. They were married before Mass. Jacquie looked very nice in powder blue dress and white hat. I took Fleur.

Cold, wet and windy. Worked in afternoon.

Had eyelid scrubbed again in evening, most painful.

Rumour that Germany has capitulated, and that the Japanese cabinet has resigned en masse.

Hospital ship came in bay and out.

8 Apr 1945

Had very bad night, eye sore and discharging a lot.

Worked in am but couldn't do much because of sight.

Benediction, then visited the de Vleeschouwers, Doreen, and Aileen Thirlwell.

Spoke to Rev Sandbach re clubs. Pasty.

9 April 1945

Worked in am. Eye bad.

To C.A. Meeting.

Lecture on Banks, I didn't go.

10 Apr 1945

Eye bad.

Doreen came for shorthand.

Went to see 'Housemaster', Kathleen Davis very good.

Zusuki (78 yrs) is Premier of Japan.

Cold, rainy, windy.

Walked round with Alice Anderson, then Gladys and Peggy.

Awa Maru missing.

11 Apr 1945

Getting warmer.

Bridge in afternoon in our room with Gladys, Marie and Vincent.

We had seconds in vegetable balls. Eyes not so bad.

Cigarettes came in today. *((We four Redwoods were non-smokers, but always 'bought' our allotment and sold them at profit to smokers who were always happy to have them – so we covered what we had paid for them and had spare money for canteen purchases.))*

Americans and Russians supposed to be meeting in Germany in about 1 month.

Another theft from Canteen (6/7th April), valued at about Yen 2,000.

Rumour that 25 Shamshuipo men killed at Kai Tak.

12 Apr 1945

Mum saw Professor Digby re ganglion on her finger which he'll probably remove.

Signed Annie's marriage certificate in Fr. Hessler's room.

German lesson outside. Worked.

3 packets cigarettes each *((if you had the money to pay for them.))*

Spent evening with Peggy, and Dorothy Wilson outside American Block.

13 Apr 1945

Raid in night – noisy, ended about 2am. Another raid started about 11 am and went on till 1.30pm when I went to hospital (to work). Then to Annie's party in Grants' room. Quite a big air raid between 1pm and 3pm. Tummy rather upset.

Worked in afternoon. Visited Mrs Grant, de Broekherts, and Burgess.

Rumour says Roosevelt died.

Card from Charles Pike (RAMC, in Shamshuipo Camp).

15 Apr 1945

Raid on.

Water in hydrant in am but not in taps yet.

Joint Communion Day. Went to see Mrs Taylor, then heard plans so left.

Rumours: the new Jap premier has committed hari kari *((harakiri, i.e. ritual suicide))* and that Japan has sued for peace: we offered 7 points, 3 of which they have accepted, 4 being considered.

Roosevelt died on 12th April.

'Church Congress' in afternoon. I read report on Girls' Clubs. Many other papers read – there wasn't time to read them all out.

Benediction in Quarry (grotto). Father Hessler's birthday.

16 Apr 1945

Went down to the nullah and did a big clothes wash, but lost my soap in nullah *((across which was barbed wire, so I couldn't get at it))*. Someone's fault for taking out the stones which someone else had put there after they too lost their soap.

Air raid alarm just as I finished; apparently a false alarm, but another about noon.

Shigometsu (or some name like that – a Jap Minister) has committed hari kari they say.

The camp expected an attack last night: now expected tonight. *((Can't remember any details of expected attack... I imagine this means the Allies were expected to attack the Japs.))*

We opened our last tin of tomatoes tonight. Had eyelashes done.

17 Apr 1945

Very hot.

No air raid.

Bridge in afternoon with Dick Cloake, Betty Drown and Mr Simmons in our room.

Kitchen staff of American and Married Quarters walked out.

18 Apr 1945

No air raid. Our turn to clean flat. Went to hospital with Mum to have her callosity on finger removed. Clifton was there with his father who is going blind.

Dick told me off about my bridge, wants me to study it properly – can't be bothered now.

Tea in quarry with Sheila and Pat (Cullinan). They tried to make me agree that we do another play but I don't think it worthwhile – can't cope with constant air raids, and lack of enthusiasm.

Sheila and I went to funeral of Mr J. Owens (RC) who died yesterday of beriberi heart.

A kitchen squad (under Mr Owen Evans) has done well so far. The main grouse from strikers seems to be that they're not allowed to draw their meals from the kitchen, but may eat them there when on duty.

Clifton made me a nice small stool (a piece of canvas across two bits of wood).

19 Apr 1945

Shorthand with Joan and Doreen. Primrose Day.

German lesson outside Block 4.

To Mrs. F. Large's first aid class (she was Clifton's mum).

20 Apr 1945

Terrific wind and storm in night. Thunder like Nimitz *((Admiral, whom we were always expecting to relieve us))*.

Much groaning of lorries, presumably bound for the Fort, in night.

We all had stew seconds. Had lovely sweet tart and ground rice in afternoon.

Bridge in evening with Marie, Alec and Gladys.

21 Apr 1945

Newspaper says raid on 17th when a ferry was bombed.

Rumour that Allies have broadcast from Berlin, and that Spain has forbidden Germans to land there.

Went to see Burgess and Pat C.

Meeting with juniors (RC clubs) in evening. Marjorie Wilkinson, Rosemary Lewis and Irene Drewery accosted me afterwards re 'going up' to next group.

22 Apr 1945

To early Mass after which air raid alarm went. All clear not until second Mass finished.

Worked in afternoon.

Danny Wilson and Mrs Bander won the raffled cakes, and Mrs Wilson (mother of Wendy) the embroidered cushion.

We had vegetable tarts, stew and salad at night – terrific meal.

Went to Open Forum in evening. I'm to transfer to new Catholic Action group.

23 Apr 1945

Rumour that Russian shells are falling in Berlin, and 'we' are 11 kilometres off.

To Dr. G. Herklots' lecture on Tropical Seas; the walking on the sea-bed bit was most interesting.

Went to new C.A. meeting in morning – Gladys, Rosaleen, Mrs Connolly, Mrs Lederhofer.

24 Apr 1945

Outside roll call.

Yesterday we were able to buy 4 ozs. wong tong at Yen 7.70.

Newspaper says that Russians are advancing along Unter den Linden into the heart of Germany.

Went to play reading of 'Flashing Stream.' June Cheape excellent in her part.

Worked in morning.

25 Apr 1945

Date of San Francisco Conference.

Shorthand to Doreen in am, worked in afternoon. Meeting (church) in our room at 1.30pm, and at 6.15pm in Grants'. Dorothy told us the sad story of her family's bombing (in the UK).

26 Apr 1945

No oil has arrived so far for ten-day period from 20th April. But salt issue free.

Watanabe and ? (Jap) have gone, and new people did roll call on Tuesday.

Worked in afternoon, then German lesson.

Went to senior girls' club meeting in A3 (Mrs D. Jenner spoke).

27 Apr 1945

Oil came, we had 2 ounce issue each.

Soap issue.

Apparently fighting still going on in Berlin and Europe – not the end yet.

Clifton's father went to hospital yesterday. Clifton not well today.

Junior club meeting on cold windy evening in Block 3 stairway.

Am forging ahead with writing 'Theo' story.

28 Apr 1945

Requiem Mass for Mr Owens.

Mr J. Graf (Dutch) was beaten up for going uphill to Japs to complain of being 'done' by a guard/dealer (black market). As a result the new boy in charge stopped guards' weekend leave – they're usually well loaded with rings etc. to sell at weekends, and 28 furious guards sought vengeance on

Graf. Three chased him up towards the CSO whither he was bound for refuge, and they hit him with rifles etc., but Kathleen Grant (who saw this) said Graf was very brave and didn't squeal, though it might have been death if Mrs. V. Armstrong (she spoke Japanese) hadn't intervened.

Bridge in afternoon, with Tom Cashman, George Davitt (policemen) and Gladys Johnson.

June Cheape's 25th birthday... gave her a typescript of The Hound of Heaven. After, Mabel, Clifton and I went to June's landing (her billet). There were Tony Sanh, June, her husband (who was in a separate billet, they appeared to be 'not together'); Fleur Cheape (4) and her little friend Maggie Seraphina (4); George Saunders, Alec Summers, Freddy Morley. Had a kind of brandy snaps, tea, lovely iced cake (with marzipan made of peanut butter and wong tong, I was so full up). Went to Rosary.

Then on to Clifton's verandah with someone's gramophone, dancing.

29 Apr 1945

Took Conchita (Mejia) to Mass with me. *((Conchita was one of the large family who lived in the room below us. She had a disabled leg, and should have been wearing a brace, walking was very difficult for her, she was a sweet child – then 5 years old)).*

Went to see Doreen (shorthand pupil), who has started writing a story of Stanley entitled 'I am hungry' which impresses me. Gave her a cumshaw shorthand lesson.

Peter Van Der Lely was beaten up yesterday as well.

30 Apr 1945

Rumour that Leopold *((King))* is released and has gone to Switzerland. Stalin's son is supposed to be held as hostage by Germans. Truman says that war is not yet over but the Americans and Russians have met.

Mrs Eileen MacLeod gave a very nice talk on 'Uganda'.

We ate our garden produce this evening – very little.

1 May 1945

Doreen Leonard and Joan Wilkinson came for shorthand.

Rations pretty grim. Daily baking allowed now, which helps oil situation.

Worked in afternoon, then to C.A. meeting in Maria Connolly's room. Mrs Nora Hillon and Elsie Bidwell have joined us.

Jean Martin's 5th birthday. *((Mabel often took Jean and other tots for walks around the camp, and made clothes for Jean.))* Mrs. Deacon gave us a piece of Jean's cake. *((Mrs Deacon was the mother of Mrs Irene Braude who as well as looking after her own toddler, Patricia, was guardian to Jean in camp.))*

Play reading of younger girls' club in evening beside railings.

Rumour that Germany has surrendered unconditionally.

Newspaper says Mussolini has been assassinated.

2 May 1945

Kris Thoresen has chicken pox.

Stye coming on my eye again.

Mr. L. Barton *((of Treasury, HK Govt.))* gave talk on street sleepers in Hong Kong, at S Teresa's club.

George and May Halligan have adopted Jeanette Madeline Clark, (born in camp, baby sister of Valerie and Margaret who were adopted earlier in camp by Mr & Mrs Thomas). *((The Clarks had problems dealing with children. Valerie's name was changed to Hazel, and Margaret became Frances. I was so pleased to meet up with them both a few years ago.))*

3 May 1945

Mr. N. C. Barber died at 1.25pm, a Christian Scientist who refused to have operation for cancer of the tongue etc.

Horrible stye again.

'Jeanette' Clark is to be called 'Helena' or similar *((handwriting in original diary too faint. Within a week or so of the adoption, Mrs Clark went to the Halligans saying 'I want my bairn back' – and took Jean. The*

Halligans were devastated. Many years later I learned that Jean had died in her early twenties.))

Walked round with Gladys and Rosaleen in evening, then play reading with girls' club.

4 May 1945

Went to stream (nullah) and washed hair and clothes. The kids were having a grand time sluicing each other.

Outside roll call. They did it with two inspecting parties.

To older girls' meeting where Mrs Joan Witham gave a talk.

Newspaper says Hitler died at his bunker, and Goebbels committed suicide.

Worked in afternoon. Wrote a little of story, beginning Chapter 8.

Sat on grass with Rosaleen and Sheila playing bridge hands (practice).

6 May 1945

Wrote talk on films for Wed. club. Worked in afternoon.

To Benediction, there was the Crowning of Mary. Lesley Eager and other children, Antony Witham and Cyril Eager renewed their pledge to Children's Eucharistic Crusade.

7 May 1945

Paper says that Northern Germany, Norway, Denmark etc. have surrendered as from 8.30am on Friday 4th May. Hitler apparently 'was deprived of his life' by a 'Red Army bullet' when coming down a staircase in his residence with a weapon in his hand – on May 1st.

Bought 4 ozs. tomatoes from the Anguses for a pound of rice. *((Mrs. M. Angus – 72, two sons Herbert 'Ginger' Angus – 37, Frank Angus – 36, daughter-in-law Mrs Hilda Angus – 41; all were in camp, but not Hilda's husband.))*

Went up to Lena and Thomas Edgar's bungalow and had a lovely tea after we'd fixed up rough ideas of C.A. Meetings, reports etc. – lettuce, tomatoes, bread and butter, bread and beancurd, tea with cube sugar, and little tarts.

Miss S. Spencer (nurse) has had some short stories published (pre-camp).

8 May 1945

((writing too faint to read))

9 May 1945

((writing too faint to read))

10 May 1945

Armistice signed 2.41pm on 7th May; the German people asked by Hitler's successor to keep calm and try to help dispel the feeling of hate – so ideal.

We all seem to take the peace so much for granted here, because it has never seemed real to us, but I try to imagine how it is – no blackouts, children coming back from overseas, no more the dread of something happening – and the prospect of being able to settle down to proper family life again.

If it were the Japanese who had surrendered we would feel differently; as it is, we are praying that she will surrender and thus save more useless bloodshed (including perhaps our own).

Dr Talbot gave me aspirins – have headache with styes.

German lesson. Father (don't remember which) invited me to go to Pacifist Circle 3.30 tomorrow.

11 May 1945

Paper says Allies have retreated from Okinawa; also that prisoners of war returning from Germany were mobbed in England – sounds wonderful, yet still unreal to us here.

I think I'll have to be a pacifist really because it's the only way I can see, yet still want to be intensely nationalistic and patriotic, therefore go to meeting to try to learn how to reconcile the two.

12 May 1945

No rations have come in; tonight we had a dry garden hash – very nice. *((I can't remember what garden hash was!))*

Doreen didn't come for lesson. Worked in afternoon.

Rumour that Hankow has fallen, Rangoon too, and a landing in Canton delta.

13 May 1945

Rumour that repatriation is in the air again – in Chinese newspapers – now that the menace of German action is no longer present, since that apparently was the fly in the ointment before – the Germans wouldn't guarantee us a safe passage.

Mass offered in thanksgiving for Peace in Europe.

Catholic Action meeting, Miss D. Pepperell gave a talk on Hong Kong poverty.

Went to Doreen and gave her shorthand lesson, then called on Asletts. Betty is home again (from hospital presumably). We talked evacuation in 1940, then walked round by the lovely rocks and sat by Indian Quarters – glorious day.

14 May 1945

Yesterday evening the Protestants had thanksgiving service in the open, and Japs made a fuss and said permission must be asked for these things, but allowed it.

Rumour of repatriation, and Okinawa gone to us.

Visited Maria, Mrs Harris and Burgess in hospital.

Peggy and I played Iris Joyce and Gladys MacNider in evening, they won.

Wrote two poems for children to recite in end of May celebration.

Peggy and I, bridge with Kerslake & Allison, and we won +3!

Then Peggy and I joined Dorothy Wilson, Sheila, Elsie and Gladys on a ledge overlooking the sea to finish the third anniversary of Elsie's reception into the Church.

15 May 1945

Had teeth filled (Dr. Lanchester).

16 May 1945

Rumour that Okinawa has fallen to us; paper says we have Rangoon.

Churchill says we have a long fight ahead against the Japs, and slangs the Irish in the newspaper.

Peggy and I, bridge with Alan and Alec at noon, they won by 5.

Garden produce now has to count as 'rations'.

Communal housing after the war under discussion.

17 May 1945

German lesson.

Air raid alarm at 12.30pm.

Bridge with Mum and Mrs K, we lost to them badly.

18 May 1945

Outside roll call.

Gave quiz at St. Agnes club.

Peggy and I played Dorothy and Sheila in evening, and had sweet tarts.

I may resign from the evening club, and Dorothy Wilson take over.

19 May 1945

To Confession.

Wendy Rossini asked me to work for her sister Winifred at hospital, which I did. *((Winifred Rossini had joined Dorothy Holloway, Norah Witchell, Olive and I doing shifts in the hospital office.))*

20 May 1945

Sewed sheet out of pillow cases. *((I now wonder where the pillow cases came from.))*

Benediction in afternoon.

'Confirmed' at church:

Anna Mejia (10)

Andree de Vleeschouwer (8)

Flossie James (8)

Francis Ward (10)

Solveig Sandberg (10)

George Halligan (33)

Humphrey Cruttwell (36)

Vincent Morrison (29)

21 May 1945

Pacifist meeting. Worked in afternoon. Pasties.

22 May 1945

Peg (Barton) and I lost at bridge to Edith Johnson and Bang Stuart.

Dr Kirk says Mum has anaemia and must rest a lot.

2 letters from Auntie Lily. Worked in am.

23 May 1945

Worked in afternoon. We did Mum's bed. *((This probably means we debugged it.))*

After St Joseph's club meeting in evening, went to supper with Dorothy Wilson (her birthday), Peggy, Sheila, and Gladys.

24 May 1945

Bridge with Fortescues, they won 35!

Went to Open Forum at American Block.

25 May 1945

Rainy.

Outside roll call. We had Mum excused (health).

Heard that majority of Rosary Hill inmates have gone to Macao.

Canteen for 4 ozs. wong tong each and 1 oz. egg yolk.

We played Baileys in evening and only lost by 6. Walked round later with Gladys, Irma, Peggy and Olive.

Newspaper says Churchill has resigned because of words with Attlee, but King apparently asked him to form a Govt. of his own which he has done. Difference of opinion was because Attlee wanted elections and Churchill thought it was a bad time for elections.

Parcel rumours again!

26 May 1945

Two engagements announced:

Muriel McCaw to J. Channing (Police)

William Watson to Doris Scourse (nurse).

27 May 1945

Went to see Annie, then Doreen who is sick. Olive wasn't feeling well so I worked for her, therefore missed the end of May celebrations at St Stephen's, where my 2 poems were recited.

Sheila is looking so animated, and Pat's eyes are shining all the time – they are engaged; he assisted at Solemn Benediction at St Stephen's.

Supper with Sheila.

28 May 1945

To church study club meeting in Veronica Willey's room.

Bridge in afternoon, against Miss Nora Bascombe and Mrs Lily Caer-Clarke; we won.

Concert, very good in parts; new song 'Some Day Soon.

((The song was composed in camp, and started:

'When the carrier plane comes to carry us Home

Some... day... soon...'))

29 May 1945

Gave shorthand test to Joan and Doreen – neither are much good, judging by results.

No parcels after all.

Worked in afternoon.

C.A. Meeting at 1pm.

We now have orders to stand to attention and bow, then at ease, at roll calls.

30 May 1945

Worked am. Swimming with Peggy in afternoon. Not feeling well.

Took minutes for Gladys at meeting in evening.

Sat with Irma, Pat Lederhofer (18) and Peggy, and learned of the latest St Stephen's romance. *((Alas, not given here... perhaps this was Billie Gill's pregnancy?))*

31 May 1945

Corpus Christi. Wendy Barton's 17th birthday.

Walked with Gladys in evening. Then bridge, Mr & Mrs Tribble beat Peggy and I – 42!

1 Jun 1945

Glorious First *((I had always tried to celebrate the Glorious 1st of June, remembering history lessons))* – but the only new thing I had to wear was a nice bright hair ribbon which was once a belt of June Cheape's ex-pyjamas!

Outside roll call in a.m. We had our first experience of (mass) bowing – had to giggle because no one seemed to be bowing at the same angle.

There was trouble in Indian Quarters where Block 15 was accused of laughing at the Japs and had to stand for some time in the sun.

Two cards from Auntie. Worked in afternoon.

2 Jun 1945

Mr. F. W. Grinter hurt when air raid tunnel fell in.

We Redwoods had spring-cleaning today.

Japs made Tony Sandberg work up the hill all day. *(('Up the hill' meant at Jap HQ in camp.))*

To St Joseph's social, went quite well, big crowd.

Did hospital library for Dorothy Holloway who is still in hospital.

3 Jun 1945

Swimming with Peggy, Gladys Johnson and Beryl Goldenberg.

Bridge with Rowell and Brown.

New ration scale on paper – meat once a week, cut in oil.

4 Jun 1945

Apologetics at Veronica Willey's room in am.

5 Jun 1945

Maria Connolly had operation.

Worked in am. Bridge against Smalley and Judah in afternoon.

C.A. meeting in evening.

No rations came in.

6 Jun 1945

Did spring-cleaning in our room, killed many cockroaches.

Mrs. Flaherty was beaten up, up the hill, and sent to hospital. Other Black Market people arrested.

One of the Married Quarters' kitchens, which were pre-war garages. The vegetable squad are shown at their work. The second person on the right is my pre-war boss, Mr B.H. Puckle, Director of Air Raid Precautions, wearing his ARP beret.

7 Jun 1945

Mr. V. Seymour in trouble up the hill, and had to stand up there some time. His wife took food up to him.

Worked in am, then Peg & I played bridge against Mr W.J. and Mrs J. Fulker, we lost.

Some people had to go up hill for putting 'reunion soon' or something like that on their postcards.

8 Jun 1945

Outside roll call in the rain – not heavy.

More beatings. Smith *((don't know which one!))* to hospital today, and H. Vanthall has just been taken in *((presumably 'up hill'))*.

Rumour – official that we get no meat.

Played bridge with Dorothy, Mrs Hall and Mrs Shields.

Peg & I played Grace Darby and Wyllie.

9 Jun 1945

Worked in am. In afternoon, to beach with Peggy, Dick and Mezger, very choppy. Big breakers.

10 Jun 1945

German with June in am.

Mabel not well. Went to see Annie, then to hospital visiting Maria Connolly and Mr MacFadyen.

To Benediction, then Catholic Action junior meeting where I recited 'Sunday Afternoon' poem.

11-18 June 1945 .

((No entries. I was in hospital for some days with a suspected 'stone'.))

19 Jun 1945

Still in hospital. Miss Batley *((either Edith or Ivy, don't remember which))* in hospital because of eating berries of castor oil plant.

On Sunday last, we had MEAT – wonderful.

To Rosary with the RC nurses in Operating Theatre on last 2 evenings, and Holy Communion in Ward 6 on two mornings. Heaps of people besides family came to visit me, Doreen in particular.

20 Jun 1945

Came out of hospital. Was given lard.

We bought wong tong in exchange for dry rice.

Annie brought us some wong tong, she thinks she's pregnant.

22 Jun 1945

16 years since we left Hong Kong in 1929.

Repatriation rumours – ship in Manila!

To club meeting. Harold Bidwell talked about Beaumont College.

Air raid alarms. We ate at 4pm because everyone had to be indoors 4.30-5.30pm. People – some of them Europeans – went out from Gaol.

Finished writing 'Balancing Jean' very badly and scrappily.

23 Jun 1945

Rumour that some of the outlying beaches have been shelled.

Social in afternoon, great success. I recited poem:-

'Is there really an England, I wonder?
Or is memory confused with a dream?
Was there ever a life without hardship and strife
Where a lazy content reigned supreme?

Does there still stand a road trim with houses,
All alike, yet a difference in one?
(Nothing frightfully great, just the creak of a gate
That's a welcome when roaming is done.)

Did I ever rush to a hot kitchen
On a raw winter's late afternoon,
And toast hunks of bread that I afterwards spread
Thick with butter that melted too soon?

Was I once in a small old-world garden,
Bright with roses and pansies and all?
And away at the end, a few Wyandottes penned,
And a cat sat in state on the wall?

There are none who can steal my illusions,
That is, if illusions they be:
And though all else may go, I have something no foe
Can appropriate – my memory.'

Letter from Margaret Todd (UK):- 'Delighted to get letter... Expecting baby in May.'

24 Jun 1945

Sheila's (Haynes) and Pat's (Cullinan) banns called for last time – as precautionary measure in case of invasion.

Tony Sandberg's and Esther Haughlands' banns called first time.

Lent Limelight book to Paulina Pemble (13), who is 'loving it.'

In evening after Benediction Peggy and I went walking to kaolin pit by Bungalow D, had drink of water from Lena Edgar, then to concert at St Stephen's. Ian Heath at piano – first recital for ages, since strict injunction re only 2 concerts per month. We called on H. Kew, then Peggy and I sat outside railings by A3 chatting, and expected Admiral Nimitz, great full moon.

25 Jun 1945

To St Catherine's meeting in morning, then we all started to pack in accordance with the latest rumour. It sounds impossible and rather grim, but that doesn't make it any the less improbable – we were caught on the hop on Dec. 8th 1941. *((Sadly, today I have no memory of what this 'latest rumour' was.))*

Olive's bed broke in the night.

26 Jun 1945

Played bridge in Peggy's room in evening.

27 Jun 1945

Lots of people ill with enteritis.

I started back at work again after illness.

IT'S supposed to be tomorrow. *((Whatever it was we expected on the 25th!))*

29 Jun 1945

Rumour that sugar and oil will stop; and that Churchill is in Singapore.

Planes over most of night.

Made emergency biscuits.

30 Jun 1945

Rumour that British fleet 20 miles from Canton.

Reverberating gun practice in morning.

Bridge against Mrs Lilian Kershaw and Mrs Ormiston – lost. Went swimming.

1 Jul 1945

Five years today since we were evacuated from HK and last saw Dad.

Bridge, we played Dr Selby and Shields, went down 16.

Worked in afternoon. Visited various people, including Mr Charles Poyntz.

Peg & I played June Cheape and George Halligan in evening, we lost.

Lovely meat pasty.

2 Jul 1945

Eileen Grant in hospital – typhus.

Had sought-by-me interview with Mr. Gordon Burnett. *((He was a journalist with Newspaper Enterprises. I was asking for advice re writing)).* He set me an exercise which he would criticise.

Worked afternoon. Pacifist meeting.

Swimming with Peggy Barton and Dick Cloake.

3 Jul 1945

Got Limelight story back from Mrs Jenner, her criticism: characterisation isn't good; it is far too long; characters subservient to the plot rather than the plot dependent on the characters; it won't sell as it is but the plot is quite good. It was a shock to hear that the conversations were confusing and garrulous.

Swimming in afternoon.

Peg and I played Mrs Smalley and Joyce (?), and called a small slam and made it.

4 Jul 1945

Doreen for shorthand. Worked in afternoon, typed much of Catholic Youth Magazine. Father Hessler sick.

Went to see Mr Burnett with my 'exercise' – 400 words about camp life. He said it wasn't bad... but to me it sounded like a school composition compared to his which he read to me as a sample. He has offered to help me with narration, and told me to report on the food queue as if writing a letter, and he will criticise it.

Clifton went into hospital.

5 Jul 1945

Worked in a.m. In afternoon, visited Clifton in hospital, and Mrs Hamilton, Mr Poyntz and Mrs Stratton.

J.J. Osborne died.

Practised bridge with Peggy and Dick Cloake at Peggy's.

Mr Ingram came for cigarettes.

Bridge.

6 Jul 1945

Outside roll call in the rain, with a lecture on how to stand from the interpreter. 2 hours outside. Japs nasty. Rainy, squally.

Rumours that Russia has declared war on Japan.

We beat Miss Newman and Finnie by 32!

Eileen getting worse.

To Mr Osborne's funeral; aged 57. Crowds there.

7 Jul 1945

Went to R.C. Children's Congress: recitation by Wilfred Ogley (12) who forgot his words and had to dive in his pocket for copy; a 'talk' on Florence Nightingale by Joe de Broekert (10); and 'two words' by Brother Grimshaw *((but many more than two!))*. Good crowd of children there. Wrote a little of 'Roll Call'. Played 'hearts' with Mum, Mabel and Peggy.

8 Jul 1945

Meat stew, delicious. Took egg white to Peggy which she will cook for Mr Nicholas. *((This was part of a scheme of Father Meyer's whereby he would get egg white to be cooked by some of his congregation, for elderly invalids mainly.))*

Visited in hospital Pat C, so glad for him and Sheila; then to Ivy Wright-Brown, Mrs Hamilton, Mr Nicholson.

9 Jul 1945

St Catherine's meeting in a.m. Bridge at noon.

Eileen Grant still very sick.

Bought 1 lb wong tong between us (Redwoods). Pacifist meeting.

Just after 8 this evening, all sorts of whistles went, meaning an outside roll call. Edward Reed (a youth) had escaped while under arrest at Jap HQ for selling white Military (Jap) sugar; the roll call was supposed to be to find him. We were there till about 9.15 – quite dark, fishing lights out in bay.

10 Jul 1945

Reed gave himself up near Bungalow C and was beaten up again. Dick Cloake said people were being taken up hill from St Stephen's (his billet) all night long.

Mabel weighs only 105 lbs.

C.A. meeting, then to work.

To St Stephen's in evening to repeat my talk on 'Films' – rather sceptically since it was originally written for younger people.

I was in the soup with Mrs. E. Longworth. *((She lived next door, among the 25 of us who shared the bathroom, and used to knock on the bathroom door when in the queue saying 'Will you be long?' – we secretly called her Mrs. Will-you-be-longworth.))*

11 Jul 1945

Black market trouble. Swotted German.

Bridge in evening against Burnett and Sully and lost 25.

12 Jul 1945

Sheila Haynes' 30th birthday, we had supper party outside in evening.

Repatriation rumours again!

Went to first lecture on Pope's Five Point Peace Plan on 'order' – the first point. About 40 there.

13 Jul 1945

Outside roll call during which it rained, but they let us go inside.

Went to see Willeys (F.J. and Veronica and daughter Barbara aged 6; their son Brian died in camp in 1943 when 3 years old), and Asletts in morning.

Swimming in afternoon with Peggy and younger sister Audrey, and Anneke Offenberg.

Air raid alarm 12-2 but heard no bombs.

Bridge in evening with Billy and Vivienne.

3 and a half packets of cigs. Each Yen 5.60.

14 Jul 1945

Confession. Worked in am, then swimming, glorious.

Rumour that we're going to Manila, and that a ship is waiting in Manila with food to rush to Hong Kong on the fall of Hong Kong.

Went to see Annie, the Van Der Lelys lavished potato leaves on everyone there. *((Anything extra to eat was welcomed.))* Abie Hardoon there too.

15 Jul 1945

Worked in a.m. Had to stay there until 1.15pm because of air raid alarm from 11 until then, but no bombs. Meat.

To meeting of British RC Club. *((This was a club planned for Hong Kong after liberation. Committee elected:- Q. Macfadyen, Harold Bidwell and Elsie Bidwell, W. FitzGibbon, F. Willey, Tom Cashman, Mrs Dorothy Wilson, Peggy Barton, Mrs Grant (probably initial E.), Elsie Bidwell. Lots of eats.))*

Benediction in evening, then Peg and I went for a walk to cemetery. Met Jim Johnson (HK Police) on way: husband of Betty nee Bone, a Govt. colleague of mine, evacuated to Australia.

16 Jul 1945

Pacifist meeting in evening – only Audrey, Charles, Father and myself. Rumours in abundance:-

1,900 Allied planes over Japan, 30 downed.

Russia has taken over Red Cross.

Foodship is coming here (within 24 hours!!) – American parcels.

We are to go to England via Vladivostok.

We are to go to Manila (a) direct, or (b) via Macau where we will be transhipped.

We will receive 4,000 Yen apiece for ill-treatment from the Japs.

A ship is waiting in Manila ready to rush up here as soon as we fall.

We cling to the repatriation rumours and the parcel ones: re the latter, argument is that the Americans can now dictate because they have Japanese prisoners in the Philippine Islands. *((We internees did in fact (in about 2002) receive £10,000 each compensation, less £1,000 each to cover cost of negotiations by a post-war society which had been pushing for compensation for years.))*

Feeling sickish and unhungry.

17 Jul 1945

Jap order is that all dry reserves of rice to be handed in to Indian Quarters Quartermaster by tomorrow morning, under threat of dire penalties.

Pasties. Feeling better now, but not perfect.

Bridge, Peg and I played Tacchi and Goldenberg in afternoon, went down 36.

18 Jul 1945

We (Redwoods) ground all our dry rice this morning. Am still not hungry.

Very brief letter from Uncle Harry (my Dad's brother in Bath, Somerset), dated 15th January 1944. Two letters from Aunt Lily, one 31st December 1943, saying 'My best Christmas gift was your card. Happy to know you are so cheerful and busy. Longing to see you.' And one 8th March 1944 saying 'Hope you and girls are keeping fit and cheerful as we. Don't worry, everything going fine. Just off to buy oranges.'

Mum got contents of her safe deposit box. *((This had been kept in Hongkong & Shanghai Bank in town. Now the Japs sent contents of boxes to owners in camp. What a generous gesture this was – having lost our home and all our possessions in the war – to receive treasured letters, policies, the last letter from my Dad before his death, certificates – including my L.G.S. Matric one, and a few snaps.))*

To lecture by Mr P.E. Witham in the Bartons' room (American Quarters) on 'The Ledo Road between Assam and Burma.'

19 Jul 1945

250 tons of firewood supposed to be brought today by lighter – but cancelled. Even Mr Gimson (Colonial Secretary & Representative of Internees) detailed to assist. We were to have pasties for meal to help men – but pasties had already been started to be cooked when cancellation of

firewood so we still got them. *((The logs of wood had to be hiked up to the camp kitchens then chopped or sawn – very heavy work.))*

Later: the wood came in later after all, and a number of women took hot tea down to the men, made from tea leaves collected – a teaspoon or so from each donor.

To Crutwell's German lesson at 12.30 – Jill Beavis, Mrs Betty Drown, and J. Oram.

Then to girls' club meeting in Rosaleen's room *((the Grant family))*. Mrs Dorothy Jenner *((a well-known Australian journalist who wrote for newspapers there under the name 'Cassandra', and who read and criticised my story written in camp))* came and talked about careers. Here is what each girl would like to be:-

Doreen Leonard – actress. *((Died in the UK in 1946.))*

Maureen Pearson – didn't know. *((Post-war she worked in an office in Hong Kong, and in 1948 was killed – thrown off back of motor-bike.))*

Teresa Cullen, Yvette Whitfield didn't know.

Rose Harris – manicurist.

Joan Wilkinson – stenographer.

Nita Olivier – journalist.

Pat Thoresen – reporter.

Yvonne Blackmore – domestic science.

Wendy Barton -domestic science.

Mary Edmonston – public relations in foreign countries.

Leilah Lois Wood – governess. *((Post-war she studied music and became a piano teacher. I am still in correspondence with her, she has a farm in Saskatchewan, Canada.))*

Ingeborg Warild – governess.

20 Jul 1945

Outside roll call, after which Mr Burnett came in and ran over my 'roll call' exercise, criticising and suggesting.

Some folk said they heard shelling and bombing last night, and some claim to have SEEN machine-gunning at 9pm last night.

Peggy and I went swimming in afternoon, later I visited Tom Cashman and Mr Nicolson in hospital.

21 Jul 1945

Went to see Annie and Kristine in morning. Planned to go swimming in afternoon but beach closed, so sunbathed under tree and read.

The de Vleeschouwer children wildly excited to see their (banker) father carrying wood, which arrived per lighter about 4pm. *((That the Japs were supplying us with so much wood for cooking was rather depressing, as it seemed to imply that we would be in camp for a much longer time than we'd hoped.))*

22 Jul 1945

The men were working all night, bringing in wood from lighter. They were given congee, and Margery Fortescue's band worked supplying tea until 3.00 am., but Mrs C. infuriated us all by growling at Margery this morning for the movement and noise – a noise outside the chlorinated water tap in the courtyard – because of waking Weir baby & Mrs. W had a temp.! Margery tired and very upset.

Clifton said Japs wouldn't let Mr Gimson carry wood but he spent the night among the men doing so.

News is supposed to have come in camp that someone called Mitchell in Macao has picked up a radio message from a Mrs Lockhart saying she's well in May 1945, and the message has been passed to Mr Lockhart in here.

Just about 9pm last night there was a sudden noise of a plane and machine-gunning: Mr. Ingram *((it must have been Mr. A. Ingram, as I didn't know the other Mr Ingram listed in camp))* saw a plane, very low, having come down with engine off, and after he heard a little bombing.

Tony Sandberg's third banns called today.

Catholic Action meeting. Mr FitzGibbon gave talk on establishment of a Catholic newspaper in HK after the war. *((Such a newspaper was established – the Sunday Examiner. I used to contribute items to it, and also used to sell it outside St Joseph's after Mass on Sundays. When attending St Joseph's Church in 2008, I noticed the Sunday Examiner was still on sale there.))*

23 Jul 1945

Mr Albert Victor Frain died this afternoon. *((Poor man, he'd gone ga-ga and had to be accommodated in a tiny room on the ground floor of the hospital, with a minder.))*

Worked in morning. Olive's beri-beri is coming back again, and her legs are septic.

Pacifist meeting in Rosaleen's room in evening, Q. MacFadyen, Gregory; and S. Carr came too.

No sugar ration – deficit by (someone: E. Reed??) stealing it has to be made up to Japs.

24 Jul 1945

To Mr Frain's funeral, taken Father Hessler there too by Rev. MacKenzie Dow.

The Formosan (guards) now living up the hill.

25 Jul 1945

No one came for shorthand – feel like throwing them both over.

About noon, a plane sounded very near and made a most peculiar noise, as if it had dropped something, then it zoomed over our heads and went slowly out to sea. A few moments later the air raid alarm went. Some say it was a sea-plane – can't be identified in camp. Mr R Mottram said it had a jagged white marking under wings. Mr Walker said it was a green plane. It appeared to be in difficulties and jettisoned about 6 of its cargo, which are either bombs, depth charges, or mines: about the size of Mimi Lau blocks, and marked '100 lbs. 1943'.

One fell near St Stephen's white cross, 3 or 4 in Bungalow A area – 2 actually on it – and one went through the roof of St Stephen's and landed on a Mr King's bed, but no serious injuries there. But at Bungalow A, the

Rev. F.R. Myhill aged 33 was seriously injured, with superficial (multiple) wounds and especially on chest – and shock.

Leilah Wood, aged 16, also badly hurt, she has multiple abrasions and wounds, one in her chest. Worrying because she vomited up a little fresh blood, she is also badly shocked.

Mavis Hamson, aged 8, also much bruised. Mavis' mother and Leilah are sisters.

All clear about 1.20pm, when I went to work.

Olive not at work because of legs (septic).

Raid alarm again between 1.45 and 2.15.

About 4.30 a party of about 7 Japs and Formosans (including interpreter) came to hospital to see the victims. Then another 2 or 3 came, including Captain Saito(?).

It's ten to 7pm and all clear hasn't gone yet.

Rumour that Churchill has made speech saying that the Japanese war will be over by April 1946!!! Which distresses us except we won't allow ourselves to take it seriously, like all the other rumours we dislike.

Bungalow A and St Stephen's evacuated pro tem.

26 Jul 1945

St Stephen's, Block 8, Bungalows A, B and C still evacuated, the ex-inhabitants are sleeping wherever they can in Blocks 9, 10 and 11, some 200 of them. Not supposed to return to their billets, but some have risked it to get essentials.

Leilah (in hospital) looking so much better.

German lesson off (Crutwell's) because air raid alarm between 11.45 and 12.10, but we had it at 4pm.

The Formosans are reputed to have stopped Tony Sandberg's wedding till Saturday because it's 'a better day'!

Irma Mejia's 20th birthday.

Peace Programme meeting in grotto in evening.

27 Jul 1945

7am Mass in Grants' room (Block 2, Married Q), then outside roll call at 8.30am, followed by a general address outside Block 2, where Married Q. people and Blocks A1, A2 and A3 assembled. (A4 and Dutch Block went to Indian Quarters for their address.)

Lieut. Kadowaki, looking like a member of the foreign legion with khaki flaps attached to his little cap with 1 star on, Mr Max Bickerton (our interpreter) and Mr Gimson stood on tables – Kadowaki had a table to himself.

Kadowaki gave some explosive words in Japanese which Bickerton translated in a low voice to Mr Gimson, who relayed message to us. First of all, Lt. Kadowaki referred to 'the raid 2 days ago by American planes', and expressed sympathy to us for damage and particularly to those injured. Remainder of the lecture concerned bowing.

We were told that after the bombing, the Adjutant from the (Jap) Governor's office visited camp and commented that we, particularly women, were lax about bowing. Lieut K appreciated that our customs are different from theirs, but we must observe the bowing, otherwise – much though he regretted it – Kadowaki would have to take action.

He then summoned a small Jap soldier who demonstrated the model salute

(a) to a soldier wearing headgear

(b) to a soldier not wearing headgear.

He showed us how to bow, beginning as if the head is going to drop off completely, but stopping suddenly as if it was controlled by clockwork *((that is my description))*.

Then we were dismissed at 10.00am.

Card from Marion Woolard (in Kent, a school friend).

28 Jul 1945

Clifton on 'bomb disposal squad', 11 bombs. The Jap experts say they're harmless. *((None of them exploded on impact, the damage was caused by their crashing down.))*

Rumour that landing in Shanghai imminent.

Eileen Grant came home from hospital today.

3 bombs were extracted, one 200 lbs, two were 100 pounders.

29 Jul 1945

Worked in afternoon. Then went to St Matthew's group party in Maria's room. Benediction in evening. Meat.

30 Jul 1945

Olive's 29th birthday – I gave her a dress hanger and hankies which got yesterday from Eve Hill (nurse) for 1 packet cigarettes. Mum gave Olive a pair of her voluminous pants to make a blouse with.

31 Jul 1945

Mrs H had stillborn baby. *((I can't remember Mrs H's name)).*

Worked in am. C.A. Meeting. Two lots of bridge, first, Peg & I v. Dick Cloake and Philip *((Appleyard?))*; second, we played Dugdale and Sewell.

1 Aug 1945

Mrs. E. Byrne, whose husband died while grinding rice last year, had news that her only son has died.

Firewood cut 25%.

News circulating round camp these last few days is that Labour Govt. has got in at Home with a big majority, Attlee in charge. It's said that Churchill and Attlee flew to Potsdam. Churchill also said to have resigned from politics to write a history of the war. Joan Wilkinson came for shorthand.

St Joseph's meeting in evening. Mrs J. Witham elected President, Mrs Edna Grant Vice, Mrs Marvin Secretary.

2 Aug 1945

Mrs Dorothy Fyffe gave talk to St Agnes club in our room. Saw her polished show some months back, when she stepped into the breach at about 2 days' notice. She went on music halls with her elder sister when she was 15, and travelled through Europe, appearing at Folies Bergere, and in Royal Command Performance in 1938, and before the King and Queen when they visited France in 1939, when Maurice Chevalier was also on the latter bill and was largely responsible for sending the sisters to Rio de Janeiro. At the time, Tyrone Power and Annabella were there. At Royal Command Performance, Gracie Fields was the big attraction. Dorothy was also with Bertram Mills' circus for some time. *((Dorothy had a daughter, Elisabeth, born in camp in July 1942)).*

There's to be draw from Welfare – 73 tins of salmon and jam between 2,500 people!

All 'refugees' except Bungalow A's allowed back to blocks after 9 days in temporary billets.

Rumour of 3 food/evacuation ships. Also rumour that some peace points accepted by Japs, etc.

4 Aug 1945

Doreen doesn't want to bother with shorthand any more. Joan W came for lesson.

Different people heard machine-gunning last night.

1.45pm, a contingent of about 10 Japs including the colonel and Captain Saito and Lieut. Kadowaki came to hospital on inspection. Mr R Zindel (Red Cross) was with them. Last night some of them inspected dispensary at the hospital, and it had already been cleaned out this morning. They had also inspected the Married Quarters kitchen (in pre-war garages) and criticised that too.

Bridge in evening, Peg and I v. Rosie Judah and Sheila.

Salt fish in rations, not meat.

5 Aug 1945

Sheila Mackinlay's banns called today, to Searle (Police).

6 Aug 1945

Not feeling well. St Catherine's meeting. Working. Went to see Doreen about shorthand – and found that Doreen's pa knew nothing about her decision to stop learning.

Pacifism meeting in our room.

7 Aug 1945

Not feeling very good. Worked.

8 Aug 1945

Went to work, then brought up breakfast.

9 Aug 1945

Having day off, though feeling much better.

10 Aug 1945

Strong rumour (which Clifton swears true) that Russia declared war on Japan and we have landed on Japan proper!

Outside roll call, then news that technicians (previously interviewed) were to go off today – no one knows where, they had to be ready to leave by 2pm.

Technicians' families allowed to go with them. But the Seraphinas and Wards were not allowed because too many children. About 199 went, including (people I knew):

T. Pritchard, C. Fuller, W. Mezger, C. Harloe,

Mr and Mrs de Broekert and 3 children,

Mr & Mrs I. Heath + 2 children,

Mr & Mrs E. Blackmore and Yvonne,

Mr & Mrs R. Lederhofer and Patricia,

Mr and Mrs Mackintyres and daughters Muriel and Ailsa,

J.J. Cameron and daughter Moira,
S. Marvin and wife, Mr & Mrs A. Black,
E. Greenwood and wife, Mr & Mrs R. Cryan,
George and May Halligan, the Langstons,
Mr & Mrs S. Chubb and Christopher.

Even Mr. A. Glanville (a patient in the TB sanitorium) was sent.

There were two instant marriages:- Sheila Bruce and Eric Humphreys, and Tamara Jex and Clifford Crofton, but the new wives weren't allowed to accompany their husbands – one Jap told Tamara she may be able to follow in 10 days' time *((he was nearly right!))*; she and Clifford had been due to have a slap-up wedding the next day. G. Padgett and Miss R. Hobbs (nurse) couldn't be married then because no banns called.

The embarkees had to line up four deep on the road outside the Gaol. Crowds of us left behind stood leaning over the Married Q. railings, some kids sitting outside the railings with legs dangling over the edge.

They were allowed to take camp beds, luggage etc. Some with knapsacks, baskets, basins, suitcases, little baskets hooked on bamboo poles. The Macintyre girls in brief sunsuits, Moira Cameron in blue serge coat 3 years too short for her, and all the little de Broekerts in white topees, Anne carrying her doll.

Japs counted them, and as names were called, they trailed off towards the Prep. School *((on way to jetty))*. Conjectures as to why they were removed were many: Japs handing over to Wang Ching Wei, and our technicians required; or needed for exchange of other prisoners, etc.

The people who went to help them with the luggage got back at 10pm and reported that they went off in a coastal boat, and apparently the only place to be was in the hold.

Everyone diving in dustbins for anything useful discarded by the absentees!

Sheila Haynes came over in evening and asked me to her wedding to Pat Cullinan!

Burnett was reasonably pleased with 'Come and Get It!' which was the title of my account of the food queue.

((More about the technicians' departure – Yvonne de Jong (nee Blackmore) was a schoolgirl in Stanley. We are still in touch; recently she published a small paperback called 'An Extraordinary Youth' with a chapter about Stanley. Her father being an engineer, he with his wife and Yvonne were in the technicians' group. Here are extracts of what she writes:-

> 'No explanation was given and we never found out why we were removed from Stanley...
>
> Our quartermasters issued some dry rations in case of an emergency...
>
> There were 177 of us... we boarded a large motorized Chinese junk and were guided into the reeking, fishy hold where we were battened down...
>
> Our destination turned out to be a former small refugee compound on Argyle Street, Kowloon. There were eight huts surrounded by high fences and barbed wire. Guards were posted at each corner...
>
> We were quite relieved finding ourselves to be still alive and not drowned in the deep blue sea...
>
> Our emergency rations proved invaluable as no food was supplied for two days.
>
> It was a time of great suspense... on the tenth morning we looked out we found there were no guards at their posts, they had disappeared overnight. Our men held a conference and decided to wait a day and see what happened next. Nothing!
>
> On August 12th U.S. airplanes dropped pamphlets signed by Admiral Nimitz advising us to stay where we were and await the arrival of the navy.*))*

11 Aug 1945

Up early and went to Bartons' room (American Block) where Sheila and Pat were married. Father Meyer took the ceremony, which was followed by a Nuptial Mass. Mr. J. Joyce was Best Man. Quentin Macfadyen gave

Sheila away. Pat looked nervous, Sheila most serene in her dark blue taffeta dress. Hugh Goldie there, Rosaleen Millar and sister Eileen Grant, and Miss M. Paterson.

((Miss Paterson was a teacher; she it was who, when a nurse at the Jockey Club wartime hospital when the Japs first entered that hospital, bravely escaped in the night and made her way via the cemetery to Bowen Road Military Hospital and reported that the soldiers were raping the young nurses; as a result the next day Dr Selwyn-Clarke, Director of Medical Services, visited the Jockey Club with a Japanese official, and the nurses and patients were then all evacuated. My mother told me about this as she too was nursing at that hospital.))

Meat today, but I still can't eat rice.

Wedding reception in the Barton girls' room. *((The Barton family occupied two rooms in American Block, one shared by Mr and Mrs Barton and their five sons Alec, Terence, Leo, John and Daniel, the other by their six daughters Marie, Margaret (Peggy), Audrey, Wendy, Jacqueline and Rosemary; Marie moved out after she married Vincent Morrison.))*

Loads of tasty eats, I only had to refuse once, and the cake was delicious – white thick cream on top. Hugh Goldie there, Boesterd, Sheila's aunt, Mrs Kella, Marie Paterson and Bartons.

Worked in am. Frank Angus' offer worth thinking about, about $400 a month – but I don't want to be working out here all my youth – what's left of it. *((Frank Angus had in mind some post-war job and asked me if I would join as secretary.*)

Margery Fortescue has my trouble (lack of appetite) too, she has gone quite thin, and gave me one and a half limes because she was given some.

13 Aug 1945

Still not well. Started writing new story.

St Agnes meeting, then C.A. Meeting.

Peggy Barton rusked rice bread for me.

Pacifism in evening.

14 Aug 1945

Lovely First Communion Service for Barbara Willey and Ronnie Harris – both looked very nice in white.

Lazing out on grass, I heard a plane in distance; it cruised along so long, then suddenly became much louder; it was a huge thing, dark and old-looking like a great evil bird swooping down sharply over the American Block, machine-gunning – it sounded like that but no one was hurt so perhaps it wasn't.

I flew into Block 2's front entrance. Children in the road started to shriek, gardeners popped out of their gardens, and everyone flew for safety. Mabel arrived back from the workshop.

While we were sheltering in our corridor, back came the plane again, and the Japs up the hill began pot-shooting at it with rifles, which made an awful frightening crack-crack. Lots of children and adults were at the beach. Four times the plane came, then it was all over and we saw the wreckage of a naval patrol boat (presumably Jap) to the left of the island in front of the hospital; and some saw – they said – survivors kicking about, poor souls. Tim Fortescue said a second boat was also sunk, all of which shows that the rumour that our war is over isn't true.

To 'Co-operative' talk by Mr. A. J. C. Taylor in grotto.

15 Aug 1945

Mr. Pederson died after operation.

Feeling a little better. Spent most of morning at hospital, trying to get medicine.

June Cheape asked me to do duplicate bridge with her, but I haven't the guaranteed time.

3 cards from Auntie.

News of the new Labour Government: school-leaving age to be raised; no one allowed to earn over £2,000 annually; essential services – railways etc. to come under Govt. control; unemployment benefits altered; expectant and nursing mothers to be fed and housed etc. It all sounds idealistic.

Meeting in Bartons' room. Mum came and other guests. I'm now President, Elsie Bidwell vice. Brother F. Grimshaw talked about papal infallibility, Alice, Mum, Peggy and I played bridge.

16 Aug 1945

Still tired and un-hungry, though taste in mouth not so foul since Dr Kirk's medicine.

Camp full of rumours and news of a truce, armistice and peace.

To choir practice to practise 'Te Deum'.

Fresh rumours have been coming in all day, viz:

That news came on radio last night that armistice and cease fire was at 4pm yesterday.

That Kadowaki smashed radio when he heard it.

That Formosans were given iron rations last night.

That there were various parties in camp last night (this last is definite – Brother Grimshaw was invited to one: there were 2 RC Brothers in camp, Bro. Grimshaw and Bro. L. Bonnici).

That Jap officials have gone into town.

That the Formosan guards are running around in civilian clothes.

That food ships are sailing from Manila as soon as peace is signed.

That peace was actually made on Monday the 13th.

Latest (at 5.55pm) that Kadowaki is now with Gimson; and that the Formosan guards say the Emperor broadcast at 3 this afternoon and gave orders to prepare lists of internees etc. for embarkation – which we presume applies to those in Japan since it's said to be one of the peace terms.

We were each given a roll of U.S. toilet paper today. *((A very welcome 'first' in three & a half years; the toilet paper supplied to camp came in large sheets of Chinese buff-coloured paper that had to be cut up)).*

17 Aug 1945

All slept badly last night.

No roll call of any description.

Carmen Hailstone (a friendly neighbour) gave us a tin of sugar. Mrs. Lambert, for what reason we know not, came and gave us a tin of York Sausage Roll which we forthwith ate. Margery Fortescue gave us some onions. Our neighbours the Hamiltons also gave us some food (diary indecipherable here).

Rev. Sandbach told us the war was over. *((To avoid drawing too much Jap attention, certain camp dignitaries were deputed to announce this news to small groups of people: in our block, lots of us congregated on the internal concrete staircase and landing.))*

Our Police went on duty patrolling this evening, with mostly their hats their only uniform.

Couldn't eat the Victory Pasty Peggy brought me.

Heard a crowd of Formosans singing gaily as they went up the hill in a lorry.

18 Aug 1945

Feel awful, so am in hospital; had some real powdered milk.

Eddie Greenwood and Mr. A. Brailsford drove into camp on fire engine! *((Presumably the only transport they could get. Eddie's pre-war job was with the Fire Brigade; he and Brailsford were among the technicians removed from camp some days ago.))* They told us they had to do (physical) work, but otherwise 'did more or less what they liked.' They saw our flags up over Shamshuipo Camp.

We are allowed to write to military camps. I have just written to Arthur, Harry Chalcraft, Pat Twitchett, and Charles Pike.

7pm. Still no sign of relieving Army, but this afternoon 3 fellows came to camp in a launch: an army fellow; a member of HKVDC, K. Robert (a PWD engineer), a Mr Owens (Wavy Navy). They said the p.o.w. in Kowloon are free and hoisted the Union Jack this a.m.

It's said that the Chinese are starving, so as the entire camp can no longer eat rice *((because better rations were coming into Stanley))*, etc., contributions were collected and taken in to town. We Redwoods gave away all our iron ration biscuits, but it was no sacrifice at all. Promise of a big sugar ration tomorrow, and an oil ration. Am still in hospital with little appetite, am longing for the day when I feel like fried bread, and potatoes.

I had a letter from Charles Pike on blue paper, dated yesterday, with an envelope to match, and sealed with sealing wax!

RAF plane came over this evening, did Victory Roll and dropped pamphlets which fell over the Fort.

Just heard a bulletin saying the atomic bomb and Russia's entry into the war caused the end.

Mabel came to hospital with sugar for me from the Hamiltons, and pineapple from Margery Fortescue.

Rumour that our men from Japan are on their way to Hong Kong.

It's said that Shamshuipo husbands won't be re-united to Stanley wives for a week.

Dr Kirk has just examined me and said 'no gallstones.'

19 Aug 1945

Still in hospital.

No fleet!

Bulletin says that 100 visitors from town (i.e. Chinese and non-interned) can come in daily, 50 per bus; and that in due course internees wishing to visit town may do so, though advised not to (and only with permission of CSO).

Two radios have been put at disposal of the camp.

No news of our release.

Prisoners (internees) from gaol will be returned to camp.

Dr I. Newton thinks the Fleet won't be here until Monday.

Apparently there's still fighting in Guadalcanal because Japs can't get in touch with their troops.

More corned beef issued today; there's to be more beans, bran, rice, meat, tea & sugar sent in.

11.30am: Report that a launch left Shamshuipo this morning for Stanley with relatives... arrival awaited here any moment.

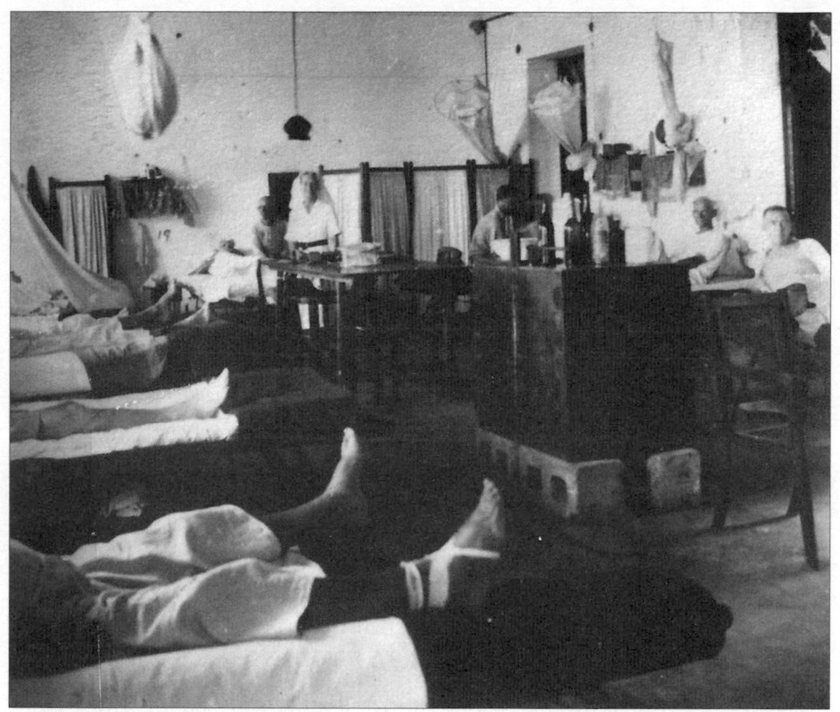

One of the wards in the Stanley camp hospital (called Tweed Bay Hospital). It shows some of the concrete breeze blocks used in the ward. We called these blocks 'Mimi Laus' because of the court case just before the war in which a young Mimi Lau was thought to be involved in securing contracts for the supply of the blocks for ARP work.

Mum had a note from Mr. Kirman who is at Central British School (wartime hospital) in Kowloon, he was a Naval Dockyard colleague of my Dad's.

A load of sweets came in, we were each given 4 ozs. sugar.

Rumour that Peace Treaty is signed either today or tomorrow.

June Cheape and Clifton brought me a lovely hot sweet drink of ground bean flour, which the Sister wouldn't let me drink because I'm starting Santonin tonight (anti-worm).

LATER: Two poor little half-starved boys have just come into camp and have been put in our ward – James and David Cameron, sons of Muriel (nee Smith). Muriel and her mother and the kids stayed out on

Irish passports, ended up in Rosary Hill. They are pale little souls, fair-haired, and the elder (about 5) is thinner than anyone I've ever seen in camp. They are well-dressed.

20 Aug 1945

8.00am. The little boys behaved very well and are thrilled with everything. *((Although they had been put in separate beds next to each other, in morning they were found to be together in one bed.))*

Again unwanted congee is collected for the sampan people, who are apparently crowding on the Indian Quarters' beach edge, and swapping fish and bananas for clothes.

Late last night, news of another pamphlet which had been dropped, addressed to Allied p.o.ws and civilian internees, saying that the end is near, telling us to stay put and be cautious till surrender of Japan – if we'd had that last week we'd have been thrilled: it was a sort of general pamphlet advising us what to do if the Japs did/did not surrender.

2pm. Half an hour ago, some 'close relatives' arrived in camp from Shamshuipo Camp.

Mrs. N. Hale's husband has arrived (at hospital), he's having tea with her on verandah now.

I witnessed the reunion between the Hamiltons – just as in films, he with his cap in one hand which was round her waist.

Among the patients in our ward was 'Tommy' – Mrs. B. Tomalin whose husband was in Shamshuipo Camp. Tommy's friend Mrs. Simon-White came into the ward and said 'He's just coming!' We all understood this to mean that Tommy's husband was on his way up the stairs.

'Don't get too excited,' she told Tommy, who wanted to get out of bed at once, but we all insisted she stay put until he arrived. Well, 'he' arrived – but it wasn't Tommy's husband, it was Mrs Simon-White's (also from Shamshuipo.)

After the Simon Whites had left, a disappointed Tommy expostulated indignantly, 'Why should she think I would be excited about seeing HIM!'

5pm. Rosaleen's husband came (Capt. Millar, Royal Scots); also Bob Cherry, Henry Eardley.

Mabel had letter from Lane of the RS Band, who is the only band member left in camp; some died, some away (Japan). He says Sid (Hale) and Arthur (Alsey) in Shanghai. *((They had been in Shanghai for a time after being shipwrecked on the 'Lisbon Maru' but ended up in Japan.))*

I had a letter from Jimmy James, he'd opened my letter to Harry Chalcraft (R.A.) and said Harry went to Japan in 1943, also Topper (Olive's fiance Sam Brown). Jimmy's letter gives vivid picture of how things are at Shamshuipo, they are all longing for a ship.

Tales that our camp isn't nearly so bad as those in Burma and Manila.

We hospital patients had an opportunity to go on lorry tonight to concert at St Stephen's, but I decided not to. Dick came to see me this afternoon.

The little boys are settling down very well in the ward.

6pm. From people (Chinese or non-British) who visited from town, terrible tales of hardship and starvation; also:

- that 3 of our own p.o.ws have been arrested for fifth column work.

- that 3 Taikoo men who died weighed 50 lbs. And under.

- that 2 Americans who are now loose in town were caught by Japs on a nearby island where they've been studying tides and weather and radioing results back in readiness for Allied attack on 21st August with 2,000 planes.

Bishop Valtorta (RC) came, told us he had to sell Cathedral bell to get money to feed the poor.

Someone is supposed to have heard the King broadcasting and saying he hoped to have all his people back in the motherland soon – SO DO WE!

There's talk of a food ship having left Manila last night *((presumably for us))*.

Apparently the Peace isn't yet signed, which is why the British and Americans can't occupy Hong Kong yet.

(Still in hospital) Felt very good all day; had corned beef.

Doris Scourse (nurse) and Willy Watson are being married in the hospital office tonight.

Clifford Crofton has come back in camp (technician who married T. Jex the day the technicians left).

There is a Protestant Service here (in hospital) this a.m. Rev. Cyril Brown took it.

Kowloon is noisy with crackers, the visitors said the Chinese are waiting with open arms for the British.

We are told to hang on to old tins, utensils. etc. as there's nothing like that in town.

Shamshuipo Camp are in disgrace because they threw the Jap guards out of the camp.

7pm. Just heard a bulletin dated yesterday which says Jap envoys are now in Manila, having the peace terms conveyed to them; that on 2 occasions US planes flying over Tokyo area since surrender have been fired on; also in Saigon.

That Hong Kong will be taken by the *((Chinese))* army in Canton area. That all pows and civilian internees will be evacuated in hospital ships available, regardless of flag. That Manila is preparing to receive 150,000 persons; that sick and aged will have preference.

No news of pows in Japan as to whether or not they have left yet: there are 112,000 British.

Clement Attlee is Prime Minister.

Siam has un-declared its independence.

Felt very good all day. We had corned beef, and I am having Santonin tonight. Congee still being collected to give to the sampan people and the poor. The kids all got 2 packets of sweets.

21 Aug 1945

Leaving hospital today.

Fishing boats bobbing up and down, close enough to barter their fish through the barbed wire on hospital embankment.

Mr F. Kelly sent me 2 hot baked sweet potatoes which I ate and hope I won't regret.

Messrs. F. Gimson, H. R. Butters, D. Sloss, R Minitt have gone to town today to confab. in Mr Zindel's office (Red Cross official).

All sorts of rumours about what happened to our U.S. parcels, but it seems that the Japs saved the food in tunnels. Rumour that milk, butter and flour being sent in today.

Visitors from men's camps came. Among them, Charles Pike RAMC. He looked quite well, though pale and hair rather moth-eaten. He brought us (in small paper pokes) sugar & salt; and soup and oil, and writing paper! We had tea of fried sweet potatoes.

Clifton brought in his friend Norman ?? and sad news that Clif's great friend Charles Kim had died.

We had news of deaths of Naval Dockyard friends in Shamshuipo: Mr Sutton, Mr. Lee, Mr. Egan and son, and Mr. Peckham. Mr Peckham had died just two days ago.

After the meal of fried sweet potatoes, we went to gates to see visitors off, saw Major Grieve (at one time pre-war Mabel had worked for him), and Mr. Harper (Naval Dockyard).

General issue of siege biscuits, and matches and soy sauce.

In evening Peggy Barton & I went to dance at St. Stephen's *((the Japs had prohibited dancing in the camp))* to look on from the gallery, but soon went downstairs and had a wonderful time dancing with Dick and Philip Appleyard (Peggy's friend). There was a big Union Jack with V through it at the back of the stage, Reg Jenner's band, and Bill Hewitt as M.C. A lot of hot tea available. Radio there, we heard it for first time.

An American announcer who hummed and hawed told us the news summary was for pows and internees in Pacific. Rather depressing... delays in signing Peace, envoy plane held up... which to our suspicious minds sounds like the Japs up to their old tricks.

22 Aug 1945

Boxer, Foy, Leiper, Roberts, Andersons *((William and James Anderson))* and others imprisoned by Japs elsewhere arrived at Central British School (hospital) last night from Canton, and are coming here tomorrow; also the technicians *((who had left camp on 10th August))* are returning.

We've had issued today: 25 cubes of sugar apiece; half a tin of evaporated milk; a tin of Chase & Sanborn coffee between 13. Everyone is full up.

Meat stew tonight.

Another batch of people came in, I saw Brian Harper of Naval Dockyard (he and parents and elder sister Joyce had been our neighbours when we Redwoods lived at 98 Kennedy Road in 1929).

10 packets of cigarettes (Japanese ones) each.

Mum went to Indian Quarters beach and bartered our old clothes and rice for bananas, one fish and 2 crabs!

A list is being prepared of sick and infirm in case a priority list is required.

Reports about occupation of Japan which starts on 26th August and that British Fleet is on its way to Hong Kong; there's trouble because China wants Hong Kong.

To St Joseph's meeting in Bartons' room – interesting talk by Mr Barton about his life.

23 Aug 1945

Ena Cochrane *((nee Penney, an old school friend of Olive and I))* had a baby girl, called Fearn. (In 1943 she had a son, Alexander Graham).

Clifton's 24th birthday.

Tiffin, fried corned beef on fried bread. We got weighed. I was 112 lbs, Peggy 117, Mum 118 (her pre-war weight was about 170 lbs.)

Peggy and I sat outside railing above main road and saw a lorryload of ex-gaol prisoners (non-British) go out, cheering.

We each received 12 ozs. demerara sugar – delicious: ate some on bread with margarine.

Bert Millar (Royal Scots officer) came in camp today *((husband of Rosaleen, nee Grant))*.

Corporal Harding called to see Mum, he was the Middlesex fellow who was a patient in Jockey Club Hospital during war. *((As it wasn't an Army hospital, the nurses had to hide his uniform when the Japs overran the place.))*

Tomorrow is supposed to be the last day for visitors, since the Allied troops will be coming soon.

A Chinese 'linen boy' came in with a handkerchief in an envelope for each of his old customers, but before opening up his rattan basket with these, he carefully unfolded and held up a small Union Jack... so touching.

Professor Digby has put Mabel's name to go on the first ship.

Met Jimmy James from Shamshuipo.

Kids received two more packets of sweets each.

Saw A. B. Allan and Mr. Kaufmann (Naval Dockyard buddies of my Dad's).

Watched troops leaving 9.30pm. They assembled around Ration Garage with friends and relations while their lorries were being used to convey rations to the Hospital and St. Stephen's, the children enjoying lifts all the time. Several cars parked nearby were also invaded by the children, some were also perched on the top of the big gate across the road.

News on notice-board indicates that there is some trouble about Hong Kong – China wants it too; we're told we shall have to be very patient for a good week yet: I'm worried about what may happen if armed control doesn't arrive soon.

Mr. F. Kelly gave us some peanut and wong tong. *((Being Police, he had had a trip into town.))*

Vague news that Chandra Bose and some high-ranking Jap officers were killed in a plane crash.

Margery F. brought Claire van Wylick, whom she taught pre-war, to see us (the van Wylicks weren't in Stanley).

24 Aug 1945

Typhoon blowing up.

Flags of Allies are being made in workshop ready for raising ceremony, lamp posts and railing stanchions have already been converted into flag staffs.

Weather far too rough for sampans to come selling. Much rain and wind, I hope that men don't come in from camps – dangerous: the conveyances are old and rickety (and only one of the two that set off from here last night had lights, then only one solitary headlight.)

6.30pm. No lorries of troops came.

Started to type new story on Mr Fantham's typewriter, because feel the need of taking on a job which will be a fight against time in these days when time seems to go so slowly.

Maria Connolly has had bad news about her Mexican friends and relatives. H. Sequeira (whom I knew through ARP) was among those released from gaol yesterday.

The Peace is to be signed aboard U.S.S. 'Missouri' and H.M.S. 'King George V'. 700 miles of sea have to be mine-swept first.

Bulletin says that arrangements are being made for surrender of Hong Kong to be taken by a British commander and for a British administration to take over.

Also that s.s. 'Queen Mary' has arrived in New York with 1,000 U.S. prisoners *((presumably from Germany?))*; and arrangements are ready at Manila to receive 35,000 pows from Japan.

Heard radio in Clifton's room – gramophone records from Radio ZBW Hong Kong!

(('Is it really true' was written on August 24th 1945, six days before Admiral Harcourt liberated us. Although I was still writing my diary then, I had this urge to record how things were during the period when we knew the war was over but had no contact with the outside world.))

IS IT REALLY TRUE?

Even a week after all this started, we still ask each other: is it really true, or is it just another of those dreams which has haunted and tortured us for three and a half years? We have been nominally free for a week, but neither envoy nor Fleet having arrived, our suspicious natures are inclined to wonder whether they ever will materialise, or whether this is all a trick. We feel we want to urge the Allies to come while the coming is good, lest the pendulum should suddenly swing the other way, leaving us in a far worse position than that in which we have been for so long. The sure knowledge that the internees and pows in other Japanese-occupied territory in the Pacific are feeling exactly the same as we are makes the situation no easier.

We look out to sea and cry 'Come on, Nimitz, or Fraser – we've been waiting for you for years – now you CAN come, what's the delay?' It's not that we don't realise the need for caution – perhaps we who have had so much experience of the way things work in this part of the globe, realise the need even more than our relatives at Home who are longing for our release; it's just one of the strange things about life that it's harder to be patient for a fortnight, knowing things will end in a fortnight, than it is to live through three and a half years which had no definite stopping-place.

Tales (in recent months) that the Russians had declared war on Japan were rife. Rumours of the Potsdam Peace Conference began to filter through to the Camp at the beginning of August; it was said that all the points save one or two had been accepted, or that all had been rejected – you could take your choice. Things, however, really started happening on Friday, August 10th (only a fortnight ago from today) when at about 10.30am news whipped round the Camp that 175 technicians and families were leaving Stanley (by Jap. order) – no details, the list of people was given out and by 2pm that afternoon, they were lining up along the main road with their luggage. We watched them going with mixed feelings – their destination and their fate were equally obscure, but one cheering thought remained uppermost in everyone's mind – their removal meant that some sort of change was pending, and we couldn't but think that it was a change in our favour. When the luggage helpers returned, they said the people left in a coastal boat.

Between the hours of notification of departure and 2pm, two weddings were celebrated, the bridegrooms being technicians; the brides were not allowed to accompany them, although a Jap. official comforted one bride with the information that she would be able to join her husband 'in about ten days' time' – he was almost right.

On Monday August 13th there were strong rumours that there would be, or was, Peace, but we didn't really believe them – according to Stanley the European war ended many, many times before it actually did.

On Tuesday morning an incident occurred which killed the peace rumours: one of our planes machine-gunned, bombed and sank a naval patrol boat just past the little island beyond the Camp hospital. I was lying on the grass reading and saw the plane come down very low over us, while the Japanese terrified us by shooting at it with rifles, the cracks of which sounded much more dangerous than they really were. Children playing around shrieked, gardeners popped out of the gardens, and everyone (including me) flew for cover. We cynics immediately started 'I-told-you-so-ing' to those who had so positively asserted that the war was over; their suggestion that the war being over, the naval boat had no right to move and was for that reason sunk, sounded far too fantastic to be true.

The next morning I arrived home from Mass to find the Camp full of 'authentic' rumours that a truce had been called. We were each donated a roll of USA toilet paper – the first real toilet roll most of us have seen for three and a half years. I went to Choir practice to practise the 'Te Deum'. Rumours continued to pour in thick and fast: that there was a Cease Fire at 4pm on the 15th; that Lieut. Kadowaki (Camp Commandant) had smashed the radio when he heard; that our Formosan guards had

had parties the previous night (Brother Bonnici, at choir, told us Brother Grimshaw had attended one of these parties); that food ships would be sailing from Manila as soon as the peace was signed.

Later in the day came news that the Emperor had broadcast at 3pm and instructed the Japanese to prepare lists of pows and internees for embarkation, as one of the first conditions of the surrender was said to be that our people in Jap-occupied places and in Japan itself were to be brought to places of safety ready for removal Home.

Hardly anyone slept that night – we all discussed the matter thoroughly and prayed that it was true. Next day was Friday 1st – our regular Roll Call Day, but when there was none, excitement grew greater. About mid-day Rev. Sandbach visited each block and, beneath a Union Jack someone unearthed, read a statement by Mr. Gimson (Colonial Secretary) informing us that hostilities have ceased, that the terms of the Potsdam Conference of July 26th have been accepted by Japan, and that we must be cautious and prudent.

Rumours were rife: an envoy would arrive that day; the troops at Kowloon were freed and running the Colony; the Fleet left Manila (for Hong Kong) at 7pm the previous evening, and the Camp chicken farm was to be exterminated. This last was the only rumour which appeared to have any foundation, since we were given chicken stew the next day...

In recent months our kitchens had made 'siege' biscuits from rice flour which were to be our iron rations if the Allies attacked Hong Kong and we were marooned in our billets. Now these were released to us, plus a small tin of bully between every four, and a bar of yellow Chinese soap between two. More rumours abounded: that a Chinese plane dropped leaflets saying General Chiang Kai-shek is to be Governor of Hong Kong; that the Allied Fleet will be arriving any minute, and that we would all be out of Stanley within three days.

That evening the lights of Stanley shone again – some brave man went to the Jap HQ and asked for the fuses. The (Hong Kong) Police started patrol-duty round the camp (mostly their helmets their only uniform). Someone told me that one of the (Jap) officials at HQ was observed sitting alone outside on the porch when his dog came up to him and nuzzled up against him. The story goes that the official stroked the dog slowly and thoughtfully, and gazed into space.

The next day, Saturday 18th, one of the technicians roared back into camp on a motor-bike, followed by another on a fire engine the bell of which was clanged furiously. Apparently the technicians had been fed on spinach and rice, and required to cut barbed wire and knock down huts.

Three British officers arrived by launch from the Kowloon camps – Colonel Field, and Owens and K. Robertson. They reported that the Union Jack had been hoisted at Shamshuipo Camp, and brought letters from the pows to which we were allowed to reply, saying exactly what we liked and as much as we liked. I had a letter from a friend in RAMC.

We learned that the Chinese in town were starving, and as the whole camp was feeding well from extra rations, many of us handed over some of our siege biscuits to be sent to town to help feed the hungry; also that day, one of our planes flew over and gave us the Victory Roll; it also dropped leaflets, but none fell in the camp. In the evening we heard that the atomic bomb, and Russia's entry into the war against Japan, had really caused the end of the war.

On Sunday 19th August, visitors (mainly Chinese) were allowed in from town, one load in morning and one in afternoon, to be continued daily. Most of them brought little presents of food, but they had grim tales to tell of conditions in town; the Bishop (RC) came to see us – he had had to sell the Cathedral bells in order to get food for the poor. Two radios were put at the disposal of the Camp. There were rumours that fighting was still progressing in Guadalcanal area, and we learned to our disappointment that the peace had by no means been signed. Another tin of corned beef between four was issued, and we were promised more beans, bran, rice, meat, tea and sugar.

There was a semi-official report that a launch had left Shamshuipo Camp with so many husbands etc. and would be coming to Stanley, but later in the day it was contradicted, the visiting party not having been allowed to leave.

(Toilet paper)

[illegible] started, we still ask each other is it really true — or is it just another of those dreams which has haunted & tortured us for 3½ years? We have been nominally free for a week, but the envoy w/ fleet having arrived, we our suspicious natures are inclined to wonder whether they ever will materialise, or whether this is all a trick. We feel we want to urge the allies to come while the coming is good, lest the pendulum should suddenly swing the other way, leaving us in a far worse position than that in which we have been for so long. The sure knowledge that the inmates of other Japanese-occupied territory in the Pacific are feeling exactly the same as we are makes the situation no easier. We look out to sea, & cry, "Come on, Nimitz, or Fraser — we've been waiting for you for years — now you can come, what's all the delay?" It is not that we don't realise the need for caution — perhaps we, who have had so much experience of the way things work in this part of the globe realise the need even more than do relatives at home who are longing for our release; it is just one of the strange things about life that it's harder to be patient for a fortnight knowing that things will end in a fortnight, than it is to live the 3½ years which had no definite stopping-place.

Rumours of the Potsdam Peace Conference (tales that the Russians had declared war on Japan were rife) began to filter through to the Camp @ the beginning of August; it was said that all the points save one or 2 had been accepted; that all had been rejected — you could take your own choice. Things, however, really started happening on Friday, August 10th (only a fortnight ago from today) when about 10.30 a.m. the news whipped round the camp that 175 technicians & [illegible] were leaving Stanley. There were no details given; the list of people [illegible] that afternoon they were lining up [illegible] with their luggage. We [illegible] with mixed feelings — their destination & their fate were equally obscure, but one cheering thought remained uppermost in everyone's mind — their removal meant that some sort of change was pending — & we could not but think that it was a change in our favour. (+)

After a few days news was received in a note from one or 2 of the technicians that they were back on their pre-war jobs; this was more cheering than ever.

(+) Between the hours of notification of departure & 2 o'clock, 2 weddings were celebrated, the bridegrooms being technicians; the brides, however, were not allowed to accompany them, altho' a Jap. official comforted one of them with the information that she would be able to join her husband in about 10 days' time; he was almost right — the bridegroom himself returned to camp as soon as possible after the surrender.

On Monday, Aug 13, there were strong rumours that there would be, or there was Peace; but we didn't really believe them — according to Stanley, the European war ended many, many times before May 8th. On Tuesday morning an incident occurred which killed the peace rumours — one of our planes machine-gunned, bombed & sank a [illegible] opposite the hospital. The plane was [illegible] low, & made 4 attacks, while the Japs. terrified us by shooting at it with rifles, the cracks of which sounded much more dangerous [illegible] started 'I told you so-ing' to those who [illegible] positively asserted that the war was over. Their suggestion that, the war being over, [illegible]

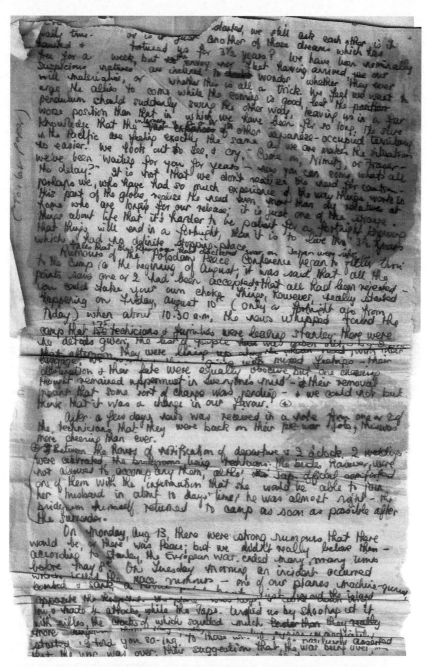

I wrote 'Is It Really True' in camp during the fortnight between the end of our war and the arrival of the British fleet. It was written on toilet paper. This is the first page.

One of the civilian visitors from town brought a pamphlet which had been dropped by plane; it was addressed to prisoners of war and civilian internees and signed by Wedemeyer (i/c U.S. Forces), and warned us to remain in our camps on the surrender of the Japanese, and that a representative was en route to deal with the food, clothes and medical supplies situation, and act as liaison between the Authorities past and present until the arrival of the Allied Forces.

Another tale was that, in town, now free, were two Americans who had been captured on a nearby island some time ago by the Japanese; they had been studying tides, weather etc., and radio-ing messages back to their base, and (now) revealed that the attack on Hong Kong was scheduled for 21st August, beginning with 2,000 planes.

Someone heard a broadcast by the King saying he hoped to have all his subjects home in the fatherland soon – we felt the King couldn't hope this any more fervently than we did!

Our Camp now stinks of fish, because many of us are bartering our meagre possessions in exchange for fish, bananas or eggs from the sampan people who are poling their tiny craft up to the barbed wire skirting the Indian Quarters beach, and below the hospital. I watched them from the hospital verandah; it was just like being on a ship anchored in a foreign port – the sampans bobbing up and down close to shore, the boatmen and women grinning and haggling. Mum, in anticipation of us all soon getting new clothes, bartered some of our clothes and rice for bananas, one fish and two crabs!

Rice was still the main basis of our diet but many people no longer needed it so a daily collection of left-over cooked food was made and taken to the Carmelite Convent near our gates for the Sisters to distribute to the needy in the village.

Two little English lads *((James and David Cameron))* on their Irish mother's passport had stayed uninterned in town with her, but she had died during the occupation. Now they were brought into Stanley, and looked half-starved, pale and rickety, and hardly able to believe the food they were now given. It was a good lesson to us, who thought we had been badly fed.

August 20th was a never-to-be-forgotten day! That afternoon, about 100 regular and HK Volunteer pows arrived in the camp. There were wonderful reunions and tears.

Most of the men looked comparatively fit, though some very thin. We girls learned that Arthur, Sid and Topper (our boyfriends) were all sent from Shamshuipo to Japan.

(Much later, we heard that Topper died in Japan, while Arthur and Sid were on the torpedoed 'Lisbon Maru' but survived.)

Every day this week (except today, 24th, when it's extremely typhoony) two more loads of troops have visited. The transport situation is acute – they arrive at all hours, and out of the two conveyances that bring them only one possesses lights, and that only has one solitary headlight; they are said to be driven on alcohol and water. The tales the troops have to tell make us realise once again how lucky we have been in Stanley. About 800 men were lost on the 'Lisbon Maru'. At one time in Shamshuipo four or five people a day were dying of diphtheria. Central blindness, dysentery and electric feet were rife, and in most cases there were no medicines to treat them. The troops surprised us by being so well-dressed, particularly their boots, but apparently these have been saved up for such an occasion, and an issue of clothes was made not so long ago. Some days they have arrived here by launch.

We heard that our camp is known as the 2nd best out here, Shanghai being the best and Burma the worst.

There had been rumours that the pows in Japan had already left for the UK but that is apparently untrue. Civilians from town have reported that some of our Red Cross parcels have been sold, unearthed in tunnels, some dumped in the harbour – no wonder we received so few. Today we had 40 lovely (commercial, not camp-made) siege biscuits issued apiece.

During this week we have also received 25 cubes of Taikoo white sugar apiece, 12 ozs. each of demerara sugar, one third of a tin of evaporated milk each, about one and a quarter ounces of Chase & Sanborn coffee, one and a half oz. Margarine, and 10 packets cigarettes.

My RAMC friend arrived with the troops on 21st. He was pale and his hair looked rather moth-eaten. He brought us small paper pokes of sugar and salt; also a tin of soup and oil!

That evening the first official camp dance was held, dancing having been forbidden by the Japanese. Reg Jenner's band played in front of a large Union Jack across which stood an enormous 'V'. Crowds attended. At 9pm came a great surprise; silence was called for, and a radio was tuned in and we heard our first broadcast from the outside world. It was from America, giving news for Pacific pows and internees. I found it rather depressing – talking of envoys being detained through plane accidents, etc., which to our suspicious minds sounded as if the Japs were up to their old tricks.

From then on we were seeing on our noticeboards daily summaries of news taken from the radio. The Japanese in camp are behaving very well. Many prisoners have been released from the gaol, waving and cheering as they went by in their lorries. Some of our troops who were for some reason delayed at the ferry on their way over here said some Japanese brought them pineapple and bread!

We have learned that there is some trouble over who should have Hong Kong as the Chinese want it as well as the British, but ostrich-like we have pushed that worry into the background.

We are a changed camp. In a week, the very scenery looks more friendly and beautiful. We have meat stew in the rations almost every day, and even that now tastes rather commonplace compared to the corned beef we sometimes have – despite the fact that it's only in the last two months that we've had meat at all, and then only Sundays. Rice is no longer being gobbled. Wong tong (Chinese sugar in bars), once the most treasured of buys from the Black Market, is completely out of date – demerara and cube sugar have replaced it; the dustbins are packed with fish bones, empty tins and banana skins; chatty days are practically over – we have unearthed our much-mended hot plates now the electricity is on again (a chatty is a tiny primitive earthenware 'cooker' fuelled by grass and twigs); the heavy aroma of coffee can often be smelt, and the children seem to be forever chewing sweets.

The events of the day are the arrival and departure of visitors; even those who lost their husbands either during the war or in camps can't resist waiting and watching.

We're not yet out of the wood; but have emerged far enough to have a taste of some of the things we have missed in the gloom of internment, and to look back and see that hard though our trials have been, there are those whose trials and rigours have been 100 times harder. Whatever may be before us, we know we have to thank God for the things that are behind us.

August 24th 1945

(Six days before Admiral Harcourt liberated us.)

---

25 Aug 1945

Typhoony and rain. No POWs from Shamshuipo could come.

Olive in bed with colic. I worked for her in afternoon.

Tomorrow a large Govt. party, including Miss Connie Murray and Nancy Grady (stenographer colleagues) are going into town to work for our officials starting the Govt. in French Mission.

In evening to dance with Peggy and Wendy, one of her sisters.

Mrs Hailstone's (Carmen?) wedding anniversary, she gave us some lovely cake.

26 Aug 1945

News on noticeboard is that supplies will be parachuted into Stanley today.

Pigs came in ration.

Last night Olive was told to see Mr R. R. Todd (of Colonial Secretary's office) today. Olive senior to me in the HK Govt, but she was ill, so I went instead. They want her to work at camp CSO instead of at hospital. I may go instead if Olive isn't better by the time they want her to start.

2 letters from Charles.

Mum and I went to Fr Hessler's talk on 'The Pope's Contribution to World Peace'.

Crowd of admin. staff going into town today. Made birthday present for Peggy.

Mrs M. Hassard died yesterday. Mum & I went to her funeral this evening (Rev. Martin took service).

Mr H. Overy died this morning.

Annie and Ronald Rennie now have a room to themselves. *((Since their wedding they had lived in a corner of the verandah of the Van Der Lely family's room in the Dutch Block: the corner had been made private by piled suitcases etc.))* I smoked a cigarette with her and Abie, then Rennie went on Police duty.

27 Aug 1945

Had instructions to work at camp CSO starting Wed. 29th.

Loads of troops from Shamshuipo came in. Saw Mr Hudson, a neighbour when we Redwoods lived in Naval Terrace.

We had LUMPS of meat – lashings.

Mr. Hall visited us *((our pre-war lodger, a colleague of Dad's who came to stay with us after Dad died, his wife being evacuated to Australia.))* One of his eyes is blind as a result of an operation, which maybe can be fixed up later. He's been working outside his camp quite a lot, and was with Arthur Alsey, Sid Hale and Topper Brown before they went to Japan.

28 Aug 1945

Large crowd of Shamshuipo folk have just come over by launch.

It is Tim Fortescue's birthday as well a Peggy's, she is 22.

We had raw meat issue – a colossal amount, some we fried.

Radio messages say that food and other supplies have been dropped on pow camps in Japan; the pilots report that some of the men were naked *((they were probably wearing just fandushis))*; it's said they are going to be taken by carrier plane to Okinawa first.

Tale that 10% of Shanghai internees have to be hospital cases.

Lord Louis Mountbatten's Order of the Day to troops who have just won back Burma is that they can't be demobilised as so much territory has to be occupied in the Pacific so that places can be cleared up for handing over to the civilians.

Bickley, the blind fellow the VADs (and Mabel) nursed at Military Hospital was brought over and came to visit us.

Spoke to a fellow from Middlesex Regiment who said that Winter was killed in the war. *((Can't remember Winter's Christian name: he was a member of the small literary group I joined in 1940, he was so interested in writing))*.

Pam Pritchard has had a perm and is being married next week.

Mr Gimson is broadcasting Home tonight, and there are to be messages from Home to us.

Peggy and I played bridge with Dick and Philip in evening.

29 Aug 1945

What a day – didn't even get time to write about it (it's 30th now).

A fighter zoomed over us very low several times – frightened me.

Men arrived from Shamshuipo about 11am, Messrs Kirman, Gill and Jenkins – all Naval Dockyard friends of Mum and Dad. Heard that Topper nearly died in Shamshuipo but recovered and was very fit when sent to Japan; he received Olive's cards in Shamshuipo and replied to them. *((But he died in Japan.))*

Also came my Army friends Pat Twitchett, Busty Harris, and Hugill. Rain began to pour down soon after they arrived. *((Pat had been my first boyfriend))*. He's 31 now; said that at one time in camp they all had to shave their heads and remain thus.

About 1.30pm a big plane came over very low, and started dropping parcels by parachute! The best sight in our lives. The plane flew very slowly and carefully above the American Block and the Indian Quarters.

The parcels were pushed out – 13 or 14 in all, we were so excited we lost count; mostly 2 at a time, sometimes 3. The parachutes were enormous, and billowed and swayed gracefully – several white ones, two shades of green, and one scarlet one.

One landed on American Block roof, one in front of the Mosque, and one on Block 13 roof, and several on the white cross on the Indian Quarters green.

One parachute didn't open, its parcel hit the Dutch Block corner (the de Vleeschouwers' room) and most of its contents were smashed... a yard one way and it would have fallen on the roof where crowds of people were gathered.

The parcels were big tin canisters, greenish like steel cabinets; mostly contained medical supplies, but also cigarettes, sweets and chocolate. When all parcels were dropped, the plane came back again 3 times, flying even lower than before, almost hedge-hopping over the Indian Quarters, and hardly any higher than we were *((on Married Quarters plateau))*. The side door was open and a fellow standing up there looking as if he might fall out any minute. It was so rainy and dull that we were surprised the plane came.

Later, we were issued with 'fandushis' (for underpants), matches & cigarettes, and toilet paper.

I had to rush off at 2 o'clock to work at CSO (in Block 2 of Married Q.), so nice to use a decent typewriter again *((the ones in the hospital office were ancient and the keys were inclined to stick.))*

The parachutes were brought in – glorious-looking things.

The boys in the office said they heard Mr Gimson's broadcast Home very plainly, and that he represented the situation here well, saying we want some sort of reassurance from the Allies. We certainly got it today! Had tea with the boys in office – they provided the cake.

In afternoon, the Fleet came into sight – some of it anyway. I couldn't see anything but specks against the hills.

Later, Peggy Barton and I helped Audrey Barton, 19, and Irene Drewery (12) take cooked rice to the Carmelite Convent (a little way beyond camp gate). It was in a container on a make-do two-wheeled cart, we had to bend down to push it along. (Father Hessler and other men brought the heavier loads of food). It was quite a long way. The Convent was lovely – red, waxy-looking tiles, sweet Sisters in black and brown; 14 or 15 little Chinese girl orphans playing around. Chapel peaceful, the orphans went in and said their night prayers (in Chinese), then to the little room where they eat, sleep and play; it had French windows opening on to a small garden; there was little furniture – 2 large cupboards, a few shelves. All the little pairs of shoes lined one shelf; all the little tin plates on top of one of the cupboards. The only light was a small blackout bulb. They sat and slept on wooden boards on trestles, no pillows. There was a Shanghai tub in another room. Most of the children were very thin; 2 had their hair shaved off, the youngest were 5 or 6 years old. One very sickly little soul called Rosa was almost transparently thin, she wouldn't smile at us. They all – except Rosa – were sucking meat bones with great relish.

We were marooned there for some time because rain coming down in torrents. Came home about 8pm, Father Hessler looking like a typical American lad, in ordinary clothes, his long-trouser-legs rolled up, and a sack over his head.

Back home, Mr. Kelly there with food he'd brought from town – real bread, cake, jam, sweets... arrangements had been made to have a birthday party for Mabel on 30th.

Dick Cloake called, Olive and I and Elliott Purves went with him to Dick's billet for a little party. Dick gave me a little taste of some rather nice wine.

30 Aug 1945

11am: Mabel's 22nd birthday, and Mary Taylor's 27th.

Tens of planes have been over all the morning, some of them zooming frighteningly. Fleet movements have been seen on the horizon.

19 heavy planes have just flown over us, and most people are up on the roof because they say the Fleet can be seen entering Lye Mun, but I can't see (well enough) so no good going.

7pm: Here I am sitting on the 4th floor of the French Mission, overlooking St John's Cathedral!

At 2pm Miss Grace Ezra (Govt. stenographer) came and told me to be ready to go to town at 5pm to work with Secretariat there. (As I write this, I can hear someone's radio playing V for Victory Symphony.) Brian Baxter (from Shamshuipo camp, a Naval Dockyard employee) was visiting us. I rushed round to see Father Hessler who gave me a blessing. Peggy Barton was running round me all the time, helping. Mum and Mabel did the packing. (Olive still not well).

Family helped carry my folded camp bed and meagre belongings down to the Ration Dump where transport was supposed to come, but when we arrived, the transport had apparently left! While I waited, hoping another transport would arrive, family brought along my share of Mabel's birthday party planned for evening, and I ate it sitting on my suitcase at the roadside.

Planes were zooming about, then a car drove through the gate, and out stepped the civil servant who was acting camp commandant now that Mr Gimson was in town (I think he was our Commissioner of Prisons).

'The Admiral will be here in a few minutes,' he called out, 'Tell everyone to assemble outside the CSO!'

Everyone in hearing rushed off with the glad tidings, everyone but me, I dared not move from the spot in case my transport arrived. People came running from all directions to get a vantage point outside Block 2, I felt so frustrated that I couldn't join them.

Then in came two cars, the first contained Admiral Harcourt in full fig, and Mr Gimson (who is now Governor.) Then some marines on small amphibians all looking so huge and healthy, their white starched uniforms gleaming, and their faces so pink that it looked as if they were wearing makeup.

Now I threw duty to the winds and dashed up the road to join the crowds. The Admiral made a short speech, short he said because he had to get to other places in the Far East. The National Anthem was sung as the flags were raised.

The Admiral and his retinue drove off and I went back to my station near the gate where I had left my luggage, and found several more government servants waiting for transport, which turned out to be an ancient bus with no glass in the windows, and holes in the wooden floor. As it drove us away from Stanley through puddles, water splashed up between the floor boards.

Among the passengers were 2 Eurasian teenage stepsons of Mrs. K. Rosselet, an ANS friend of Mum's. They had not been interned but had today been visiting their stepmother. Stubbs Road in an awful mess. The Gap Road flats *((where we Redwoods had lived until the Jap. attack))* had been bombed. Japanese were visible in Wellington Barracks (Queen's Road). British sailors were in Naval Dockyard barracks, throwing cigarettes down to Chinese children. We all waved frantically.

The bus stopped at the steps up to Battery Path opposite HS Bank. The Rosselet boys carried my bed and luggage up the path to the French Mission. This building had now been commandeered for Government quarters and offices. *((It was outside this French Mission during the fighting that I had been waylaid by an Irish priest who was asking all who passed by if they were RC, and offering Confession and Holy Communion in the building. I had joined a short Confession queue on the ground floor.))*

Now I was directed to the top floor. The two Rosselets kindly carried my luggage up to a room already occupied by Mrs. D. Mathias, Nan Grady and Barbara Budden, all Govt. employees.

We had dinner downstairs, served by Boys! Lovely, comfortable chairs with arms; flowers on table; soup, mashed potato, hamburger, fried eggplant. Sweet course I couldn't face, but had room for coffee with milk and sugar.

Listened to radio at 10.30pm, hearing Charles Moorad of U.S. broadcasting from Hong Kong – rather frightening perhaps to families in the UK: "You can recognise an internee a block away," i.e. gaunt appearance, sunken eyes etc. *((We didn't think we looked like that!))*

There's a huge Japanese shrine on the Peak.

Tim Fortescue broadcast 'Good Night' on radio.

31 Aug 1945

Slept fitfully, heard the bugle call from Naval Dockyard.

Glorious day, planes about, and 3 Chinese are doing shadow boxing in Cathedral porch. The trams are making their old creaking noises.

Have upset tummy, praying it won't continue lest I get sent back to camp again. Sent my sugar ration to Mum in camp last night by Joan Walkden who with Lorraine Money had been over to Shamshuipo camp (I don't need it here!)

Lovely breakfast!

((I wrote the following to my Mother in Stanley.))

> 'Nonchalantly we read the daily paper while waiting to be served. Who said that congee tastes like porridge? I honestly didn't recognise porridge when it appeared, with milk and sugar ad lib. We also had pineapple, then a fried corned beef cake, with a few chips; there was bread and butter and jam ad lib, but I'm going easy on everything, because I don't want to upset my tummy and be sent back to Stanley! Being served is wonderful, there are boys even to light one's cigarette, if one smoked; I almost wished I did, just for the luxury of being thus waited on.
>
> Had you forgotten that cups of tea and coffee usually sit on saucers? I had! And honestly, I couldn't think what to do with a serviette when I saw one sitting on the table in front of me – then I remembered. A boy has just come round the office (it's 11am) serving coffee, but all I fancy is a drink of water, as I'm getting up an appetite for tiffin. We can have tea and cake in the afternoon, dinner is between 7 and 8pm.
>
> The Japanese gendarmes are still keeping law and order. We are quite safe here, and sleep on the very top floor of the French Mission. The fan is going in the office, and it just seems as if we've never had to shift for things the way we did at Stanley. The luxuries of the meals are just too too lovely – last night when first I sat down to dinner, I was almost afraid to take the first spoonful

of creamed asparagus soup with crackly toasted bread bits inside, because that is usually the stage in dreams at which one wakes up. Would you believe it, I couldn't even touch the sweet, which was pineapple on pastry, and my coffee I couldn't finish because it was too sweet.

Tonight at tiffin time we had peanuts on plates to nibble between courses – only about Military Yen 1,000-worth every two yards down the two long tables!

Just received your note. I hope we do all go to Australia, as you suggest, but haven't really much hope that Olive and I will get away with the rest of you (so busy). Anyway, maybe we won't be very long after you. So funny to hear trams groaning past, and dogs barking etc. But the best sight of all is the Fleet anchored out in the stream.

Mabel was right, I don't need my plate and spoon and mug, and will try to send them in to you. Planes are zooming over us all day long. I'm working in particular for Mr. Megarry, but we stenos are all apt to have any work shot at us by anyone who comes in.

Did I leave the nut from my camp bed at home? One is missing – it's the bit that goes on the end of the screw securing the legs. If you find it, perhaps you'd send it.

I learned that the hospital ship is leaving tomorrow and am all agog to know whether you and Mabel are to go too. We can't ring Stanley unless they ring us.'

Took dictation from Mr C. Perdue (Commissioner of Police) and Mr T. Megarry (Secretariat). Eyes are sore.

Dorothy Holloway arrived from camp but rooming at Hong Kong Hotel, whither Nan Grady, Barbara Budden and I visited her this evening. Rather eerie going out at night. We had an escort back. *((Can't remember who that was.))*

Just received your letter and glad to hear you managed to be in the lime-light for the photos - however did you manage it? Or were they taking practically everyone?

I've just come back from a shopping expedition with ncy. The only thing I bought was a tin of Dutch Baby milk, which I'm sendi ither tonight or tomorrow. It cost Y.100, I was given that as an advance, id it won't buy anything I really need, like pants. Actually, I think I can manage for clothes, as someone said we were assured that plenty of clothes will be arriving, women's underwear included. We went into the Asia Company, which haven't very much stock, it is mostly a restaurant. If there's anything you would like me to try and get there, let me know; they will let us sign for anything. Prices seem to be coming down a little, if anything. In another shop I priced a tin of pears, they were Y.300! Pineapples are 50 yen, and bananas fairly reasonable. Tins of Del Monte salmon are 300 Yen. We didn't get time to go to Shiu Tai, but if you let me know if you want me to try to get anything in particular, I will visit them when next we go out. Saw NO cheese!

While we were in the Asia Coy (where a Russian woman seems to be in charge) a voice hailed us, and seated at a table were Mr. Allan, Mr. Ebbage and two friends. They made us sit down with them, and we had ICE CREAM! It was delicious; then a glass of cider, complete with gas. Mr. Allan is moving in to the Dockyard tomorrow and has promised to scrounge me some magazines. I'm dying to see photos of Shirley and Deanna, etc. With Mr. Allan was a R.Scots fellow called Campbell, and I asked him about Alsey. He says that on the casualty lists of the Lisbon Maru were two names Allison, but as there weren't two Allisons on board, they think one may be meant to be Alsey, as it is so near. He has promised to let us know if he can find out anything definite. He is going to tell Mr. Allan who will relay the news either to me or to you. If he writes and tells you that Arthur is definitely lost, don't go trying to pretend he isn't, because although I mind, 3 years is such a long time that our time together only seems like a dream, and I've never placed very great hopes on his having survived, as so many of them have gone.

Did you get the chocolate all right? And if so, wasn't it nice? If you haven't received it, go and see Tony Sanh, as he promised to deliver it, but was probably very loaded up with parcels and messages and may have forgotten.

Mr. Ebbage is going to try to have alook at his flat soon and I've asked him to take a whip round ours while he is there. He says that the other day they picked up a morse signal from Captain Ottway (whom I don't know) but who is apparently Royal Engineers and who went away with the draft in which Topper was included. Ottway said they were all well and safe and sound.

The funny thing about town is the lack of traffic, especially buses; a few stray crackers are being let off from time to time; not many people about, but quite a number of troops, Shamshuipo and otherwise, are about.

I saw Mr. Mottram this morning, but neither Kelly nor Clif. I espect they will roll in here some time - nearly everybody seems to appear sooner or later. 3 of the Nurses off the Hospital ship had dinner with us, and were very interested to know how we had been treated. They looked so fresh and well-covered.

I hope this will catch an evening delivery, if any, so will conclude for time being. Any parachute issues yet? Don't forget to keep my letters, please - I'm relying on them for diary which is rather neglected these days. I've managed to scrounge a copy of yesterday's and today's newspapers and mean to hang on to themif possible.

My love to you all, and God bless,

Yours in haste,

Barb.

P.S. Send replies in the big envelope I sent you - we can use it for some time then.

I was taken to town on 30th August 1945 to work with the Secretariat there. This is the letter I wrote to family in Stanley the next day.

1 Sep 1945

Worked busily in morning. *((The large room on the ground floor of the French Mission became the general office, where we girls typed among telephones and noisy comings and goings of various Govt. people who were working there too. Some of the rooms on the first floor were offices for our bosses. The top-floor rooms served as billets for us staff)).*

A relieving forces fellow (Yeoman of Signals) presented us with two 4oz packets chocolate each. Sent one packet into family via Tony Sanh.

Letter from Olive saying she's been sent to work at camp hospital again, and that some internees have been in movies which are taken at Stanley.

In afternoon, shopping with Nancy. We bought Dutch Baby Milk (Yen 100). In Asia Company *((in Des Voeux Road, our family's pre-war compradore, i.e. grocer))* met Mr. A. B. Allan and Mr Ebbage. Mr. Allan (Naval Dockyard, a great buddie of my Dad's) insisted we had an ice cream and a glass of cider with him. Also at table was Mr Campbell of Royal Scots, he said it's feared that Arthur Alsey may have been lost on the 'Lisbon Maru' *((we learned later that he was rescued))*.

Letter from Mum saying that 66 folk are going on the hospital ship from Stanley, she is lying off jetty.

((The following is from a letter I sent to my Mother:-))

> 'Mr Allan is moving into the Dockyard tomorrow and has promised to scrounge me some film magazines. Did you get the chocolate I sent, and if so, wasn't it nice? The funny thing about town is the lack of traffic, especially buses. A few stray crackers are being let off from time to time; not many Chinese people about, but quite a number of troops, ex pows.'

2 Sep 1945

(Sunday) Got up early and went to St Joseph's Church (Garden Road) but it appeared to be closed, not even any handles on the doors. Went round back to Grotto, Our Lady's statue still there and OK.

Knelt on the marble prie-dieu but there were mosquitoes and ants so couldn't concentrate. There met a man in military uniform, Mr. Sherry (I didn't know him), he said Mass would be at 8.30am but I couldn't stay as due in office.

Very busy in office, even though Norah Witchell from camp is also helping. The phones ringing continuously and one is forever dashing up and downstairs trying to find people.

Bottle of milk each at tiffin and dinner.

Mary Taylor arrived last night and working with Police Dept.

Eric Himsworth is Food Controller and dashed in to get someone (me) to type something, just as I received a note from Olive pleading 'try to get me out of this dump.' I asked Himsworth if he had a steno, and he hadn't, so he dictated to me a note to Stanley requesting Olive to come and work for him.

Hospital ship 'Oxfordshire' is at Kowloon.

Was given a tablet of soap today.

Our office is moving to Hong Kong Bank building tomorrow.

Surrender signed in Japan today.

3 Sep 1945

Started work on first floor of HK. Bank Building, and this morning scrounged this book (a thin black notebook with headings in Chinese characters; it became my diary).

Olive arrived on the morning bus from Stanley, sleeping and eating at Gloucester Hotel. She says Stanley meals very poor.

The Oxfordshire left Kowloon Wharf but hasn't departed for good yet.

Things much easier in office as we typists have a room to ourselves, and only one telephone.

Mr T. Megarry's office next to ours (I was working for him).

Olive and I in evening went to Asia Company and had ice cream and cider. It was good! Cost us Yen 160 each; also bought 1 lb bread which, with some chocolate we were given, we sent to Stanley for Mum and Mabel, via George Watt (Police) whom we met there.

A sailor was accidentally injured at Stanley, operated upon, and died last night.

Tony Cole is now at French Mission, driving for H.E. the Governor.

After dinner, Barbara B and I went for a walk down Garden Road, by Cricket Club and Naval Yard, along waterfront up Pedder Street. I wasn't very happy, it was getting dark and there was much cracker-firing. Chinese flags out. Roads in bad state, and great stones and piles of earth in the fairway.

4 Sep 1945

'Empress of Australia' arrived in, with 3,000 RAF troops, also another hospital ship.

We town girls received each two 4 oz packets of Cadbury's milk choc, and a pkt of 20 Craven A cigs from parachute supplies from Stanley. And someone came in office with 4 dozen 2 oz. pkts of Nielson's choc, we had 6 each.

Visited Olive's quarters after work, then she came to see mine.

After dinner, Nan (Grady), Barbara B and I walked via CSO to Government House, which has been partly rebuilt, redecorated and furnished, massive armchairs and sofas. Really lovely, except for a strange tower on the top.

One part upstairs has been rebuilt as a Japanese residence: a little wooden springboard for taking off gitas and leaving them, then up to a wooden flooring which had some sort of soft material on as well, covered with straw matting; ceilings very low, room divided into partitions by sliding screens covered with traditional paper; small alcoves, a very low wooden table, and small cushioned stools.

Bathroom queer, the bath built-in, but wooden, with a little seat, like a boat.

There was also a little shrine; the floor was sandy and earthy and stony with big stones strewn here and there; a minute pool no bigger than the page of this book, and a kind of confessional and little temple, complete with roof. Mr. S. Marvin showed us round. *((Barbara B had a particular interest in Government House, as she had worked there for H.E. (Governor) pre-war.))*

Pam Turnbull married R. Sleap.

EXTRACT FROM LETTER of 4th September from me to my Mother still in Stanley:

> 'Hope you enjoyed the bread and butter and choc. we sent. Olive and I have decided to draw a certain sum of Yen each and buy food right away to send you. I can get you a jar of pickles for 50 Yen...
>
> Both Olive and I are coatless – what happens in wet weather I don't know. *((We had left them in the camp))*.
>
> Things are rapidly becoming organised, but most of the men are pretty tired, working very hard, with very little rest, and so many of them aren't fit to do so. Three weeks ago, we would never have believed it possible to do so much in present conditions.
>
> I'm feeling in fine fettle. Judging by my white skirt I think I've put on a little weight. Things aren't nearly so hectic now, as in the new offices (HK Bank) we have a typing room to ourselves, with only one phone, whereas in the French Mission, a large number of staff shared one big room and we were always having to answer the phones and chase up and down stairs trying to find people we didn't know...
>
> Our meals have been getting slightly more substantial these last few days, tho we're getting blasé enough to say 'corned beef again!' as if it was rice and stew...
>
> The Chinese are still celebrating with fire-crackers; more and more shops are getting ready to open, by sticking a cardboard notice on their shutters or in the window, with their name. It's intriguing to see things becoming more and more normal every day...
>
> Still haven't had a hot bath, our ambition is to dine on one of the ships and see their movies – some of our men have done this...
>
> I enclose a piece of paper for reply – don't use it for bridge scores!

Did I leave the nut from my camp bed at home? One is missing, it's the bit that goes on the end of the screw securing the legs.'

((Imagine calling 'Stanley' home!!))

5 Sep 1945

Peggy Barton arrived today and is to work for Medical Department pro tem.

Eileen Grant's American boyfriend *((F.N. Merritt junior))* who was repatriated in 1942 has re-appeared... swept into camp in the middle of her engagement party to Lewin Benn *((who'd been in Shamshuipo Camp))*. Now Eileen and Merritt are engaged.

Clifton appeared in office looking very nice in white shorts and shirt *((his camp wear was usually just khaki shorts as in the photo of him grinding rice with another internee))*. He brought me things from Stanley.

Olive acquired a lot of umbrellas from her office, we have been dishing them out to all and sundry, sent 2 to Mum and Mabel. Peg & I went to Asia after office, had cider and ice-cream. Lots of fleet there, also Mr. Pine and Mr. Hurst, dockyard colleagues of my Dad (they'd been in Shamshuipo) and had more ice-creams each, with them, the men had beer; great to see Mr Pine tucking into a plate of steak and onions and chips.

The Fleet men are big and pink and fresh, clothes beautifully white. One large Irishman kept saying 'Shucks!' every time we tried to explain how difficult it would be for us to come on board his hospital ship which is said to be the finest-fitted hospital ship in the world.

The Asia Co. has now acquired a gramophone; the atmosphere was as on the films – amid loud chatter, Chinese boys dashing around, serving, sailors everywhere, clatter of plates etc. from kitchen; different flags displayed inside the entrance to the shop.

Peggy and I then went to Olive's room (in hotel); she had acquired in her office, shoes, lovely housecoats, hankies, diaries! Haven't eaten any choc today (except Una's fudge) – mouth still sore.

6 Sep 1945

Went to Stanley on lorry. Olive came for a quick visit. I stayed overnight. Camp seemed very changed. Empty hooch bottles stacked up in yard. Many people have changed billets *((due to vacancies caused by internees going into town to work))*. There were even some camp additions.

Mum & Mabel had issues of bread, 3 tins milk, tin lambs' tongues, fresh butter, oats etc. – wallowing in food.

Mrs Large (Clifton's mother) gave me a dress – nice of her.

Mum, Mabel & I went to P.O. Club where men of 'Kempenfelt' *((HMS Kempenfelt, one of the ships that came in with the Fleet))* gave a cinema show – 'Shine on Harvest Moon' – our first films since December 1941, apart from a short Jap propaganda one in 1942. *((The show was held in the Central Recreation Club, also called the Prison Officers' Club, in Stanley.))*

Slept on Olive's camp bed.

7 Sep 1945

Got bus from Stanley, at 8.30am, came round Shaukiwan way. Much damage, a lot due to looting, the structure of the buildings seeming intact but insides were bare. I was dumped outside HK & Shanghai Bank where I left most of my luggage.

Very busy at work, didn't leave till 6. Went to Olive's room and acquired knitting wool, scent and books.

We girls have now acquired a wash amah, Ah Kit, who met me coming up Battery Path steps and insisted on carrying my case.

In evening with Nan Grady and others to cinema show at Hong Kong Hotel – 'Three Comrades' – a terrible choice. We thought everyone in film looked too fat.

Peggy had a perm today. *((No hairdressing salons in Stanley!!))*

Curfew is now 10pm instead of 9pm. We girls had lemon squash with Jim Johnson, Bicky (B.I. Bickford), Max Bickerton. Jim Johnson told us the story of the cat-catchers in Stanley.

8 Sep 1945

Mum came in from Stanley, up to my office. She looked very nice in blue and white dress (from some unknown source), and hollows in her face seem to have filled in already.)

Pears for breakfast, and lovely cold meat for tiffin, and pasty for dinner.

The new administration arrived (Brigadier MacDougall.)

Mum visited Naval Dockyard and Naval Terrace. *((Naval Terrace was an enclosed block of six lovely flats (ground, first and second floor) adjoining the Naval Dockyard, the entrance being in Queen's Road. All occupied by key Dockyard personnel who needed to be near the Dockyard. My Dad had been Superintending Electrical Engineer. We had a ground-floor flat, spacious rooms, verandahs on each side. Lovely garden all around, with trees – and a hard tennis court. There was a door in the wall through which employees could walk into the dockyard, but we used the main door which opened on to Queen's Road. Every night a Dockyard Policeman (Indian I think) used to patrol round our flats. We had lived there until Dad died)).*

Barbara B. & I to hotel, met Mum and Olive, then to King's Theatre, free show. Saw 'The Lodger' and new Gaumont British News, retaking of Rangoon etc; had a glimpse of Princess Elizabeth.

Mum staying overnight with Olive. Mum and Mabel may be off on the Empress of Australia.

Had a sort of medical exam today – I was put down 'to leave HKong early' (i.e., not immediate or delayed).

9 Sep 1945

To St Joseph's, plus Mum and Olive. Very few people there. Revolver shots nearby while in church.

To work, busy; Megarry said I could have afternoon off, so collected Mum and Olive, we had tiffin at Olive's hotel.

Then Mum and I trammed to Happy Valley, but had to walk from Tin Lok Lane. There's an overgrown shelter/pillbox beside ARP School & HQ (my old office.) *((I can't remember anything more about the overgrown 'shelter' or 'pillbox' beside the ARP School. At one time post-war it was Harcourt Health Centre.))*

Went to No. 19 Gap Road, our pre-war flat. Stairs in very bad state, no wood on them. No door on our flat, the floors completely bare – and empty. The only recognizable thing was a dead plant lying on verandah, minus pot.

Some of next door's front windows were dangling into our verandah, a bomb must have caught that flat.

In the bedrooms there were odds and ends of broken glass; a few books in Chinese writing, and 2 lampshades, one of which we think was ours. No woodwork of any kind – no partition, no cupboard door, no lavatory, but the bath was there; the remains of the lav. cistern was lying in our bedroom (Mabel's and mine). Many bricks lying in bathroom. There was nothing to show that Mum, Olive, Mabel and I had once lived in that flat.

A well-spoken Indian, who was a sort of caretaker living downstairs, came up and very pleasant.

Mum & I went to cemetery, very overgrown but undamaged except for the top area where parts of some crosses are buried in rubble – either a landslide or else been blasted. Dad's grave all right. We couldn't find Mr Cole's grave (George Cole of Naval Yard, killed during the fighting at Aberdeen), the area where it might have been was very much overgrown.

We trammed to Asia Co., had ice cream and cider, I left Mum at hotel (for bus) and returned to office... where Eileen Grant and husband (!) rolled up for registration of their marriage, which had just taken place at Wah Yan College Chapel. She looked very lovely, with a perm, large picture hat, and powder blue georgette dress, with corsage. Klaus and Lundy (friends of Grant family), and Eileen's sister Kay and mother Mrs Grant were in attendance.

Peggy, Tony and I had lemonade at Canadian Cafe; one of the relieving forces there asked Tony if he was from Stanley, did he know J. Joyce (which we did); it transpired that he was a young brother of J.J., on the

'San Feugh', had been here 5 days but hadn't yet got in contact with him.

Mrs M. Budden found family photographs in her pre-war flat.

10 Sep 1945

After work, got air-line bus to Stanley. *((The air-line bus was obviously a cut above the old Vulcan orange buses but can't recall anything more about it.))* Arrived in camp about 6.30pm, saw Clifton who was also visiting, he said Mum and Mabel had embarked about 3pm. No sign of E. of Australia, apparently anchored very far out – could only see corvettes and launches.

Margery Fortescue and Adrian are in 'our' room (Tim in town). Picked up remainder of my camp possessions.

Had a lift back to town on a Volunteer lorry; was dumped at foot of Garden Road. *((I knew there was a film show at Queen's Theatre.))* Left my luggage with a surprised sentry outside HK & S. Bank, rushed to theatre, saw 'When Irish Eyes Are Smiling' – (technicolour). Mr J.A. Bendall came part way back with me and collected my luggage from sentry.

Afterward, to Mrs. Budden's birthday party (French Mission) – Xmas pudding from tin, and tomato sandwiches... lovely.

11 Sep 1945

Father Xmas came to us – comfort parcels. We girls each received one, full of the most lovely things: knitting wool & needles & pattern; S.T.s, writing pad & envelopes; Johnsons baby powder, cold cream, box with darning wool, cotton, safety pins, deodorant, adhesive plaster, lipstick, face flannel, comb, real toilet paper, hairnet, hairbrush, soap, mirror, face towel, toothpaste and brush; hair brush; sunglasses, pencil, bandage, tape, thimble – all really thrilling. *((None of those items had been supplied to us in Stanley!))* Also an envelope with a lucky number we were supposed to keep – competition to expire 28th February 1943!

A Miss Archangelsky is working with us at present.

In afternoon Mr Megarry asked me to do some work for Colonel Strickland, for which I had to go to the rather deserted Supreme Court, first floor, my typewriter following me carried by a coolie.

Shots were going off periodically.

Out on the Cricket Club ground (opposite Supreme Court) the Navy & Army were playing cricket. As dusk began to fall, the men disappeared and sounds of 'The Maiden's Prayer' was tinkled out, presumably on piano in the pavilion.

Left Supreme Court just before 8pm, went to Canadian Cafe, which was lit only with an oil lamp. Two or 3 'relieving forces' were trying to balance a debt for a bottle or brandy with 5 Yen and 25 gold cents; I was very happy to provide the extra Yen 75. Had a quick cider.

11 Sep 1945

((An extract from a letter dated 11 Sep 1945 that I wrote to a friend in the UK. Many years later they handed the letters back to me.))

> 'So far we have had no inward mail and are longing for same. Yesterday, Mum and Mabel embarked on the 'Empress of Australia', but their destination is at present unknown, they aim eventually to get to England. I didn't see them on board because they boarded from Stanley. I'm very glad they have got away because, although we expect to follow in a few weeks, there's always the possibility of a hitch, and Olive and I wanted to be sure that Mum and Mabel got out of this place soon. The bunch who left yesterday were told they would be maintained in England or Australia, wherever they wanted to go, and that their passage back to HK in due course would be guaranteed. At present, I'm quite prepared to leave the East for ever!
>
> It's much hotter in town than in Stanley, and we are feeling the heat pretty badly, with all the unaccustomed running about (between offices). Some 700 ex-internees are working in town – mostly men, Government servants and essential services. Some

650 women and children had cabin accommodation on the E. of A., and a few hundreds of Stanley men were given deck accommodation; all the ex-pows from the men's camps are also aboard in deck accommodation.

Last night we saw our first fairly up-to-date film; it was 'When Irish Eyes are Smiling', and our only regret was that it wasn't in modern costume; of all the films we have been shown this past week not one has been a modern one... we are dying to see what the world of today looks like, fashions, etc. At present we feel like country cousins; you should have seen us all stare and exclaim the other night when one of the relieving forces produced a perfectly ordinary cigarette lighter! Some of our makeshifts would make you laugh. I suppose things have been pretty short in England during the war, but I wonder if the school children had to rely on cigarette papers on which to do their home and school work? Our men have had to cut grass sometimes to get fuel with which to cook our rations. Life at Stanley was so communal that there was even a communal coffin, a huge affair with a false bottom, so that each corpse would be carried therein to the cemetery, the coffin lowered into the grave, the false bottom removed by a fixed rope, and returned for the next victim.

A couple of days ago, Mum came in to visit us from Stanley (about half an hour's journey by road from town) and we ventured to our old flat in Happy Valley. That block of flats had been bombed fairly recently, ours was knocked about but not too broken except for a pile of bricks in the bathroom. No wood in the flat at all, even the staircase had been bereft of wood. No doors or cupboards, the whole place was absolutely bare; only things left were an old plant, out of its pot, which was lying on the verandah, two old lampshades on the floor. The bath remained, although the lavatory had vanished, and the cistern, broken, was on the floor of one of the bedrooms. I looked among little heaps of rubbish for papers or something that looked like home, but such papers there were in Chinese. If there had been one thing that reminded us of home, I think we would have wept, but the absolute lack of reminders made it seem impossible that it was once our home. We also visited Dad's grave, the tombstone was OK.

Life is rapidly getting back to normal; many people have had perms in the last week, but my hair is too short for one at present. We had swimming at Stanley – a lovely beach, but it was such a drag there and back, we hadn't much energy to go there very much, and the whole experience of wallowing in the water or swimming – though fantastic – gave us too much of an appetite which couldn't be satisfied on rice and greens. Still it seems too much to realise that we are really free and can eat decent food; I'm only sorry that I can't eat all we are offered, my stomach seems to have shrunk; it breaks my heart to have to refuse food or leave anything on the plate, after the many dreams of food we have had.

We still have had no news of or from the boys *((soldiers))* we knew pre-Dec. 8th, we thought some of them were sent to Japan.

Things have happened so quickly – it is only a month ago since we were all in a flap in camp because the Japs sent for 170 technicians and their families and sent them off to an unknown destination, later proved to be Kowloon. That was the first sign we had that something might be happening, though we had no idea what; coincident with that was the rumour that Russia had come into the war. On the 14th August the rumours that the war with Japan was over seemed contradicted, because a plane zoomed down very near Stanley and sank a couple of small ships – so the news of the 15th was doubly surprising... we can still hardly believe it! Please excuse incoherence, I think all internees and pows are slightly mental in some way or another, we have poor memories and repeat ourselves, and find life very, very sweet after so much seclusion and restriction.'

12 Sep 1945

Worked all day for Col. Strickland. Went to Canadian Cafe for cider at 12.30, then bought note books at China Products, now have a new plot book.

We are to receive Red Cross clothing.

Lovely meals – apricots, sausage, pork etc.

Invitation for HMS Vindex tomorrow, and Swiftsure on Saturday.

There's supposed to be a ship leaving Saturday, I bet I'm on it! Want to be.

13 Sep 1945

Saw 'Coney Island' at Queen's, in technicolour, really lovely.

The weekend boats (if any) are for Australia.

Still working at Supreme Court, and finished too late to go on HMS Vindex.

We girls (stenos) have put our names down for the next boat, I hope it's soon because am feeling very weary and ready to go from this rather uncertain atmosphere.

Mr Gimson is leaving by plane at weekend.

14 Sep 1945

New currency started. Newspaper free this morning because Yen were obsolete and HK dollars weren't available first thing. Tonight I received HK$200.

Now moved into office with clerk at Supreme Court. Furious rain and an ugly storm in morning.

HMS Duke of York is in harbour now, very near and large.

Olive had good time on Vindex last night, they came home in a Jeep. *((The Jeep, developed while we were interned, was new to us!))*

15 Sep 1945

Not feeling well in evening.

Got Australian Red Cross clothing – a set of everything,very nice.

16 Sep 1945

(Sunday) To Mass at St. Joseph's, also Confession, Holy Communion and Benediction. Then went shopping, bought a dress-length *((enough material to make a dress))*, then went to work.

Was released about 3pm but couldn't get out (of Supreme Court) because the road between Queen's Pier and Government House lined with sailors and soldiers because it was Signing of Surrender ceremony. Went up on verandahs and watched it all from there with Mr. Castilho, the clerk.

The sailors looked very clean in white shorts and bibs; an Air Force Pipe Band and a Military Band. The ships in harbour fired noisy salutes, 3 planes roared across the tram wires.

When I eventually came out, passed the Jap delegates, uniformed, coming away in their car; they looked stony-faced.

I was whisked to Stanley and back by Clifton (in car) and George Saunders after 5pm. Had some food with the Larges (Clifton's parents were still in camp.)

Olive, Peg Barton and her sister Marie went on HMS Swiftsure yesterday, and Indomitable at tiffin time. Fireworks, rockets, lights etc. in whites and reds and greens from Dockyard and ships at night. We were all up on roof (of French Mission) watching.

17 Sep 1945

Couldn't eat much (not feeling well).

F. Gimson, B. Bickford, Mrs. Hardie, Mr. & Mrs R. Minnitt, Max Bickerton & others left by plane for UK. Tony Cole and Jim Johnson sailed on 'Vindex' to Australia. Hope it's our turn next.

Went to Bank to draw $200 – so glad it was there (and had been all during internment).

Went to see Dr J. Selby who is dosing me for worms.

Olive & Peggy & I went to Queen's and saw 'The Way Ahead' – it was inspiring, even though I am a sort of pacifist.

18 Sep 1945

Ate a little, I am in the middle of worm treatment – castor oil last night, and Santonin this evening.

Still working at Supreme Court. Bought hair curlers. Dorothy Kennard etc. left for UK today. A plane came down and lost mail from Australia.

19 Sep 1945

Feeling miserable, general neuralgia through a cold; unhungry. No worms.

There are ships leaving this weekend probably. Dying to go. A new clerk – Lee Wing Kit – appeared in the office, he is a steno, and Miss Grace Ezra is coming in from Stanley and doesn't want to leave HK till Spring, so that simplifies my departure.

Olive and I went to Dairy Farm for mineral, met there Miss McLellan, Miss Brett (nurses), Doctors Alan Barwell and Mark Erooga, and Mr Skinner.

Still no one knows where the Empress of Australia is.

20 Sep 1945

This morning before going to Supreme Court, I went to see Dick Maynard to make sure he had us down for as early as possible departure, then to work.

On arrival at French Mission for tiffin, Nan Grady said 'Have you heard? We're going on the 'Smiter' tomorrow.' I thought she meant just for a social visit – but it means sailing!!! Later, departure delayed to the 22nd, but I've left work, having handed over this afternoon to Grace Ezra, got away at 4pm.

Olive doesn't want to go on Smiter *((she was having too good a time these days!))* but will go.

Went shopping and had hair cut.

Clifton and parents are also down for this ship.

22 Sep 1945

REPATRIATION DAY.

(Diary was packed last night (21st) so couldn't write anything then. Went shopping.)

Had a cable from Aunt Lily, she had received ours, thank God she is still alive.

Assembled at Queen's Pier at 9.30am, launch to 'Smiter' which is out in mid-stream. Assembled on hangar deck.

Olive and I have the Paymaster's cabin (one bunk and one camp bed), everything pale green. Most of the Nursing Sisters (all from Tweed Bay Hosp) are in bunk layers of 4 on the Mess Deck. Olive has given her bunk to Miss E. Riley *((aged 52, we thought of her as elderly!))*, Olive will sleep on camp bed, and I've taken Miss Riley's stretcher (the topmost of the 4) on the Mess Deck, very near the ceiling.

So far we are supposed to be going to Trincomalee (Ceylon), about 6-7 days, then transhipping.

The Stanley folk came round in a minesweeper.

We have to climb over enormous steps every section of below decks; the bathroom queue is reminiscent of Stanley – no time for baths. We had a lovely meal of mutton chop served by white stewards.

As we sailed about 7pm I really thought 'This is the last of Hong Kong.'

As we passed the 'Duke of York' she bugle-called us, the men on board stood to attention, and then everybody cheered everybody else.

23 Sep 1945

To picture show last evening, on hangar deck. It was 'In Old Oklahoma' with John Wayne and Martha Scott. Clifton and I sat on a ladder at the side and told each other how ludicrous it was to be sitting on an aircraft carrier, watching a film. It was rather rough.

I slept very well, although felt a little rocky till I got off to sleep. I'm on the top layer, quite near the hatch, supplied with one blanket, lucky I'd packed a sheet. My immediate neighbour was Nan Grady, much to our surprise when we climbed aloft and met each other. We have 4 sittings for meals.

We're awakened by piercing oscillating whistle which means the tannoy is going to work, then a bugle, then 'Rise and shine, you've had your time.' Then 'Dress of the day is tropical rig.'

So far I've felt very well today. Breakfast was lovely but I didn't tempt tummy too much – skipped eggs and bacon, had just grapefruit, shredded wheat, bread and marmalade. Doreen also on board.

Had prayers led by a Brother in the Pilots' Ready Cabin.

Captain gave a nice little speech on hangar deck; we had canteen vouchers given us. Clifton, Tim Fortescue, etc. are sleeping on camp beds on deck.

Weather rather rough.

24 Sep 1945

Haven't been on Flight Deck much because pretty windy. Sat on sponson most of morning with Doreen Leonard and Clare Van Wylick.

We were allowed 5/3d spending power in the canteen. I bought ovaltine, washing soap, choc and fruit salts. There were also cigarettes which could be bought at the expense of the sailors' rations – they agreed to have only half they were entitled to so that we might have some. Gradually getting into things English, I now have 2 shillings and a halfpenny, just glimpsed how the English life will become the normal, and HK$ a thing of the past. Have a few regrets.

Terribly happy on board, and trying to remember all the time to thank God, whatever may happen, for giving us all this – freedom, a ship, and time to enjoy ourselves and relax, and to be going HOME, however long it takes. It's said there's a 75% chance of our going all the way to UK on this.

Grand happy film in evening, Gloria Jean in 'She's My Lovely'.

25 Sep 1945

Got sunburnt on Flight Deck, when we had a display of AA fire, straight, orange flashes streaking into a puff put in the sky by one of the 5-inch guns.

Paravanes (one on each side of the ship) were let down, like great blue fish.

Intriguing little transports 'Clarkat' moving about the ship. Moving decks which go up from hangar to flight deck. We are supposed to sight Singapore tomorrow.

In evening our ship picked up an SOS and answered it, thought they had it, turned on the searchlights and discovered it was a junk – and not the ship that was in trouble.

26 Sep 1945

Anchored Singapore about half past 12. Passed a convoy of small naval craft convoying a large 3-funnelled transport. In harbour were many naval ships, including the aircraft carrier 'Trumpeter' which is a sister ship to us, and the flagship 'Nelson'. We stayed for about 3 hours. We left about 4pm. The little islands around are bristling with trees and bushes sprouting thick and green out of the sea.

Dance on Flight Deck at night. The deck was lit up, the band came up on the lift; 2 very nice singers, and we learned some of the latest (to us) songs. Flags were arrayed on the ropes round the band group. The officers looked very nice, some in black, some in white, and lovely smart cummerbunds. The MC kept saying 'Come along, ladies and gentlemen' because most of the seamen were very bashful.

The Captain looked like a film version of a bandit chief, in white silky shirt which billowed in the breeze, black cummerbund and black trousers. He made a little speech, said this was probably a unique occasion. Clifton gave a turn which went down very well. *((Clifton and friend Eric MacNider had often appeared on the Stanley stage together.))*

27 Sep 1945

Wind getting up. Porpoises about.

Got talking to a ginger-haired steward. I think they are overworked with us being on board. He says we're the third lot of passengers they've carried, they carried 100 evacuee children from Canada back to the UK. *((Clifton was anxious that Mabel 'won't wait for him.' We prayed that she would.))*

28 Sep 1945

Wakey Wakey earlier this morning. We had stopped at Sabang, on the northern tip of Sumatra. Water looked very deep – we were anchored quite close to land, and took on about 100 Marines who had only been there ten days ago from Penang. Low-lying hills, luxuriant in trees, could see absolutely no sign of habitation at all. Stayed about a couple of hours.

Pitching and rolling rather upsetting.

The ginger steward said Empress of Australia had dumped her passengers in Madras.

30 Sep 1945

Too bothered by weather and rocking to write yesterday. Couldn't eat dinner.

Film 'Gentleman Jim' in evening.

Rough again.

1 Oct 1945

Out on deck early to see hazy coastline of Ceylon, lots of small catamarans bobbing up and down. The harbour choc-a-bloc with ships. We're anchored rather far out.

Clifton got one of officers to signal Block House re 'Empress of Australia', to find it is due here tonight or tomorrow – but whether or not the original passengers from HK (including Mum and Mabel) have been dumped elsewhere we don't know.

At 2pm we were standing by. Fyffe *((David Robert Fyffe, Canadian, repatriated from Stanley in 1943 though British wife Dorothy and baby daughter stayed in camp))*, turned up on board.

We went ashore in landing barge, thence into Red Cross buses, taken to Echelon Barracks, to a sort of marquee and sat down in comfortable chairs drinking tea or lemonade and eating biscuits. Red Cross workers, very smart in uniform, were buzzing round doing all they could. There were magazines, books etc. Red, white and blue bunting draped the ceilings. There was a corner roped off, made like a toyshop for the kids, and they had a wonderful time. At different venues in Echelon, we received toilet things, underclothes, shoes, second-hand summer dress and skirt and blouse. We had HOT BATHS (with bath salts) and some folk had hairsets and face massage! Everything was taken care of. *((Heaps of released POWs around, looking pale and ill, hair in tufts. We found we people had a name, RAPWI, I think it stood for Returned Allied Prisoners of War and Internees.))*

((There were no billets for us at Echelon, we were siphoned off to various places to sleep.)) Olive and I learned that a Mr & Mrs Best had invited us to stay with them. *((We had met the Bests in 1938 as they travelled on the 'Kaisar-I-Hind' to Ceylon when we were aboard on our way to Hong Kong.))* She and I were put in a bus driven by an Indian, with among others the Mills family, the Buddens, Mr Megarry, Mr. J. Pennefather-Evans (Commissioner of Police, HK), and a Wren who was in charge of us.

Some were dropped at Kent House, we were taken to the Bests' house. Mrs. B came out to receive us. *((Although the Bests asked just for Olive and I, we airily took with us our best friend Nan Grady, who was happily welcomed too.))* They gave us a lovely bedroom, they are so very very kind, and have 3 other lodgers. We want to stay here for a while – it's all so grand – and I hope we never forget to thank God for it.

2 Oct 1945

8.30am. Slept beautifully, had hot baths, then delicious breakfast of bacon and egg and porridge.

10.30pm. Mabel and Clifton are married!

Olive, Nan and I went to town to try to find whereabouts of everyone, and met Dr. and Mrs. Valentine (from Smiter) who said Clifton was on board 'Empress of Australia' in the harbour. Later, I saw Mabel and Clifton on the other side of the road, swinging along as if walking on air, arms entwined. We rushed over to them. 'Hey, we're married!' Mabel announced – they had been married this morning, in cabin on ship, by Father Green, the padre who was in Shamshuipo Camp; Clifton in shorts and shirt, Mabel in shorts and blouse, with wedding ring made in camp out of a ten-cent coin.

Mabel has jumped ship, and as Mrs. C. T. Large, will travel with Clifton, who was in an absolute daze, I don't think he even realised we were there. They went in to Echelon Barracks and I haven't seen them since, though I met Mrs Greenwood who said she saw Mabel after the Red Cross had fitted her out and she looked fine. I'm terribly happy for them, I'm sure they were made for each other. *((They had over 60 years together. Clifton died in 2006, and Mabel is now 93.))*

Olive and I, Nan Grady and Van (H. Vanthall), Elliott (Mr. M. E. Purves) and a few others hired a rowing boat to take us out to the Empress. We weren't allowed on board at first as none of us had any passes. Eventually, Mr. W. J. Carrie – an HK official at the gangway – arranged things. Mum appeared, so smart in a newish dress, she is fatter.

Some of our pows from Japan are on board, others got off at Manila to go to Rest Camp there. News that Arthur Alsey is alive and well, and sent his regards. Topper (S. Brown, Olive's fiance) died of dysentery in Japan in 1944. About 3,000 on board.

I'm trying to get berth on Empress of Australia in Mabel's place.

3 Oct 1945

Am aboard the Empress!

Up at crack of dawn (to find officials who would give me Mabel's berth); set off Jawattea Road, a lorry stopped and Indian driver offered me a lift and dropped me at 'Slave Island'. Saw very few Europeans, but

Indians were helpful. Found 'Sub-Area HQ, junction of Parsons Road and Malay Street'; a Col. Johnston proved helpful, and said OK.

Another lorry gave me a lift to Echelon Barracks. Busloads of internees from E. of Australia coming in (to get their clothing); met up with Mum, and Olive and Nan, and also the Bests. We lost Mum for hours – even broadcast for her over tannoy – she eventually re-appeared, having had to go elsewhere to get her glasses fixed.

Colombo is lovely. The town is busy, the traffic alarming; their rickshaws are higher than Hong Kong's. Petrol and whisky are rationed, and clothing is going to be. Mrs Best told us the services are still mobilised, but gradually being demobbed. The place is teeming with WRNS and FANY, in plain but very snappy uniforms, cute hats. Loads of Europeans cycle all over the place, which seems very clean. Straight roads and many avenues. Houses nearly all bungalows, with big grounds; beautiful big open spaces, gorgeous flowers and trees and lake. They only had one air raid – Whitsun 1942.

I left Echelon in a taxi at 3pm to pick up my belongings from Bests, then take me to Melbourne Jetty (but taxi not allowed into Naval area, so transferred to a rickshaw as it would have been a long hot walk to the jetty.) W. Kinlock (Police) also waiting on jetty and some Nursing Sisters I knew, all for the Empress. We were taken by launch to the Empress.

((I was delighted with Mabel's berth, a top bunk with porthole beside it. There were about seven of us in the cabin which was reported to have been part of the accommodation the King and Queen had occupied on their pre-war trip to Canada.)) All the other passengers were ex Stanley.

4-13 Oct 1945

((Diary very sketchy, having such a good time on ship: film shows, dances, bridge – and new boyfriend. Called briefly at Aden.))

7 Oct 1945

Shocked to learn that Norman Hellevick died on board a few days out of Hong Kong (a Dutch diabetic from Stanley, he was 15 years old.)

8 Oct 1945

Radio news said the p.o.ws liberated who arrived in the s.s. Corfu at Southampton were given a roaring welcome and taken into camp, given roast beef and Yorkshire pudding, and are going to their homes today. 600 more are arriving at Liverpool, so impatient for it to be us.

This afternoon we are in sight of the island of Socotra, off Somaliland.

10 Oct 1945

Arrived Aden about 10.45am. Rocky, the colour of used plasticine, a few trees in evidence. New jetties, one with 4 submarines alongside. Lots of hawks circling around.

Mrs E. Barron disembarked as result of a cable from her husband who is stationed not far off... what a thrill! The Governor's wife is aboard sitting in the lounge.

Local paper has news of 'longer queues, shorter rations' at Home.

Edward Frith (a school friend at the Garrison School, Hong Kong, in 1928/9) came aboard to see his sister Iris Prew who was in Stanley.

Played bridge with Tony Sanh and Mr and Mrs Rosselet.

13 Oct 1945

Bridge again. Was vaccinated.

14 Oct 1945

Arrived at Suez, for Adibaya, at 10am, ship lay very far out. *((We were told we would be supplied with clothes here.))* The first 'clothing parties' went ashore soon after.

Entertainers came aboard: a crack RAF band, and 3 shows, the 'Fiddlededees' with Eileen Lawson, a Mr. Edge on piano with Suzette Odell singing, and a Shakespearean actor. I had a cigarette!

15 Oct 1945

Breakfast 6.30am, went ashore 7.00am. We were driven in buses past docks and cranes decorated with little flags – everything was done to try and put a welcome into the arid desert scene.

There was quite a wide strip of barren-ness before the mountains which were dark, sandy-coloured, bleak, bare and ridged – as if they'd been chiselled and you could see the marks. We saw camels.

10 minutes' journey to the Clothing Centre at Adibaya. This was Kentville Camp. German pows, wearing grey with a dark diamond patch on back of shirt and trousers, were working within camp on roads.

We were disembarked into a Rest Room – a converted hangar, with carpeted floor, tables with flag-tableclothes; shell cases with roses, and lovely cushioned chairs; and a nursery place for kids, sort of fenced off with artificial green ferns – chute, rocking horses, seesaw, swing etc.

We could buy cosmetics, and have free lovely cakes, sandwiches and drinks. Then to another hangar where we waited in lovely chairs, and were taken in groups of twenty *((to get our clothes))*. Each given a sheet of items, which were ticked thereon as we received them.

A.T.S. girls and others were in attendance at each counter. Got large grip, small blue Red Cross bag with lovely odds and ends inside; dressing-gown, nightie, green coat, brown skirt and jumper, grey gloves and scarf, corsets *((!!))*, stockings, 2 sets underwear, and lovely shoes. *((All these items were new, whereas what we'd received in Colombo were second-hand.))*

I have bad styes. Laval executed.

16 Oct 1945

Left Suez early and entered Suez Canal. Mainly desert wastes on Arabian side, and a very good road on British side. Troops swimming in canal & sitting on embankment. They waved and yelled at us, 'You're going the wrong way!' Was told the Turks tried to cross the Canal in 1915, only one barge got across – they carried barges on their shoulders, having brought them for miles over the desert.

Passed remains of ships sunk by Germans in war – mass of rusty twisted metal parked on the side of the canal. Tannoy announcer gave details: it's about 40 feet deep where we entered. The Italians didn't bomb the canal much in this war.

In 1968 it reverts to the Egyptian Govt. but apparently we are building another canal in this part of the world. The Pharaohs started on the canal. It now costs 8/4d per person to come through the canal.

Arrived Port Said in evening. Some mail came on board, but none for us. Men were given different forms to fill in, reporting war casualties, details of escapes etc.

17-19 Oct 1945

Eyes bad. Hair curled fairly well (used pipe cleaners which I bought in Adibaya.)

Bridge. Lifeboat drill. Dance at 7.30pm. Tony Sanh and I danced all the time, we won the spot Waltz – he a pipe and tobacco, me, eau de cologne. Then danced with Charles Rosselet.

Painted our names on our newly acquired grips *((hold-alls))*.

20 Oct 1945

Passed land on African coast; a mine spotted about 100 yards away, which a corvette came and exploded.

Confession. Then to dance with Tony etc. Later, he, Kay and Charles Rosselet and I sat on stairs and ate rolls with meat.

22 Oct 1945

Broke glasses yesterday. Rolled into Gibraltar early, anchored fairly close, took on mail, then off. We had gifts of odds and ends, I got lipstick and vanishing cream. Glasses repaired, thank God.

25 Oct 1945

Very rough after we left Gib. Hence no diary then.

26 Oct 1945

Gale still in progress so we had to stay anchored off Liverpool. Wrote poem 'Homecoming.'

Dock strike still on.

Tombola in evening.

HOMECOMING

'I woke at six; excited, thrilled.
The ship's pulsating heart was stilled.
I leapt out from my bunk, bright-eyed
And wrenched the porthole open wide.
In swept a rush of icy air:
I shivered, not too cold to stare
Enraptured, at an English sea
With grey waves dancing angrily,
And interlaced with spitting foam.
Beyond were stretched dim hills of Home
Beneath a sky wind-racked and dull;
And as I gazed, a lonely gull
Swooped by, a smooth white rhapsody,
And screamed a welcome in at me.'

27 Oct 1945

Early morning, moved off up the Mersey, over the Bar – very muddy, and came into view of Liverpool.

A launch brought along a crowd of dull, well-dressed men (each carrying a little suitcase) who climbed ladder to ship. A crowded ferry circled round us, people waving to us. As we pulled alongside, there were loads of people waving and cheering on a raised sort of stage; a band was playing 'Now it can be told'. The Mayor and other folk made speeches. Mr. Roe's son Martin *((from boarding school in England))* was there at dockside.

((Mrs Roe and daughter Barbara were in same cabin as Mum and I. We all had to see the UK officials in the public saloon to get travel documents etc. Looking back, the logistics were awesome. I guess there were between 2,000 and 3,000 of us aboard. Every one was interviewed. Somehow the UK had got information from any relatives any of us we might have in the UK; a destination had been organised for every one.

Mum and I were told that Aunt Lily in Gillingham, Kent, had offered to have us; so had Mrs. I. Cole (pre-war family friend) whose husband Lieut. G. Cole was killed during the HK fighting; she now lived in Devon. What kindness!

Of course we chose to go to Aunt Lily, and then and there were issued with railway warrants to Gillingham. These interviews took all day, so we spent another night on the Empress, all packed up.))

28 Oct 1945

Up with the lark. Breakfast, then given a half pound slab of York choc. each, cigs and matches. As we went down the gangway, each given a scran bag with sausage rolls etc.

To nearby Riverside Station. Train already waiting, we sat in long coaches with sets of 4 seats. Mum and I were with Miss M. Ward and Miss Betty Chart (both nurses).

Tea and biscuits served on the platform. Shunted off 10.30, long journey – 5 or 6 hours. Notices painted on back of hen coops, fences etc. with 'Welcome home!' and 'Well done boys!' – touching reminders that the war was not long over.

It was dark when we drew into Euston and got out. Mum told me to stay put while she went to claim our luggage. Aunt Lily suddenly materialised out of the melee on the platform, saying 'It's Barbara, isn't it?' (We'd last met 7 years ago). She'd been brought to meet us in an ambulance from Kent – those fantastic organisers deserved a medal! Now our luggage was heaved on board the ambulance. Also passengers with us were parents with small children, and a Royal Scot.

Aunt Lily had been waiting for us in London almost all day. She produced sandwiches for us, and letters which had been addressed to us at Gillingham. We dropped the Royal Scot at Greenwich, outside his house which was decorated with a flag and a sign saying 'Welcome Home Alf' over the door. The other folk got out at Chatham.

The St John's ambulance drivers were voluntary workers, they were kindness personified.

And so back to the Gillingham house where the Redwood family had said goodbye to Aunt and Uncle in January 1938 to go to Hong Kong 'for three years' which turned out to be seven and a half... we still could hardly believe we were home.

Afterword: Life after internment

Getting used to life in England, out of camp

Imagine the enormous feeling of relief and delight in being safe back in the UK! At first we stayed with my Aunt and Uncle in their neat little semi-detached house in Gillingham, Kent, as we had no home of our own.

We had visited the Gillingham house before going to Hong Kong. Now its opulence compared with Stanley was awe-inspiring: the lovely thick carpeting throughout and on the stairs, the charming little 'best room', the running hot water, the kitchen equipment; the lovely soft beds with patterned eiderdowns – everything seemed too good to be true. Never mind that we were really homeless and practically penniless (apart from small balances in HK$ in Hong Kong); our penury and paucity of belongings didn't worry us at all then: we had survived, we were free, we were Home, and heart-warming love and affection was lavished on us by our relations.

Aunt Lily took us to the local shops to introduce us – the assistants had been hearing about us for years! In Pearks Stores, the girl produced a little packet of Smith's crisps she had been keeping for me. We had to visit various offices to get ration books, medical cards etc. Aunt Lily had advised us that many things in the shops were 'in short supply', but to us the counters of Woolworths looked like an Aladdin's cave.

It was quite a confusing time. Although I was aged 26, I was not used to traffic, so even crossing a road took time and care. I was also very apprehensive making my first train journey alone to visit a school friend in Bromley: would I manage to recognise the station name in time to get up and leave the train, or would I be borne off to central London?

Nor were we used to the quietness that descended around 6pm every night. In Stanley, apart from the compulsory rest hour between 1 and 2pm, it was always noisy (except perhaps in the more isolated bungalows.) People were always coming and going, we led a very outdoor life. In the evenings there was intermittent conversation between the occupants of every room, and in the corridors and the queues for the bathroom. During mealtimes in the Married Quarters, some 600 people queued in the courtyard beneath our room, so there was a continuous buzz of chatter.

It seemed strange now to walk in the quiet early evening through streets lined with look-alike houses, all in darkness except for the skylight above the front door lit by a beam of light from the kitchen or back room (most houses bereft of the iron railings at front gardens which had been given for conversion to war use.)

Setting up house

My sister Olive arrived in England in November on the 'Highland Monarch' and joined Mum and I at Gillingham – she and Mum and I had to share a double bed. Soon after, my young sister Mabel, her husband Clifton and Clifton's parents arrived on the 'Athlone Castle'; all four of them, together with many other ex-internees who had nowhere else to stay, were installed in a hostel at Baginton Fields near Coventry.

Feeling we were overcrowding the Gillingham house (another aunt lived there too), we rented an even smaller house in nearby Sheerness, where we'd lived from 1929-1935 and still had several friends.

Mum was so happy to be running a home again, while Olive and I, chores done, crouched over the fire, reading our many letters. We three took it in turns to be first up in the morning, making tea to take to the others in bed. One then pulled up mats from both downstairs rooms and shook them out in the tiny back yard; raked out the cinders from the fireplace and kitchen range, then sieving the cinders to conserve the meagre coal ration; swept up and dusted, then put the porridge on for breakfast. Some cold mornings when it was either my turn or Olive's, Mum used to call plaintively from her room 'Aren't you girls ever going to get up?'

Mum was asked to give talks on internment at various venues in the area. Everywhere she went she took her exhibits: the teapot, made out of a Cowbell dried milk tin, complete with handle and spout; the tea cosy made from offcuts of khaki from our issue jerkins, and the top of a large thermos flask in which she used to collect her meals. (This flask top is now in the Heritage collection in Stanley.)

We spent Christmas Day with the family at Gillingham, the table graced with a rare turkey supplied (for 39/3d) by the butcher for whom Olive had worked as cashier in 1932-5.

Missing Stanley

After the first excitement of our return, we began to miss our fellow internees and the communal life, and exchanged letters with many of them who also felt a bit lost in their new environment. We looked forward so eagerly to the arrival of the postman twice a day.

There was a joyful reunion of Stanleyites at Covent Garden, preceded by a crowded thanksgiving service at St. Martin's-in-the-Fields. Among others, we met up with Kay Rosselet, the Joffes, Miss A. Davies (who'd been Matron of Tweed Bay Hospital), Charlie Whitfield, Dr. Herklots, Joan and Cynthia Sanh and Fred Kelly.

Another day I visited a friend, Arthur Alsey of the Royal Scots, who had been with hundreds of other soldiers from Shamshuipo Camp en route to Japan on the 'Lisbon Maru' when it was torpedoed. He said little about the horrors of the shipwreck, but was still alight with delight at having been brought back from Japan to the UK via Canada. He showed me a map of his train route across Canada; he'd scribbled round the margins the wonderful meals he had had in different places – a vivid ex-p.o.w. reaction which almost brought tears to my eyes.

Another ex-p.o.w. army friend, Harry Chalcraft, got in touch and couldn't wait to visit us in Sheerness and introduce us to his recently-acquired wife. They came from London, and had to change trains at Chatham, but missed their connection; to save time they came the rest of the way by taxi. This expensive gesture illustrates so well the great bond between ex-p.o.w.s and internees: we were so touched.

In the New Year we made numerous train journeys round England to visit other relatives and friends. On several occasions in London we bumped into other ex-internees; some of them we hadn't known very well in camp, but all fell on each other like long-lost friends, and risked losing train connections by prolonged chats.

At a school reunion in Sittingbourne, there were still three staff members of my days although I'd left 10 years before; one took my hands and said 'I KNOW YOU!' In fact, everyone we Redwoods met, even strangers to us, treated us with such overwhelming kindness and awe that even now, after 67 years, I still feel teary when I remember it.

The time came to think of our future

Olive, whose fiancée had died a p.o.w. in Japan, longed to get back to her Govt. job in Hong Kong. As Clifton's job with the HK Govt. was still open, he and Mabel would also be returning there after recuperation. But I didn't intend to return. I'd always yearned to be a school teacher; it was too late for that now, so I planned to get a job as a secretary in a girls' boarding school.

Before Christmas, Olive and I were summoned to the Colonial Office in London and asked to work there temporarily because stenographers were badly needed. We were prepared to do so, but this would have meant getting hostel accommodation in London; all the hostels the Office recommended were fully booked, so we had to give up the idea.

Instead, Olive and I were called to have medicals in London to see if we were fit to think about returning to work in Hong Kong. I passed but Olive failed.

Olive was still not in good health. In camp when my Mother was seriously ill, she had assumed the position of head of the family, and still did so – so much so that when, back in the UK, we set off on a visit to Suffolk, she took charge of our tickets. The train from King's Cross was just about to leave as we ran on to the platform. I was ahead and scrambled on first. Olive pushed her luggage on board, then bundled Mum on but before she could board herself the train began to move. She fell forward on her knees and was left behind on the platform trying to get her balance. Someone in the carriage closed the door, and we watched in horror lest she should fall between the carriages. Luckily others on the platform managed to pull her backwards – but there were Mum and I speeding off to Suffolk with no tickets. The last we saw of Olive, she was standing up and waving to us. The station master phoned the next stop to expect two passengers without tickets, saying Olive was OK and would follow by the next train.

Soon after, she had spent three weeks in Scotland with Nan Grady, our camp friend, and returned in much better health, so insisted on returning to the Colonial Office to try again to get back to Hong Kong. On hearing that the Fisheries Dept. there urgently needed a secretary, she begged to be sent there immediately, by air if possible. Off we went to Harley Street for her to have another medical – to her huge disappointment, she failed again.

In between our visits out of Kent, life now inclined to monotony relieved by the prodigious letters. The only heating in the house was the kitchen range, and coal fires in both downstairs rooms – never both at once as coal was severely rationed. Maybe it was the monthly pay cheques from the HK Govt., maybe I missed the Hong Kong life and climate more than I'd ever expected... somehow I never got round to seeking a secretarial job in the UK.

Olive had yet another medical, which she passed this time. We both received letters saying we should hold ourselves in readiness to return to Hong Kong.

Passage to Hong Kong is confirmed

Olive and I were quite well off now, we'd each received about £400 back pay covering internment. Mum on the other hand had only the widow's pension of ten shillings a week. In any case, we enjoyed the coming of Spring as never before, loving the snowdrops and crocuses and daffodils and tulips not seen in Hong Kong, and the trees bursting into leaf, and lambs leaping in the fields.

Then on 11th May a telegram arrived addressed to 'Redwood', offering passage to Hong Kong per 'Otranto' sailing from Tilbury 23rd May: an immediate reply was awaited by the telegraph boy. Not knowing if this applied to both of us, or just one, and if so which one, we both replied accepting passages; then went out to the post office and phoned the Colonial Office... the passage was for me only. Olive was devastated, her earlier medical reports had counted against her early return.

She came with me to Tilbury, where I linked up with my dearest camp friend Peggy Barton who was also a passenger. Then off I sailed to Hong Kong to resume my career as a stenographer, with the prospect of Home leave with pay and free passage every four years, and a pension at retirement, never dreaming of the future that was to become mine.

Sailing to Hong Kong

'Otranto' had about 400 passengers, a number of which were ex-Stanley; those I knew included Rene Razavette, Mrs Ida Ormiston, Quentin MacFadyen, Sheila Searle, George Saunders, Edith Johnson (Stuart), and Mrs Eager and her four young children Joan, Cynthia, Lesley and Cyril. Also aboard were five R.C. priests; I asked if there would be Mass the next day. 'There will be five Masses tomorrow,' one replied.

Another passenger was John Braga, a gifted violinist whom I knew from childhood piano lessons in Kowloon from his elder sister Maud.

Being Portuguese, John had spent the war in Macao; he had a wife and two young daughters, Rosemary and Joan; to get enough money to buy food in Macau he told us he resorted to playing his violin in the streets.

I shared a cabin with two ladies I didn't know, plus Mrs Eager and her children, one of whom announced, 'When we get back to Hong Kong, I'm going to the ration dump.' (Presumably to see if any bits of vegetable had dropped off the ration lorry!)

Apart from somewhat crowded accommodation, life on board was very luxurious after the restrictions in the UK. The only sign of austerity in food was at breakfast: on alternate days, we had dried egg with our bacon instead of the real thing. Peggy and I spent our time sun-bathing, playing deck games, and daily sessions of shorthand speed practice to prepare for our return to office work.

Ashore at Port Said, we bumped into other internees Dr K. Uttley and Mr R. Lederhofer; they were travelling to Hong Kong on the 'Glenstrae'. At Colombo we enjoyed shopping for dress materials – no coupons needed here, but I was strapped for money as one was only allowed to take a very limited amount (I forget how much) of sterling out of the country. Luckily Peggy had had the forethought to bring travellers' cheques, so I borrowed from her.

Arrival at Hong Kong – feeling homesick

I was officially met in Hong Kong by a young Government clerical officer, Ray Lawrence (ex-Stanley who two years later was best man at my wedding), and billeted at the Repulse Bay Hotel, freshly decorated and painted after being used by our Forces for rest and recreation. I shared a room with another internee, Agnes Berzin.

After the noisy streets of the city, which seemed to be buzzing again as much as pre-war, Repulse Bay was almost too peaceful in the evenings. I knew very few of the hotel inmates and was very, very homesick, even though during the day at work in the Secretariat I was among ex-Stanleyites I knew.

Happier times

It was a great relief after a week to be transferred to the French Mission in town which was in use as a hostel for Government employees – women on the top floor, men on the first, dining room and lounge on the ground floor. I knew this dignified red-brick building opposite the Hong Kong & Shanghai Bank well, having stayed and worked there for some weeks between leaving Stanley and sailing for the UK in 1945.

This time I shared a room with Dorothy Cavill, a school teacher whom I'd known before she was evacuated to Australia in 1940. Most of the other residents were fellow internees, among them Edward Hopkinson, Jimmy Barnes, T. Carr, Francis (Golly) Anslow, Bob Bates, Bunny Bickford, Eric Kennard, C. Roe, Barbara Budden and Mrs Lisa Jones.

Happy in the hostel with friends, I soon got over the homesickness. I was secretary to Major Williams at the Secretariat – by coincidence his office was the very same room occupied by my pre-war boss the Director of Air Raid Precautions when I was his secretary.

One of Major Williams' remits was quartering for Government folk. When he and a small committee had to travel round Hong Kong and Kowloon inspecting damaged Government quarters to decide if they were worth renovating, I was taken along to take notes – a lovely few days out in the open, especially when I got to ride in Major Williams' jeep.

Post-war Hong Kong

Our room in the French Mission was stark compared to the one at Repulse Bay, the only furniture being chairs, high white hospital beds with calico sheets, a chest of drawers and one large shelved cupboard. There being no wardrobe we hung our dresses on the mosquito net rails round our beds; later, we turned the cupboard on its side so that the shelves were vertical, screwed in hooks and hung our clothes there. We bought cheap bright chintz from Cloth Street to drape over our trunks.

One night I heard a strange sound: it turned out to be a rat nibbling through the cardboard of the box of sugared almonds I'd bought at

Suez. In the men's rooms, rats devoured the buttons on their jackets and trousers until traps put a stop to their feasts.

The wives of some of the married men among us had not yet returned to Hong Kong; they joined us unattached men and women in the communal lounge in the evenings. When someone could borrow a Government car, we would drive to Shek O or Repulse Bay at weekends; it was strange to see groups of servicemen driving their jeeps right up on to the beaches.

Trams were running, but there weren't many taxis or private cars and only a few buses. My friend Peggy and I travelled in Kowloon on the double seat at the front of a tricycle. Sometimes she travelled on the back of a single bicycle – much cheaper than on a tricycle; many professional cyclists were doing good trade, providing comfortable little seats.

The Catholic Centre, which Father Meyer had planned when in Stanley, was already up and running on an upper floor of a large building on the sea front. It had a tiny chapel, a small bookshop, a library and restaurant for snacks. He had set it up, together with a centre for servicemen on another floor, before returning to the USA.

There was a ferry strike. The Royal Navy took over operating the ferries, one day managing to damage one pier and put two ferries out of action, so the Govt. had to run a launch at rush hours for their employees; some people had to cross the harbour in walla wallas (small motor boats) – fortunately only for one day.

Most of the houses and flats we saw with Major Williams had to be written off; many had war damage and had then been thoroughly looted; in one we saw just the steel bones of a piano. (All that remained of our pre-war flat in Gap Road was the lavatory cistern and an empty plant pot; all woodwork – floor, cupboards, doors etc. had been looted for firewood. Mrs. K. Grant of Stanley was luckier: she discovered that her flat was in almost the same condition as she had left it, as some Third Nationals had lived there during the occupation.)

My salary was HK$320 a month, less $40 for accommodation. Some examples of the cost of living at that time:

- meals at the French Mission cost $165 a month, laundry $35
- cinema tickets cost $2.50
- the Star Ferry was 20 cents (against 10 cents pre-war)
- imported fruit was very expensive; an orange cost 70 cents, an apple 50 cents
- nylon stockings cost $22
- cables to the UK cost $1.00 per word (transmission time 17 hours), or 50 cents per word (transmission time one and a half days.)

We celebrated VJ Day on 15th August with champagne in the office and a party in the evening. The 30th August was a public holiday to celebrate the first anniversary of the arrival of the British Fleet and our Liberation.

More evacuees and internees return to Hong Kong

In August 1946, the Government brought the 1940 evacuees in Australia back to Hong Kong on the 'Duntroon'. When I met the ship I was struck by how overdressed most of the ladies were, most sporting white hats. Goodness knows where they were all accommodated, despite the speed with which damaged flats etc. were being repaired. The Peninsula Hotel charged $8 a day but you had to pay for your meals.

Most male internees returned to Hong Kong with their families because their jobs were there, and you couldn't compare life in the UK with the climate, beaches, servants and relaxed living that made even immediately post-war Hong Kong so attractive. Many families had been living with relatives in the UK but couldn't expect to stay there indefinitely; relocating in the UK and finding another job didn't appeal.

My elder sister Olive returned to Hong Kong in early September and joined me in the French Mission. She became secretary to Mr C. Followes, who was then Financial Secretary. I transferred to the Dept. of Supplies, Trade & Industry and worked for Mr. J.J. Cowperthwaite, then Director.

When we learned that the HK Govt. would give ex-internees in the UK free passages back to Hong Kong, we got Mum to apply; we both thought she should come here as soon as possible to avoid another winter in the UK on poor rations, and get a job here. Our camp friends Mr and Mrs Kopeczky rented a flat in Kowloon, and offered to have Mum as a lodger. To our great delight, Mum was allotted passage on the aircraft carrier 'Victorious', as was Mabel, then four months pregnant. (Mabel's husband Clifton had returned earlier by air.)

At the beginning of December 'Victorious' sailed into Hong Kong. By an amazing circumstance, a few days earlier Olive had bumped into Ah Ding, our family amah at the time of the Japanese attack, so we took her to the wharf to meet Mum. We were all so relieved that she and her husband and two young children had survived the Occupation; now Ah Ding was working as housekeeper to an Army family, at a wage far above what we could afford to employ her – even if we had a home of our own. She spoke very good English, having been brought up in an English household where her mother was an amah. In later years she often visited us; one of her daughters when grown up came to England to work (not as an amah though!)

Looking to the future, Stanley fades into the past

So now our family was back together again. The Government opened more hostels, and Mum became the manager of one in Macdonnell Road (with accommodation.) Mabel and Clifton, and baby Jane when she arrived, lived in the Peninsula Hotel until they were allotted a flat.

Both Olive and I married inmates of the French Mission – Olive in 1949 to Bill Darby, who had spent the war in the Army in China, I in 1948 to Francis (Golly) Anslow whom I'd first met in Stanley.

By then, Stanley seemed to belong to the past. This was probably because we were all now so occupied with our present lives, and many of us raising children; also, we were in the company of internees' wives who had been away in Australia, and others who had post-war married girls they'd met in England or Australia, so you couldn't be continually harking back to an existence they could not share. Nor did Frank or I ever feel the need to take a look at Stanley before our retirement in

1959. In 2008 my five children took me on a memorable visit to Hong Kong (including Stanley) for my 90th birthday. Amazingly, the Married Quarters building where we Redwoods had been billeted was still there, still occupied by prison officer families, and looking exactly the same as in 1945 when we'd left camp 63 years earlier!

As new expatriates filtered into the colony over the years, the Stanley experience was less and less mentioned. I didn't think post-war Hong Kong very different from pre-war, except that the Japanese menace was no longer hanging over us. One of the most noticeable changes which crept up during the ensuing years was that more Chinese and Eurasian nationals were being employed in posts which pre-war would only have been filled by Europeans; people were now being judged by their abilities instead of by their colour.

In the 1960s my mother wrote her memoirs, mainly about the war and internment in Hong Kong, but could not find any publisher who was interested in them; perhaps it was too soon after the end of the war. Some 40 years later my sisters and I published them at our own expense, then the book was published in large print by Isis of Oxford, and earned us over £1,000.

Re-awakened interest

Perhaps the BBC 'Tenko' series awakened the interest of the country in war-time and internment in the Far East. There was a happy and highly successful Stanley Reunion at Leamington Spa in 1997, with many of us meeting up with people we hadn't seen since 1945, and a few years later another reunion in Warwick was attended by people from Stanley and other internment camps in the Far East.

My children were brought up to know all about the camp: how could they not, with both parents, grandmother, two aunts, and my husband's parents all being ex-internees. However, they did not show any real interest until they were much older, when their children began to ask us questions in connection with history projects they were doing at school.

Up to about 10 years ago, I used to give talks on the subject to various local clubs which were well received.

Now, of course, the Stanley Group online has stirred up much more interest in the camp. I am so grateful to the originator, as emails from members have brought me into contact with so many relatives of internees I knew; also, through the tireless investigations of some members, I have learned things about the camp that I didn't know when I was there.

How did the time in camp affect my life?

It altered my outlook on racism and religion.

Pre-war I had no Chinese, Portuguese or Eurasian friends or acquaintances; our ways didn't cross. In Stanley I had close connections, mainly through R.C. church activities, with all three races and made many friends among them, especially one, Peggy McMahon (nee Barton). Sadly she passed away in 2016, aged 92.

Pre-war I was a weekly Mass goer, but my only religious reading was the 'penny catechism'. In Stanley, Father Meyer and Father Hessler organised study clubs for their flock and encouraged discussion. I had never heard of 'Apologetics'! Of course there were many other men of the cloth in Stanley who similarly tended their flocks – we were a captive congregation.

I like to think camp made me more tolerant... something you have to be when sharing a room at close quarters with at least four other people, with their irritating habits, their snores and burps. I can feel special compassion for crowds of refugees on TV, and for starving African babies with all their bones showing.

Above all, if I hadn't been in Stanley, I would not have met my dear husband, although I didn't know at the time that he would become my husband six years later.

Index

New Territories
Kowloon
Lantau Island
Hong Kong Island

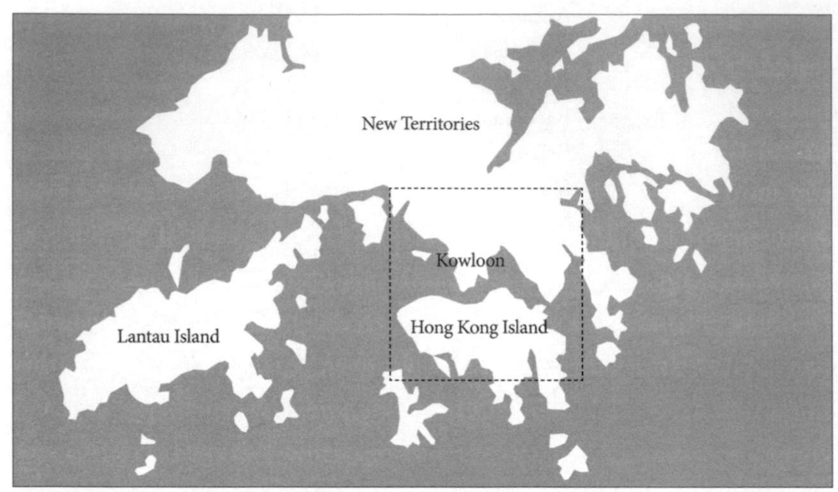

HONG KONG, 1941

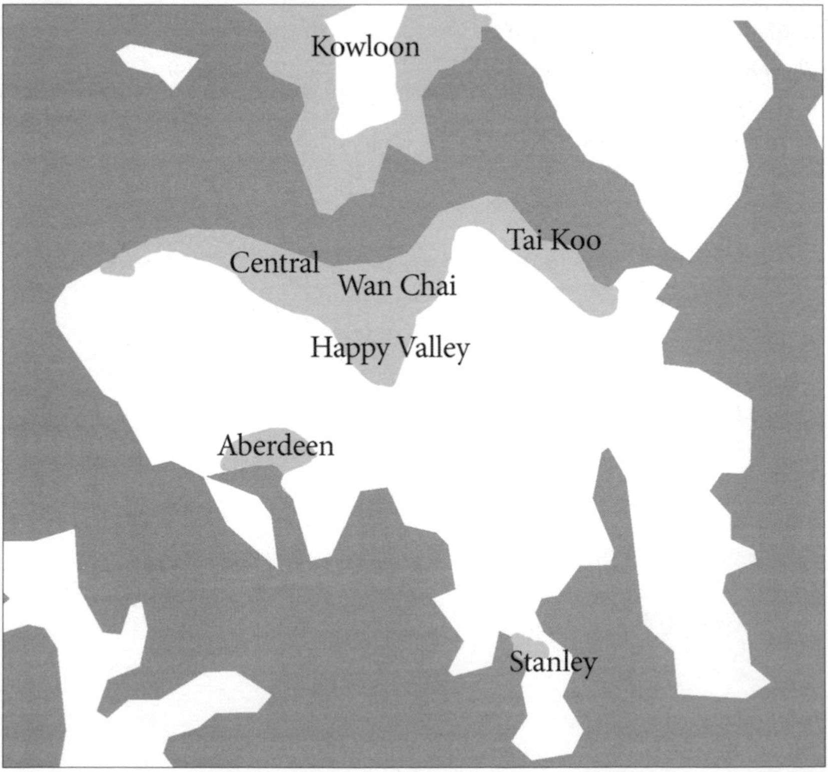

Kowloon
Tai Koo
Central
Wan Chai
Happy Valley
Aberdeen
Stanley

STANLEY CAMP

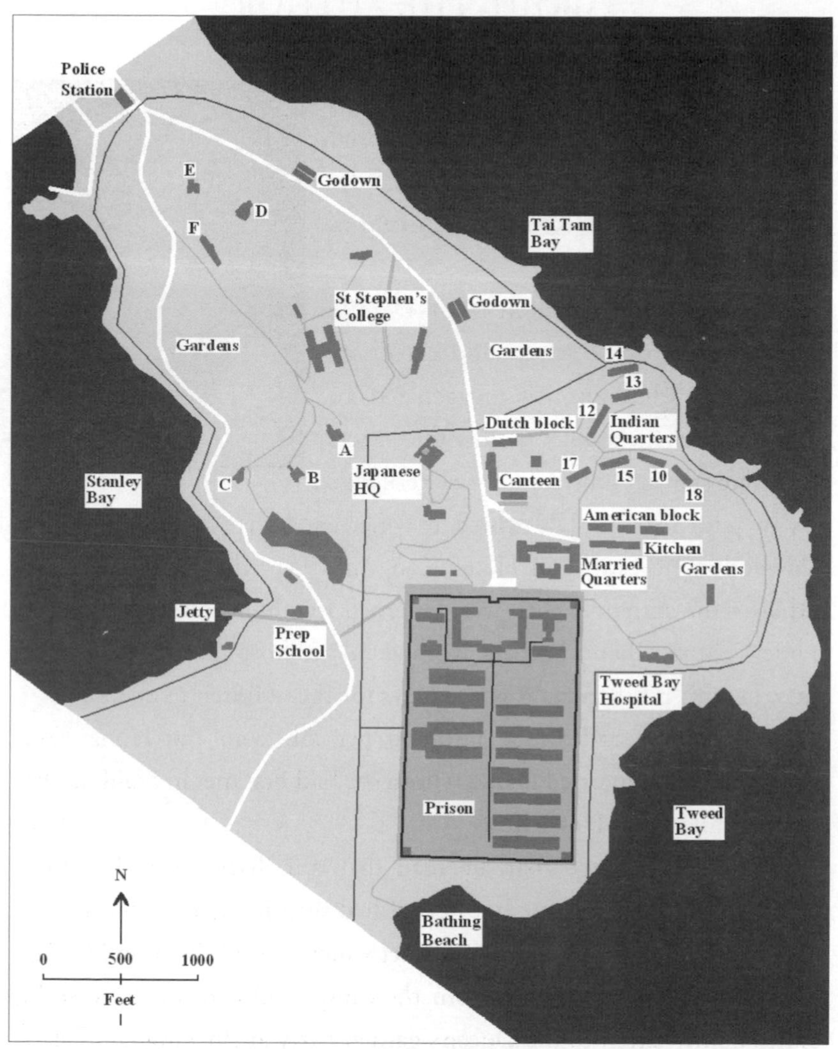

Map from *We Shall Suffer There* by Tony Banham, published by Hong Kong University Press

About the author

Barbara Anslow (née Redwood) was born in Scotland in 1918. In 1938 her family moved to Hong Kong where Barbara and her elder sister joined the Hong Kong Government as shorthand typists.

Her father William died in 1940. Despite the risk of a Japanese attack, and expatriate women and children being evacuated to Australia, Barbara and her mother and sisters decided to stay in Hong Kong; the alternative was to return to the UK which the Germans were bombing. So the Redwoods were caught in Hong Kong in 1941 when Japan attacked, and after the surrender they were interned for three-and-a-half years in Stanley Camp. There, Barbara worked in the hospital office, kept her diary, taught shorthand and wrote plays for the children to enact.

After the war ended, she resumed her job with the Hong Kong Government and married Frank, whom she had first met in Stanley. They had five children in Hong Kong.

About ten years ago, Barbara read that war diaries were becoming popular: until then, no one but herself had seen her diaries. So she sent them to a Stanley group on the internet which posted them online. This reunited her with old friends from the camp, and had some incredible results: an invitation to the Queen's garden party at Buckingham Palace; a television interview on the 70th anniversary of VJ Day, after which she recited a war poem before Prince Charles and hundreds of Pacific War veterans; a parade through London streets lined with cheering and waving crowds; and this book. She lives in Essex.